Crossword
DICTIONARY

Crossword DICTIONARY

GEDDES & GROSSET

This edition published by Geddes & Grosset,
David Dale House, New Lanark, ML11 9DJ, Scotland

© 2004 Geddes & Grosset

First published 2004

ISBN 1 84205 396 5

Printed and bound in Poland

Contents

3-Letter Words

abb	auk	bum	dab	eel	fid
aby	ave	bun	dad	e'en	fie
ace	awe	bur	dag	e'er	fig
act	awl	bus	dak	eft	fin
add	awn	but	dam	egg	fir
ado	axe	buy	dan	ego	fit
adz	aye	bye	dap	eke	fix
aft	baa	cab	daw	eld	flu
aga	bad	cad	day	elf	fly
age	bag	cam	dee	elk	fob
ago	bah!	can	den	ell	foe
aha	ban	cap	dew	elm	fog
aid	bar	car	dey	emu	foh
ail	bat	cat	did	end	fop
aim	bay	caw	die	ens	for
air	bed	cay	dig	eon	fox
ait	bee	cit	dim	era	foy
alb	beg	cob	din	ere	fro
ale	ben	cod	dip	erg	fry
all	bet	cog	doe	ern	fun
alp	bey	col	dog	err	fur
alt	bib	con	don	eve	gab
and	bid	coo	dor	ewe	gad
ant	big	cop	dot	eye	gag
any	bin	cor	dry	fad	gam
ape	bis	cot	dub	fag	gap
apt	bit	cow	dud	far	gar
arc	boa	cox	due	fat	gas
are	bob	coy	dug	fay	gat
ark	bog	coz	dun	fed	gay
arm	boo	cry	duo	fee	gel
art	bot	cub	dux	fen	gem
ash	bow	cud	dye	feu	gen
ask	box	cue	ear	few	get
asp	boy	cup	eat	fey	gig
ass	bud	cur	eau	fez	gin
ate	bug	cut	ebb	fib	gnu

gob	hug	kin	met	oft	pit
god	huh!	kip	mew	ohm	pix
got	hum	kir	mid	oho!	ply
gum	hun	kit	mix	oil	pod
gun	hut	kye	moa	oke	poh
gut	ice	lac	mob	old	pop
guy	icy	lad	moo	one	pot
gym	ilk	lag	mop	ope	pox
gyp	ill	lap	mow	orb	pry
had	imp	law	mud	ore	pub
hag	ink	lax	mug	ort	pug
hah!	inn	lay	mum	our	pun
ham	iou	lea	nab	out	pup
hap	ire	led	nag	ova	pur
has	irk	lee	nap	owe	pus
hat	ivy	leg	nay	owl	put
haw	jab	leo	neb	own	pyx
hay	jag	let	nee	pad	qua
hem	jah	lid	net	pah	rag
hen	jam	lie	new	pal	ram
her	jar	lip	nib	pan	ran
hew	jaw	lit	nil	pap	rap
hex	jay	lob	nip	par	rat
hey	jet	log	nit	pas	raw
hid	jew	loo	nod	pat	ray
hie	jib	lop	nog	paw	red
him	jig	lot	nor	pax	rep
hin	job	low	not	pay	ret
hip	joe	lug	now	pea	ria
his	jog	lye	nun	ped	rib
hit	jot	mac	nut	pee	rid
hob	joy	mad	nux	peg	rif
hod	jug	mag	oaf	pen	rig
hoe	jut	mam	oak	pep	rim
hog	kaw	man	oar	per	rip
hop	kay	map	oat	pet	rob
hot	keg	mar	obi	pew	roc
how	ken	mat	odd	pie	rod
hoy	kex	maw	ode	pig	roe
hub	key	may	o'er	pin	roi
hue	kid	men	off	pip	rom

rot	sin	sup	toe	via	woe
row	sip	tab	tom	vie	wok
rub	sir	tag	ton	vim	won
rue	sit	tan	too	vis	woo
rug	six	tap	top	viz	wop
rum	ski	tar	tor	vow	wot
run	sky	taw	tot	wad	wry
rut	sly	tax	tow	wag	yak
rye	sob	tay	toy	wan	yam
sac	sod	tea	try	wap	yap
sad	sog	ted	tub	war	yaw
sag	sol	tee	tug	was	yea
sal	son	ten	tui	wax	yen
sap	sop	the	tum	way	yes
sat	sot	tho'	tun	web	yet
saw	sou	thy	tup	wed	yew
say	sow	tic	tut!	wee	yon
sea	soy	tie	two	wen	you
see	spa	tin	ugh!	wet	zap
set	spy	tip	una	wey	zax
sew	sty	tis	urn	who	zip
sex	sub	'tis	use	why	zit
she	sue	tit	van	wig	zoo
shy	sum	tnt	vat	win	
sic	sun	tod	vex	wit	

4-Letter Words

abba	alas	arni	bald	bell	boar
abbe	alee	arum	bale	belt	boat
abed	alfa	asci	balk	bema	bode
abet	ally	ashy	ball	bend	body
abib	alma	asia	balm	bent	boer
able	alms	asps	band	bere	bogy
ably	aloe	atom	bane	berg	boil
abut	alow	atop	bang	berm	bold
aces	alps	aunt	bank	best	bole
ache	also	aura	bant	bevy	boll
acid	alto	auto	barb	bias	bolt
acme	alum	aver	bard	bice	bomb
acne	amah	avid	bare	bide	bond
acre	ambo	avis	bark	bier	bone
adam	amen	avon	barm	biff	bony
adar	amid	avow	barn	bigg	boob
adit	amir	away	base	bike	book
adry	amok	awed	bash	bile	boom
adze	amyl	awry	bask	bilk	boon
aeon	anal	axes	bass	bill	boor
aero	anew	axil	bast	bind	boot
aery	anna	axis	bate	bine	bore
afar	anon	axle	bath	bing	born
affy	ante	ayah	bawd	bird	bort
aged	anti	ayes	bawl	bise	bosh
ages	anus	azym	bead	bisk	bosk
agio	apex	baal	beak	bite	boss
agog	apse	babe	beam	bitt	both
ague	aqua	babu	bean	blab	bott
ahoy	arab	baby	bear	blae	bout
aide	arch	bach	beat	bled	bowl
aids	area	back	beau	blew	bozo
airy	aria	bade	beck	blob	brad
ajar	arid	bags	beef	blot	brae
akee	aril	bail	been	blow	brag
akin	arms	bait	beer	blue	bran
alar	army	bake	beet	blur	brat

bray	calk	chic	coir	crow	data
bred	call	chid	coke	crum	date
brew	calm	chin	cola	crut	daub
brig	calp	chip	cold	crux	dauk
brim	calx	chit	cole	crwd	davy
brio	came	chop	colt	cube	dawk
brow	camp	chow	coma	cues	dawn
bubo	cane	chub	comb	cuff	daze
buck	cant	chum	come	cull	dead
buff	can't	ciel	cone	culm	deaf
buhl	cape	cist	conk	cult	deal
bulb	card	cite	cony	curb	dean
bulk	care	city	cook	curd	dear
bull	cark	cive	cool	cure	debt
bump	carl	clad	coon	cur,	deck
bund	carp	clam	coop	curl	deed
bung	cart	clan	coot	curt	deem
bunk	case	clap	cope	cusp	deep
bunt	cash	claw	copt	cuss	deer
buoy	cask	clay	copy	cute	deft
burg	cast	clef	cord	cyma	defy
burl	cate	cleg	core	cyme	delf
burn	cauk	clem	corf	cyst	dell
burr	caul	clew	cork	czar	delt
bury	cave	clip	corm	dace	deme
bush	cavy	clod	corn	dado	demi
busk	cede	clog	cose	daff	demo
buss	ceil	clot	cost	daft	demy
bust	cell	cloy	cosy	dago	dene
busy	celt	club	cote	dais	dent
butt	cent	clue	coup	dale	deny
buzz	cere	coal	cove	dame	derm
byre	cess	coat	cows	damn	desk
byte	cham	coax	cozy	damp	deva
cade	chap	coca	crab	dane	dewy
cadi	char	cock	crag	dank	dhak
cafe	chat	coco	cram	dare	dhal
cage	chaw	code	cran	dark	dhow
cain	chay	coif	craw	darn	dial
cake	chef	coil	crib	dart	dibs
calf	chew	coin	crop	dash	dice

dick	dorp	dune	enid	fang	fish
dido	dorr	dung	enow	fare	fisk
died	dory	dupe	envy	farl	fist
diem	dose	dusk	epha	farm	fits
dies	doss	dust	epic	faro	five
diet	dost	duty	epos	fash	fizz
dike	dote	dyad	ergo	fast	flag
dill	doth	dyer	erin	fate	flak
dime	dour	dyke	erne	faun	flam
dine	dout	dyne	eros	faux	flan
ding	dove	each	erse	fawn	flap
dint	dowl	earl	erst	fays	flat
dire	down	earn	espy	fear	flaw
dirk	doxy	ears	etch	feat	flax
dirt	doze	ease	etna	feed	flay
disc	dozy	east	etui	feel	flea
dish	drab	easy	even	fees	fled
disk	drag	ebon	ever	feet	flee
diss	dram	echo	evil	fell	flew
diva	drat	edda	ewer	felt	flex
dive	draw	eddy	ewes	fend	flic
dixy	dray	eden	exam	fent	flip
doab	dreg	edge	exit	feod	flit
dock	drew	edgy	exon	fern	floe
dodo	drip	edit	eyas	fete	flog
doer	drop	eels	eyed	feud	flop
does	drub	efts	eyes	fiat	flow
doff	drug	egad!	eyot	fibs	flue
doge	drum	eggs	eyre	fico	flux
doit	dual	egis	eyry	fief	foal
dole	duan	eire	face	fife	foam
doll	duck	,lan	fact	figs	foci
dolt	duct	elmo	fade	file	foes
dome	dude	elmy	fail	fill	fogy
done	duel	else	fain	film	foil
don't	duet	elul	fair	find	foin
dool	duke	emeu	fake	fine	fold
doom	dull	emir	fall	finn	folk
door	duly	emit	fama	fire	fond
dope	dumb	ends	fame	firm	font
dora	dump	enew	fane	fisc	food

fool	game	give	grin	harp	hing
foot	gamp	glad	grip	hart	hire
ford	gamy	glee	grit	hash	hiss
fore	gang	glen	grog	hasp	hist
fork	gaol	glib	grot	hate	hive
form	gape	glow	grow	hath	hoar
fort	garb	glue	grub	haul	hoax
foss	gash	glum	grue	haum	hock
foul	gasp	glut	gulf	have	hold
four	gate	gnat	gull	hawk	hole
fowl	gaud	gnaw	gulp	haze	holm
foxy	gaul	gnoo	guru	hazy	holp
fray	gaur	goad	gush	head	holt
free	gave	goal	gust	heal	holy
fret	gawd	goat	guts	heap	home
frit	gawk	goby	gyal	hear	hone
frog	gaze	go-by	gybe	heat	hood
from	gean	goer	gyre	heed	hoof
fuel	gear	go-go	gyri	heel	hook
full	geat	gold	gyve	heft	hoop
fume	geck	golf	hack	heir	hoot
fumy	geld	gone	hade	held	hope
fund	gens	gong	hadj	hell	hops
funk	gent	gonk	ha-ha	helm	horn
furl	germ	good	hail	help	hose
fury	gest	gore	hair	hemp	host
fuse	ghat	gory	hake	herb	hour
fuss	ghee	gosh!	hale	herd	hove
fuze	gibe	goth	half	here	howl
fuzz	gift	gour	hall	hern	hued
fyrd	gigo	gout	halm	hero	huff
gaby	gild	gowk	halo	herr	huge
gael	gill	gown	halt	hers	hulk
gaff	gilt	grab	hame	hest	hull
gage	gimp	gram	hand	hewn	hump
gail	ginn	gray	hang	hick	hung
gain	gird	grew	hank	hide	hunk
gait	girl	grey	hard	high	hunt
gala	giro	grid	hare	hill	hurl
gale	girt	grit	hark	hilt	hurt
gall	gist	grim	harm	hind	hush

husk	jarl	keep	lace	lend	list
hymn	jaws	kelp	lack	leno	lite
hype	jazz	kelt	lacy	lens	lith
hypo	jean	keno	lade	lent	live
iamb	jeer	kent	lady	less	load
ibex	jehu	kept	laic	lest	loaf
ibis	jerk	kerb	laid	levy	loam
iced	jess	kerf	lain	lewd	loan
icon	jest	kern	lair	liar	lobe
idea	jibe	keys	lake	lias	loch
idem	jilt	khan	lakh	lice	loci
ides	jinn	kibe	laky	lich	lock
idle	jobs	kick	lama	lick	lode
idly	join	kill	lamb	lido	loft
idol	joke	kiln	lame	lied	loin
idyl	jole	kilt	lamp	lief	loll
ikon	joll	kind	land	lien	lone
ilex	jolt	kine	lane	lier	long
imam	joss	king	lank	lies	look
iman	jove	kink	lard	lieu	loom
impi	jowl	kino	lark	life	loon
inca	jube	kirk	lash	lift	loop
inch	judy	kiss	lass	like	loot
inky	july	kite	last	lilt	lope
inly	jump	kith	late	lily	lops
into	june	kiwi	lath	limb	lord
iona	junk	knag	laud	lime	lore
iota	juno	knap	lava	limn	lorn
iran	jury	knar	lave	limp	lory
iris	just	knee	lawn	limy	lose
iron	jute	knew	lazy	line	loss
isis	kadi	knit	lead	ling	lost
isle	kail	knob	leaf	link	lote
itch	kaka	knop	leak	linn	loth
item	kale	knot	leal	lino	loto
iwis	kali	know	lean	lint	loud
jack	kate	knub	leap	lion	lout
jade	kava	kohl	leek	lips	lots
jail	keek	kola	leer	lira	love
jamb	keel	kook	lees	lire	luce
jape	keen	kris	left	lisp	luck

luff	mast	mini	mumm	noon	once
lull	mate	mink	mump	nore	oner
lump	math	mint	murk	norm	only
luna	matt	minx	muse	nose	onto
lune	maud	miny	mush	note	onux
lung	maul	mire	musk	noun	onyx
lure	maxi	miry	must	nous	ooid
lurk	maze	miss	mute	nude	oose
lush	mazy	mist	myth	nuke	ooze
lust	mead	mite	naif	null	oozy
lute	meal	mitt	nail	numb	opal
lynx	mean	mity	name	nuts	open
lyre	meat	moan	nape	oaks	opus
lyse	meed	moat	nard	oaky	oral
ma'am	meek	mock	nave	oars	orby
mace	meet	mode	navy	oary	orgy
mach	mega	moil	neap	oast	orts
made	melt	mold	near	oath	oryx
mage	mend	mole	neat	oats	otto
magi	menu	moly	neck	obey	ouch
maid	mere	monk	need	obit	oust
mail	merk	mood	ne'er	oboe	oval
maim	mesh	moog	neon	odds	oven
main	mess	moon	nerd	odic	over
make	mete	moor	nero	odor	ovum
male	mewl	moot	ness	ogee	owed
mall	mews	mope	nest	ogle	owns
malm	mica	more	nett	ogpu	oxen
malt	mice	morn	news	ogre	oyer
mama	midi	moss	newt	ohms	oyes!
mane	mien	most	next	oily	oyez!
manx	miff	mote	nice	oink	paca
many	mild	moth	nick	oise	pace
mare	mile	moue	nigh	okay	pack
mark	milk	move	nine	okie	paco
marl	mill	moya	nisi	okra	pact
mars	milt	much	node	olaf	page
mart	mime	muck	noel	olio	paid
mash	mina	muff	nome	olla	pail
mask	mind	mule	none	omen	pain
mass	mine	mull	nook	omit	pair

pale	peri	pock	pulp	rash	risk
pali	perk	poem	puma	rasp	rite
pall	pert	poet	pump	rate	rive
palm	peso	poke	punk	rath	road
palp	pest	pole	punt	rave	roam
palt	phew!	poll	puny	raze	roan
paly	phiz	polo	pupa	read	roar
pane	pica	pome	pure	real	robe
pang	pice	pomp	purl	ream	rock
pant	pick	pond	purr	reap	rode
papa	pied	pony	push	rear	roil
para	pier	pooh!	puss	reck	role
pard	pike	pool	putt	reed	roll
pare	pile	poop	pyre	reef	rome
park	pill	poor	quad	reek	romp
parr	pimp	pope	quag	reel	rood
part	pine	pore	quay	rein	roof
pass	ping	pork	quid	rely	rook
past	pink	porn	quip	rend	room
pate	pint	port	quit	reno	root
path	piny	pory	quiz	rent	rope
paul	pipe	pose	race	repp	ropy
pave	pipy	post	rack	rest	rose
pawl	pise	posy	racy	rhea	rosy
pawn	pish!	pour	raff	rice	rota
peak	piss	pout	raft	rich	rote
peal	pith	pram	rage	rick	rou,
pear	pity	pray	rahu	ride	roup
peat	pixy	prey	raid	rife	rout
peck	plan	prig	rail	rift	rove
peel	plat	prim	rain	rile	ruby
peen	play	proa	rake	rill	ruck
peep	plea	prod	ramp	rime	rudd
peer	plim	prop	rand	rimy	rude
peke	plod	prow	rang	rind	ruff
pelf	plop	puce	rank	ring	ruga
pell	plot	puck	rant	rink	ruin
pelt	plow	puff	rape	riot	rule
pend	plug	puke	rapt	ripe	rump
pent	plum	pule	rare	ript	rune
peon	plus	pull	rase	rise	rung

runt	seal	shun	slim	song	stow
ruse	seam	shut	slip	soon	stub
rush	sear	sice	slit	soot	stud
rusk	seat	sick	sloe	soph	stun
russ	sect	side	slop	sorb	stye
rust	seed	sift	slot	sore	such
ruth	seek	sigh	slow	sorn	suck
ryot	seel	sign	slub	sort	suds
sack	seem	sikh	slue	so-so	suer
safe	seen	silk	slug	soul	suet
saga	seep	sill	slum	soup	suez
sage	seer	silo	slur	sour	suit
sago	sein	silt	slut	soya	sulk
said	self	sine	smee	span	sump
sail	sell	sing	smew	spar	sung
sake	semi	sink	smit	spat	sunk
sale	send	sire	smug	spay	sunn
salt	sent	sist	smut	spec	surd
same	sept	site	snag	sped	sure
samp	serb	sitz	snap	spew	surf
sand	sere	size	snip	spin	swab
sane	serf	sizy	snob	spir	swag
sank	seta	skew	snot	spit	swam
sans	sexy	skid	snow	spot	swan
sard	shad	skim	snub	spry	swap
sark	shag	skin	snug	spud	sway
sash	shah	skip	soak	spue	swig
sate	sham	skit	soal	spun	swim
save	shaw	skua	soar	spur	swop
scab	shea	skye	sock	stab	swum
scad	shed	slab	soda	stag	tach
scam	shew	slag	sofa	star	tack
scan	shia	slam	soft	stay	tact
scar	shin	slap	soho	stem	tael
scat	ship	slat	soil	sten	ta'en
scot	shod	slav	sold	step	tail
scow	shoe	slay	sole	stet	take
scud	shog	sled	soli	stew	talc
scum	shop	slew	solo	stir	tale
scut	shot	sley	soma	stoa	talk
scye	show	slid	some	stop	tall

tame	this	tore	twig	veil	wait
tamp	thou	tori	twin	vein	wake
tang	thro'	torn	twit	vela	wale
tank	thud	tort	type	veld	walk
tape	thug	tory	tyre	vena	wall
tare	thus	toss	tyro	vend	wand
tarn	tied	tour	tzar	vent	wane
taro	tick	tout	ugly	verb	want
tart	tide	town	ulan	vert	ward
task	tidy	tram	ulna	very	ware
tass	tier	trap	umbo	vest	warm
ta-ta	tiff	tray	unco	veto	warn
taut	tike	tree	undo	vial	warp
taxi	tile	trek	unit	vice	wart
teak	till	tret	unto	vide	wary
teal	tilt	trig	upas	view	wash
team	time	trim	upon	vile	wasp
tear	tine	trio	urdu	vill	wast
teat	tint	trip	urea	vine	watt
teem	tiny	trod	urge	viny	waul
teen	tire	trot	uric	viol	wave
teil	tiro	trow	urim	visa	wavy
tell	toad	troy	ursa	vise	waxy
temp	to-do	true	urus	vis,	weak
tems	toed	tsar	used	viva	weal
tend	toft	tuba	user	vlei	wean
tene	toga	tube	utah	vley	wear
tent	toil	tuck	uvea	voce	weed
term	told	tufa	vail	void	week
tern	toll	tuff	vain	vole	ween
test	tolu	tuft	vair	volt	weep
text	tomb	tuna	vale	vote	weft
than	tome	tune	vamp	wadd	weir
that	tone	turf	vane	wade	weld
thaw	tong	turk	vary	wadi	well
thee	tony	turn	vase	wady	welt
them	took	tush!	vast	waft	wend
then	tool	tusk	veal	wage	went
thew	toon	tutu	veda	waif	wept
they	toot	'twas	veer	wail	were
thin	tope	twee	vega	wain	wert

west	wick	wiry	wore	yawl	yule
what	wide	wise	work	yawn	ywis
when	wife	wish	worm	yaws	zany
whet	wild	wisp	worn	yean	zeal
whew!	wile	with	wort	year	zebu
whey	will	wive	wove	yelk	zend
whig	wilt	woad	wrap	yell	zero
whim	wily	wold	wren	yelp	zest
whin	wimp	wolf	writ	yoke	zeus
whip	wind	womb	wych	yolk	zinc
whir	wine	wont	xmas	yomp	zion
whit	wing	won't	x-ray	yoof	zoea
whiz	wink	wood	xyst	yore	zone
whoa!	winy	woof	yard	your	zoon
whom	wipe	wool	yare	yowl	zulu
whop	wire	word	yarn	yo-yo	

5-Letter Words

aalii	adder	agrin	altar	angle	argil
abaca	addle	agued	alter	anglo	argol
aback	adept	ahead	alula	angry	argon
abaoi	adieu	aheap	alway	anile	argot
abaft	admit	aider	amain	anim,	argue
abase	admix	aired	amass	anise	argus
abash	adobe	aisle	amate	anker	arian
abate	adopt	aitch	amaze	ankle	ariel
abbey	adore	alack!	amber	annex	aries
abbot	adorn	alarm	ambit	annoy	arise
abeam	adown	alate	amble	annul	armed
abele	adsum	album	ambon	anode	armor
abhor	adult	alder	ambry	antic	arnee
abide	adust	alert	ameer	antre	aroma
abies	aegis	algal	amend	anura	arose
abode	aerie	algid	ament	anvil	arran
abort	aesop	algum	amice	aorta	arras
about	affix	alias	amide	apace	array
above	afoot	alibi	amigo	apart	arris
abuse	afore	alien	amiss	apeak	arrow
abysm	afrit	align	amity	apery	arsis
abyss	after	alike	ammon	aphis	arson
acerb	again	alive	among	aping	aryan
ached	agami	allah	amort	apish	ascus
achor	agape	allay	amour	appal	ashen
acorn	agate	alley	ample	apple	ashes
acred	agave	allot	amply	apply	ashet
acrid	agent	allow	amuck	appui	asian
acted	aggro	alloy	amuse	april	aside
acton	agile	almug	ancle	apron	asked
actor	agist	aloes	ancon	apsis	asker
acute	aglet	aloft	andes	aptly	askew
adage	agnel	alone	anear	arack	aspen
adapt	agnus	along	anele	arbor	aspic
adays	agony	aloof	anent	areas	assay
addax	agora	aloud	angel	areca	asses
added	agree	alpha	anger	arena	asset

aster	ba'ath	bated	belly	blare	bogus
astir	babel	bathe	below	blase	bohea
astra	baboo	baton	bench	blast	boiar
ataxy	bacon	batta	benne	blaze	bolar
a-team	badge	batty	berme	bleak	bolas
atilt	badly	baulk	berry	blear	bolus
atlas	baggy	bavin	berth	bleat	boned
atoll	bairn	bawdy	beryl	bleed	bonne
atone	baize	bayed	beset	bleep	bonny
atony	baked	bazar	besom	blend	bonus
atrip	baker	beach	besot	bless	bonce
attar	balas	beads	betel	blest	booby
attic	baler	beady	beton	blind	books
audit	balmy	be-all	betle	blink	boose
auger	banal	beamy	bevel	bliss	boosy
aught	banco	beano	bezel	blite	booth
augur	bandy	beard	bhang	blitz	boots
aulic	banjo	beast	bible	bloat	booty
aural	banks	beaus	bidet	blobs	booze
auric	banns	beaux	bifid	block	boozy
avail	barbs	bedad!	bight	bloke	borax
avast	bared	bedel	bigly	blond	bored
avens	barge	bedew	bigot	blood	borer
avert	baric	bedim	bijou	bloom	boric
avion	barky	beech	biker	blown	borne
avoid	barmy	beefy	bilbo	blows	boron
await	baron	beery	bilge	blowy	bosky
awake	basal	befal	bimbo	blues	bosom
award	based	befit	binge	bluff	bossy
aware	basel	befog	biped	blunt	botch
awash	bases	began	birch	blurb	bothy
awful	basic	beget	birth	blurs	bough
awned	basil	begin	bison	blurt	bound
awner	basin	begum	bitch	blush	bourg
axial	basis	begun	biter	board	bourn
axile	bason	beige	black	boast	bouse
axiom	basse	being	blade	bodle	bouts
axled	basso	belay	blain	bogey	bowed
azyme	basta	belch	blame	boggy	bowel
azote	baste	belie	bland	bogie	bower
azure	batch	belle	blank	bogle	bowie

boxen	brize	buses	canon	chaff	chine
boxer	broad	busby	canto	chain	chink
boyar	brock	bushy	canty	chair	chirk
brace	broil	bussu	caper	chalk	chirm
brach	broke	butte	capon	champ	chirp
bract	brome	butty	capot	chank	chive
braid	brood	buxom	carap	chant	chode
brail	brook	buyer	carat	chaos	choir
brain	broom	by-end	cared	chape	choke
brake	brose	bylaw	carer	chapt	choky
braky	broth	byssi	caret	chard	chord
brand	brown	byway	carex	chare	chose
brank	bruin	caaba	cargo	charm	chuck
brant	bruit	cabal	carib	charr	chuff
brash	brunt	cabas	carle	chart	chump
brass	brush	cabby	carob	chary	chunk
brave	brute	caber	carol	chase	churl
bravo	budge	cabin	carom	chasm	churn
brawl	buffo	cable	carry	chaya	chuse
brawn	buffy	cabob	carse	cheap	chute
braxy	buggy	cacao	carte	cheat	chyle
braze	bugle	cache	carus	check	chyme
bread	build	cacti	carve	cheek	cibol
break	built	caddy	caste	cheep	cider
bream	bulge	cadet	catch	cheer	cigar
breed	bulgy	cadge	cater	chela	cilia
brent	bulky	cadre	cates	chert	cinch
breve	bulla	caeca	catty	chess	cippi
briar	bully	cairn	caulk	chest	cirri
bribe	bulse	cairo	cause	chian	civet
brick	bunch	calid	cavil	chica	civic
bride	bunny	calif	cavin	chich	civil
brief	burgh	calve	cd-rom	chick	clack
brier	burin	calyx	cease	chico	claim
brill	burke	camel	cedar	chide	clamp
brine	burly	cameo	celts	chief	clang
bring	burnt	canal	cense	child	clank
brink	burry	can-do	cento	chill	clary
briny	bursa	candy	ceorl	chimb	clash
brise	burse	canny	chaco	chime	clasp
brisk	burst	canoe	chafe	china	class

clave	colly	cower	crook	cymar	demon
clean	colon	cowry	croon	cynic	demos
clear	color	coyly	crore	czech	demur
cleat	colza	coypu	cross	daddy	dense
cleek	comer	cozen	croup	daily	depot
cleft	comet	crack	crowd	dairy	depth
clepe	comic	craft	crown	daisy	derby
clerk	conch	crake	crude	dalek	derma
click	condo	cramp	cruel	dally	deter
cliff	coney	crane	cruet	daman	deuce
climb	conge	crank	crumb	damar	devil
clime	conic	crape	crump	dance	dhole
cling	cooee	crash	cruse	dandy	diana
clink	cooie	crass	crush	daric	diary
cloak	coomb	crate	crust	darky	diced
clock	co-opt	crave	crwth	datum	dicer
cloff	copal	crawl	cryer	dauby	dicky
cloke	coped	craze	crypt	daunt	dicta
clomb	copra	crazy	cubeb	davit	didst
clone	copse	creak	cubic	dazed	dight
close	copsy	cream	cubit	deary	digit
cloth	coral	credo	cuddy	death	digyn
cloud	corky	creed	cuish	debar	diked
clout	corny	creek	culch	debit	dilly
clove	corps	creel	cully	debut	dimly
clown	corse	creep	cumin	decad	diner
clubs	corve	crepe	cupel	decay	dingo
cluck	cosen	crept	cupid	decoy	dingy
clump	cosey	cress	curdy	decry	dirge
clung	couch	crest	curer	dedal	dirty
coach	cough	crick	curia	defer	disco
coact	could	cried	curio	deify	ditch
coaly	count	crier	curry	deign	ditto
coast	coupe	crime	curse	deism	ditty
coati	coup,	crimp	curst	deist	divan
coble	court	crisp	curve	deity	diver
cobra	coved	croak	cutch	delay	divot
cocoa	cover	crock	cutis	delft	dixie
codex	covet	croft	cycad	delta	dizen
coign	covey	crone	cycle	delve	dizzy
colic	covin	crony	cyder	demit	docks

dodge	dress	dying	elogy	erato	faced
dogal	drest	eager	elope	erect	facer
doggo	drier	eagle	elude	ergot	facet
dogma	drift	eagre	elvan	erica	faddy
doily	drill	eared	elves	erode	fadge
doing	drily	early	email	erose	faery
dolly	drink	earth	embay	erred	fagot
donna	drive	easel	embed	error	faint
donor	droit	eaten	ember	eruct	fairy
dooly	droll	eater	emend	erupt	faith
doric	drone	eaves	emery	eskar	fakir
dorse	droop	eblis	emmet	esker	false
dotal	drops	ebony	empty	essay	famed
doter	dross	,clat	enact	estop	fancy
dotty	drove	edema	ender	etern	farad
doubt	drown	edged	endow	ether	farce
dough	druid	edict	endue	ethic	farcy
douse	drunk	edify	enema	ethos	fatal
dowdy	drupe	edile	enemy	ethyl	fated
dowel	druse	educe	enjoy	etwee	fatly
dower	dryad	educt	ennui	eucre	fatty
dowle	dryer	eerie	enrol	evade	fatwa
downy	dryly	egest	entia	evens	faugh
dowry	ducal	egger	ensky	event	fault
dowse	ducat	egret	ensue	every	fauna
dozen	duchy	eider	enter	evict	favor
dozer	dully	eight	entry	evoke	favus
draff	dulse	eikon	enure	exact	feast
draft	dummy	eject	envoy	exalt	feaze
drain	dumpy	eland	eolic	excel	fecal
drake	dunce	elate	epact	exeat	feces
drama	duper	elbow	ephah	exert	feign
drank	duple	elder	ephod	exile	feint
drape	durra	elect	ephor	exist	felly
drave	durst	elegy	epoch	expel	felon
drawl	dusky	elemi	epode	extol	femur
drawn	dusty	elfin	epopt	extra	fence
dread	dutch	elide	epsom	exude	fenny
dream	dwale	elite	equal	exult	feoff
drear	dwarf	elmen	equip	eyrie	ferae
dregs	dwell	,loge	erase	fable	feral

24

ferny	fjord	fluty	frock	gassy	glass
ferry	flail	flyer	frond	gated	glave
fesse	flair	foamy	front	gaudy	glaze
fetal	flake	focal	frore	gauge	gleam
fetch	flaky	focus	frost	gault	glean
feted	flame	fogey	froth	gaunt	glebe
fetid	flamy	foggy	frown	gauze	gleby
fetor	flank	foist	fruit	gauzy	glede
fetus	flare	folio	frump	gawky	gleed
fever	flash	folly	frush	gayal	gleet
fewer	flask	foray	fudge	gayly	glide
fibre	flawy	force	fugal	gazel	glint
fichu	flaxy	fordo	fugue	gazer	glitz
field	fleam	forge	fully	gecko	gloat
fiend	fleck	forgo	fumid	geese	globe
fiery	fleer	forky	fungi	gelid	gloom
fifer	fleet	forme	funky	gemma	glory
fifth	flesh	forte	funny	gemmy	gloss
fifty	flick	forth	furor	genet	glove
fight	flier	forty	furry	genie	gloze
filch	flies	forum	furze	genii	gluey
filer	fling	fossa	furzy	genre	glume
filly	flint	fosse	fusee	genus	gnarl
filmy	flirt	found	fusel	get-up	gnarr
filth	float	fount	fusil	ghaut	gnash
final	flock	frail	fussy	ghost	gnome
finch	flood	frame	fusty	ghoul	godly
finer	floor	franc	fuzee	giant	going
finis	flora	frank	fuzzy	giber	goods
finny	floss	frank	gabel	gibus	goody
fiord	flour	fraud	gable	giddy	goose
firer	flout	freak	gaily	gigot	gorge
firry	flown	freed	galea	gipsy	gorse
first	fluff	freer	galop	girth	gorsy
firth	fluid	fresh	gamey	given	gouda
fishy	fluke	friar	gamin	giver	gouge
fisty	flume	fried	gamma	glade	gourd
fitch	flung	frill	gamut	glady	gouty
fitly	fluor	frisk	gaper	glair	gowan
fives	flush	frith	gappy	gland	graal
fixed	flute	frizz	garth	glare	grace

grade	growl	halve	herse	house	ileum
graff	grown	hanch	hewer	hovel	iliac
graft	gruel	handy	hider	hover	ilium
grail	gruff	haply	hight	howel	image
grain	grume	happy	hilar	huffy	imago
graip	grump	hards	hilly	hulky	imaum
grand	grunt	hardy	hilum	hullo	imbed
grant	guano	harem	hindu	hully	imbue
grape	guard	harpy	hinge	human	impel
graph	guava	harry	hinny	humid	imply
grapy	guess	harsh	hippy	humor	inane
grasp	guest	harum	hired	humph!	inapt
grass	guide	haste	hirer	humpy	incog
grate	guild	hasty	hitch	humus	incur
grave	guile	hatch	hives	hunch	incus
gravy	guilt	hater	hoard	hunks	index
graze	guise	hatti	hoary	hurly	india
great	gulag	haugh	hobby	hurra!	indie
grebe	gular	haulm	hocus	hurry	indue
greed	gulch	haunt	hodge	hurst	inept
greek	gules	haven	hoick	husky	inert
green	gully	hawse	hoist	hussy	infer
greet	gumbo	hazel	holla!	hutch	infix
grice	gummy	heady	hollo!	huzza!	ingot
gride	gunny	heald	holly	hyads	inkle
grief	guppy	heard	homer	hydra	inlay
grill	gusto	heart	homey	hydro	inlet
grime	gusty	heath	honor	hyena	inner
grimy	gutta	heave	hoofs	hymen	inset
grind	gypsy	heavy	hooky	hyoid	inter
gripe	gyral	hedge	hoppy	hyper	inure
grist	gyrus	heigh!	horal	hyrax	inurn
groan	habit	helix	horde	hyson	iodic
groat	hades	hello!	horny	iambi	ionic
groin	haily	helot	horse	ichor	irade
groom	hairy	helve	horsy	ictus	irate
grope	hakim	hemal	horus	ideal	irish
gross	halal	hence	hotel	idiom	irons
group	hallo!	henna	hough	idiot	irony
grout	halma	herby	hound	idler	islam
grove	halos	heron	houri	idola	islet

issue	juror	laden	leavy	lithe	lunch
istle	jutty	ladle	ledge	litre	lunge
itchy	kaaba	lager	ledgy	lived	lupus
ivied	kafir	laird	leech	liver	lurch
ivory	kalif	laity	legal	lives	lurid
ixtle	karob	lamed	leggy	livid	lusty
jabot	kauri	lance	leman	livre	lying
jaggy	kayak	lande	lemma	llama	lymph
jalap	kebab	lanky	lemon	loach	lynch
japan	kedge	lapel	lemur	loamy	lyric
jasey	keeve	lapse	lento	loath	macaw
jaunt	kelpy	larch	leper	lobar	macer
jawed	kerne	lardy	lepta	lobby	macho
jelly	ketch	large	letch	lobed	macle
jemmy	keyed	largo	lethe	local	macro
jenny	khaki	larum	levee	locus	madam
jerid	kinky	larva	level	lodge	madia
jerky	kiosk	laser	lever	lofty	madly
jesus	knack	lasso	levin	logan	madre
jetty	knarl	latch	lewis	logic	magic
jewel	knave	later	liana	logos	magma
jewry	knead	latex	libel	lolly	mahdi
jiffy	kneed	lathe	liber	looby	maize
jigot	kneel	lathy	libra	loofa	major
jingo	knell	latin	licit	loose	maker
jinks	knelt	laugh	liege	loris	malar
joint	knife	laura	lieve	lorry	malay
joist	knock	laver	ligan	loser	malic
joker	knoll	lawny	light	lotus	mamma
jolly	knout	laxly	liken	louse	maned
jorum	known	layer	lilac	lousy	manes
joust	knubs	lazar	limbo	lover	mange
judas	knurl	leach	limit	lowed	mango
judge	kodak	leady	linen	lower	mangy
juice	kooky	leafy	liner	lowly	mania
juicy	koran	leaky	lingo	loyal	manis
julep	kraal	learn	links	lucid	manly
jumbo	kudos	lease	lisle	lucky	manna
jumpy	label	leash	lisse	lucre	manor
junta	labia	least	lists	lumpy	manse
junto	labor	leave	liter	lunar	manus

27

maori	mezzo	moose	muzzy	night	oases
maple	miaul	moper	myope	nimby	oaten
march	micro	moral	myops	ninny	oaths
marge	midge	morel	myopy	ninon	obeah
marly	midst	morse	myrrh	ninth	obese
marry	might	mossy	nabob	niobe	occur
marsh	milan	motet	nacre	nisan	ocean
maser	milch	mothy	nadir	nitre	ocher
mason	milky	motif	naiad	nitry	ochre
massy	mimic	motor	naive	nival	ochry
match	mince	motto	naked	nizam	ocrea
mater	miner	mould	namer	nobby	oddly
matin	minim	moult	nandu	noble	odeon
matte	minor	mound	nappy	nobly	odeum
matty	minus	mount	nasal	nodal	odium
maund	mirth	mourn	nasty	noddy	odour
mauve	misdo	mouse	natal	noils	offal
mavis	miser	mouth	natch	noise	offer
maxim	misty	mover	natty	noisy	often
mayor	miter	mower	naval	nomad	ogham
mazer	mitre	mucky	navel	nonce	ogler
mealy	mixed	mucus	navew	nones	oiled
means	mixen	muddy	navvy	noose	oiler
meant	mixer	mufti	nawab	norse	olden
mease	mizen	muggy	needs	north	oleic
mecca	modal	mulch	needy	nosed	olive
medal	model	mulct	neese	notch	ombre
media	modem	mulsh	negro	noted	omega
medoc	modus	mummy	negus	novel	onion
melee	mogul	mumps	neigh	noway	onset
melon	mohur	munch	nerve	noyau	oozed
mercy	moire	mungo	nervy	nudge	opera
merge	moist	mural	netty	nulla	opine
merit	molar	murex	never	nurse	opium
merle	monad	murky	newel	nutty	optic
merry	monde	murry	newly	nylon	orach
meshy	money	muser	nexus	nymph	orang
mesne	monte	muses	niche	oaken	orate
metal	month	music	nidor	oakum	orbed
meter	moody	musky	nidus	oared	orbit
metre	moony	musty	niece	oasis	order

oread	paddy	payer	piked	pocky	prize
organ	padre	peace	pilau	podgy	probe
oriel	paean	peach	pilaw	poesy	proem
orion	pagan	peaky	pilch	point	promo
orlop	pains	pearl	piles	poise	prone
ormer	paint	pease	pilot	poker	prong
ornis	palea	peaty	pinch	polar	proof
orpin	palmy	pecan	piney	polka	prose
orris	palpi	pedal	pinna	polyp	prosy
oscan	palsy	pekoe	pious	poppy	proud
oscar	panda	penal	piped	porch	prove
osier	paned	pence	piper	porer	prowl
otary	panel	penis	pipit	pores	proxy
other	panic	penny	pique	porgy	prude
otter	pansy	peony	pitch	porno	prune
ought	papal	perch	pithy	porte	psalm
ouija	papaw	perdu	pivot	poser	pseud
ounce	paper	peril	pixel	posit	pshaw
ousel	pappy	perky	pixie	posse	psoas
outdo	parch	perry	pizza	pouch	psora
outer	pared	petal	place	poult	pubes
outgo	parer	petit	plack	pound	pubic
outr,	parry	petto	plaid	power	pudgy
ouzel	parse	petty	plain	prank	puffy
ovary	party	pewee	plait	prase	pukka
ovate	pasha	pewit	plane	prate	pulpy
overt	pass,	pharo	plank	prawn	pulse
ovine	pasta	phase	plant	preen	punch
ovoid	paste	phial	plash	press	punic
ovolo	pasty	phlox	plate	price	punka
ovule	patch	phone	plead	prick	pupae
owing	pated	photo	plica	pride	pupal
owlet	paten	phyla	pluck	prier	pupil
owner	paths	piano	plumb	prima	puppy
ox-eye	patin	piaza	plume	prime	purge
oxide	patty	picra	plump	prink	purse
oxlip	pause	picul	plumy	print	pursy
ozone	paver	piece	plush	prior	pussy
paced	pavid	piend	pluto	prise	putid
pacer	pawed	piety	plyer	prism	putty
pacha	payee	pigmy	poach	privy	pygmy

pylon	raged	recto	rifle	rowan	salse
quack	rainy	recur	right	rowdy	salts
quaff	raise	redan	rigid	rowel	salty
quail	rajah	redly	rigor	rower	salve
quake	raked	reedy	riled	royal	salvo
quaky	raker	reefy	rinse	ruble	sambo
qualm	rally	reeky	ripen	ruche	sandy
quark	ramee	reeve	risen	ruddy	sapan
quart	ramie	refer	riser	rugae	sapid
quash	ranch	refit	rishi	ruler	sapor
quasi	range	refix	risky	rumba	sappy
quean	raphe	regal	rival	rumen	sasin
queen	rapid	reign	rivel	rummy	satin
queer	raspy	reins	river	runic	satyr
quell	ratch	relax	rivet	rupee	sauce
quern	rated	relay	roach	rural	saucy
query	ratel	relet	roast	rushy	saved
quest	rater	relic	robin	rusty	saver
queue	rathe	relit	robot	rutty	savin
quick	ratio	remit	rocky	saber	savor
quiet	ratty	renal	rodeo	sable	savoy
quill	raved	renew	roger	sabot	sawer
quilt	ravel	rente	rogue	sabre	saxon
quint	raven	repay	roman	sacre	sayer
quire	raver	repel	romeo	sadly	scala
quirk	ravin	reply	rondo	sahib	scald
quite	rawly	rerun	rooky	saiga	scale
quits	rayed	reset	roomy	saint	scall
quoin	rayon	resin	roost	sajou	scalp
quoit	razor	retch	rooty	saker	scaly
quota	reach	retro	roper	sakia	scamp
quote	react	revel	roric	salad	scant
quoth	ready	revet	rosin	salep	scapa
rabbi	realm	rheum	rotor	sales	scape
rabid	reast	rhomb	rouge	salic	scapi
raced	reave	rhumb	rough	salix	scare
racer	rebec	rhyme	round	sally	scarf
radar	rebel	riant	rouse	salmi	scarp
radii	rebus	rider	roust	salon	scart
radio	rebut	ridge	route	salop	scatt
radix	recap	ridgy	rover	salsa	scaup

scaur	sepal	shear	shunt	skiff	slung
scena	sepia	sheen	shyly	skill	slunk
scene	sepic	sheep	sibyl	skink	slurp
scent	sepoy	sheer	sided	skimp	slush
scion	septa	sheet	sider	skint	slyly
scoff	serai	sheik	sides	skirl	smack
scold	serge	shelf	sidle	skirt	small
scoop	serif	shell	siege	skive	smalt
scope	serum	sherd	sieve	skulk	smarm
score	serve	shewn	sight	skull	smart
scorn	setae	shiah	silex	skunk	smash
scots	seton	shift	silky	skyey	smear
scott	set-to	shily	silly	slack	smell
scour	seven	shine	silty	slain	smelt
scout	sever	shiny	silva	slake	smile
scowl	sewer	ships	sitar	slang	smirk
scrag	sexes	shire	since	slant	smite
scram	shack	shirk	sinew	slash	smith
scrap	shade	shirt	singe	slate	smock
screw	shady	shive	sinks	slaty	smoke
scrip	shaft	shoal	sinus	slave	smoky
scrub	shake	shock	sioux	sleek	smolt
scrum	shako	shoes	siren	sleep	smote
scudi	shaky	shoon	sirup	sleet	snack
scudo	shale	shoer	sisal	slept	snail
sculk	shall	shone	sissy	slice	snake
scull	shalm	shook	sitar	slick	snaky
scurf	shaly	shoot	sit-in	slide	snare
seals	shame	shore	sit-up	slily	snarl
seamy	shank	shorl	sivan	slime	snary
sedan	shan't	shorn	sixth	slimy	sneak
sedge	shape	short	sixty	sling	sneer
sedgy	shard	shout	sizar	slink	snick
seedy	share	shove	sized	sloid	sniff
seems	shark	shown	skain	sloop	snipe
seine	sharp	showy	skald	slope	snood
seize	shave	shred	skate	slopy	snoop
semen	shawl	shrew	skean	slosh	snore
senna	shawm	shrub	skeet	sloth	snort
se¤or	sheaf	shrug	skein	sloyd	snout
sense	sheal	shuck	skied	slump	snowy

snuff	spasm	spots	stead	stove	swamp
soaky	spate	spout	steak	strap	swang
soapy	spats	sprat	steal	straw	sward
sober	spawl	spray	steam	stray	sware
socks	spawn	spree	steed	strew	swart
socle	speak	sprig	steel	stria	swart
soddy	spear	sprit	steep	strip	swash
sofas	speck	spume	steer	strop	swath
softa	specs	spumy	stela	strow	swear
soken	speed	spunk	stele	strum	sweat
solan	spell	spurn	steps	strut	swede
solar	spelt	spurt	stern	stuck	sweep
soles	spend	sputa	stich	stubs	sweet
sol-fa	spent	squab	stick	study	swell
solid	sperm	squad	sties	stuff	swept
solon	spice	squat	stiff	stump	swift
solos	spick	squaw	stile	stung	swill
solus	spicy	squib	still	stunk	swine
solve	spies	squid	stilt	stunt	swing
songs	spike	stack	sting	stupe	swink
sooth	spiky	stade	stink	style	swipe
sooty	spile	staff	stint	suave	swirl
soppy	spill	stage	stipe	suede	swish
sorry	spilt	stagy	stoat	suety	swiss
sorts	spine	staid	stock	sugar	swive
sorus	spiny	stain	stoic	suint	swoon
sough	spire	stair	stoke	suite	swoop
souls	spirt	stake	stole	sulci	sword
sound	spiry	stale	stoma	sulks	swore
souse	spite	stalk	stone	sulky	sworn
south	splay	stall	stony	sully	swung
sowar	split	stamp	stood	sumac	sylph
sower	spode	stand	stook	sunny	sylva
space	spoil	stare	stool	super	synod
spade	spoke	stark	stoop	surah	syrup
spain	spook	stars	store	sural	sythe
spait	spool	start	stork	surfy	tabby
spake	spoon	stash	storm	surge	tabes
spank	spoor	state	story	surgy	tabid
spare	spore	stave	stoup	surly	table
spark	sport	stays	stout	swain	taboo

tabor	tazza	thill	tinny	totem	troll
tache	teach	thine	tipsy	touch	tromp
tacks	tears	thing	tires	tough	troop
tacit	tease	think	tiros	touse	trope
tafia	techy	third	tisan	towed	troth
tails	teens	thole	tisri	towel	trout
taint	teepe	thong	titan	tower	truce
taken	teeth	thorn	tithe	toxic	truck
taker	teind	thorp	title	toxin	trull
takes	telic	those	tizri	toyer	truly
tales	tempo	thowl	toady	trace	trump
tally	tempt	three	toast	track	trunk
talon	temse	threw	today	tract	truss
talus	tench	thrid	toddy	trade	trust
tamed	tends	throb	toffy	trail	truth
tamer	tenet	throe	toils	train	tryst
tamil	tenon	throw	toise	trait	tubby
tamis	tenor	thrum	tokay	tramp	tuber
tammy	tense	thumb	token	trape	tudor
tango	tenth	thump	tolls	traps	tufts
tanks	tepid	thyme	toman	trash	tulip
tansy	terce	thymy	tonal	trass	tulle
tapas	terms	tiara	toned	trave	tumid
taper	terra	tibia	tonga	trawl	tumor
tapir	terse	ticks	tongs	tread	tuned
tapis	testy	tidal	tonic	treat	tuner
tardy	thane	tie-in	tonka	trend	tunic
tares	thank	tiers	ton-up	tress	tunny
targe	thaws	tiger	tools	trews	turbo
tarot	theca	tight	tooth	triad	turfs
tarry	theft	tiled	topaz	trial	turfy
tarsi	thegn	tiler	topee	trias	turns
tasse	their	tiles	toper	tribe	turps
taste	theme	tilth	topic	trice	turvy
tasty	there	timed	topsy	trick	tusks
taunt	therm	timer	toque	tried	tusky
taupe	these	times	torch	trier	tutor
tawer	thews	timid	torsk	trill	twain
tawny	thick	tinct	torso	trine	twang
taxed	thief	tined	torus	tripe	twank
taxer	thigh	tinge	total	trite	tweak

tweed	unsay	verso	vying	weigh	wince
twerp	unset	verst	wacke	weird	winch
twice	unsex	vertu	waddy	welch	windy
twill	untie	verve	wader	welsh	wings
twine	until	vesta	wafer	wench	winze
twins	unwed	vetch	wafts	wersh	wiped
twirl	upper	vexed	waged	whack	wiper
twist	upset	vexer	wager	whale	wired
'twixt	urban	viand	wages	wharf	wiser
twyer	urges	vibes	wagon	wheal	wispy
typic	urine	vicar	wails	wheat	witan
tyros	usage	video	waist	wheel	witch
udder	usher	views	waits	whelk	withe
uhlan	usual	viewy	waive	whelm	withy
ukase	usurp	vigil	waked	whelp	witty
ulcer	usury	vigor	waken	where	wives
ulnar	utter	villa	waker	which	wizen
ultra	u-turn	villi	wakes	whiff	woful
umbel	uvula	viola	waltz	while	woman
umber	vague	viper	wanly	whims	women
umbra	valet	virgo	wares	whine	woods
unapt	valid	virtu	warms	whirl	woody
unbar	value	virus	warns	whisk	wooer
unbid	valve	visit	warps	whist	woozy
uncap	vapid	visor	warty	white	wordy
uncle	vapor	vista	washy	whizz	works
uncut	varix	vital	waste	whole	world
under	vatic	vitta	watch	whoop	wormy
undue	vault	vivid	water	whore	worry
unfit	vaunt	vixen	waved	whorl	worse
unfix	vedic	vizor	waver	whort	worst
unhat	veiny	vocal	waves	whose	worth
unify	velar	vodka	waxed	whoso	would
union	veldt	vogue	waxen	widen	wound
unite	velum	voice	weald	widow	wrack
units	venal	vomer	weary	width	wrapt
unity	venom	vomit	weave	wield	wrath
unlit	venue	voter	webby	wigan	wreak
unman	venus	vouch	wedge	wight	wreck
unmew	verge	vowel	weedy	wiles	wrest
unpin	verse	vulva	weeds	willy	wring

wrist	xebec	years	yogis	yucca	zinco
write	xylem	yeast	yoick	yummy	zincy
wrong	yacca	yeats	yokel	zambo	zonal
wrote	yacht	yield	yonks	zamia	zoned
wroth	yager	yodel	young	zebec	zooid
wrung	yahoo	yodle	yours	zebra	zoril
wryly	yearn	yogin	youth	zibet	zymic

6-Letter Words

abacus	achene	aerify	air-gun	always	anneal
abaser	aching	aerose	airily	amadou	annual
abated	acquit	affair	airing	amazon	anoint
abater	across	affect	air-sac	ambler	answer
abatis	acting	affeer	airway	ambles	anthem
abbacy	action	affirm	aisled	ambush	anther
abbess	active	afflux	akimbo	amende	antiar
abbeys	actual	afford	alalia	amends	antler
abduce	acumen	affray	alarum	amenta	antlia
abduct	adagio	affuse	albata	amerce	anyhow
abject	adamic	afghan	albedo	amidst	anyway
abjure	addict	afield	albeit	amnion	aorist
ablaze	adduce	aflame	albino	amoeba	aortal
abloom	adhere	afloat	albite	amorce	aortic
aboard	adieus	afraid	albugo	amoret	apache
abound	adieux	afreet	alcaic	amount	apathy
abrade	adipic	afresh	alcove	ampere	apepsy
abroad	adjoin	agamic	aldern	amulet	aper‡u
abrupt	adjure	agaric	aldine	amuser	apexes
abseil	adjust	ageism	alegar	amylic	apiary
absent	admire	ageist	algine	ananas	apical
absorb	adnate	agency	algous	anarch	apices
absurd	adnoun	agenda	alight	anchor	apiece
abuser	adonis	aghast	aliped	ancone	aplomb
acacia	adorer	agnail	alkali	andean	apnoea
acajou	adrift	agnate	allege	anemia	apodal
acarus	adroit	agoing	allied	anergy	apogee
accede	advene	agouta	allies	angina	apoint
accent	advent	agouti	allude	angled	apollo
accept	adverb	aguish	allure	angler	appall
access	advert	aiglet	almond	angora	appeal
accord	advice	aigret	almost	anight	appear
accost	advise	airbag	alpaca	animal	append
accrue	adytum	air-bed	alpine	animus	aptote
accuse	aedile	airbus	alumni	ankled	arabic
acetic	aerate	air-dry	alveus	anklet	arable
achean	aerial	air-gas	alvine	annals	arbour

arcade	ascent	attend	azotic	bardic	beagle
arched	ashame	attest	babble	barŠge	beaked
archer	ashlar	attire	babies	barely	beaker
archil	ashler	attorn	babish	bargee	bearer
archly	ashore	attune	baboon	barium	beater
archon	askant	aubade	backer	barley	beauty
arctic	aslant	auburn	back-up	barman	beaver
ardent	asleep	augean	badger	barony	becalm
ardour	aslope	augite	baffle	barque	became
areola	aspect	augury	bagman	barrel	beckon
argala	aspick	august	bagnio	barren	become
argali	aspire	auntie	bagwig	barrow	bedaub
argent	assail	au-pair	bailie	barter	bedeck
argive	assent	aurate	bakery	baryta	bedell
argosy	assert	auriga	baking	basalt	bedlam
arguer	assess	aurist	balata	basely	bedrid
argute	assets	aurora	baldly	bashaw	bedrop
aright	assign	auteur	baleen	basket	beechy
armada	assist	author	balkan	basnet	beetle
armful	assize	autumn	ballad	basque	beeves
armlet	assoil	avanti	ballet	basset	befall
armour	assort	avatar	ballot	bateau	befell
armpit	assume	avaunt	balsam	bather	befool
arnica	assure	avenge	bamboo	bathos	before
aroint!	astern	avenue	banana	batist	befoul
around	asthma	averse	banded	batlet	beggar
arouse	astony	aviary	bandit	batman	begird
aroynt!	astral	avocet	bandog	batoon	begone
arrack	astray	avoset	bangle	batten	behalf
arrant	astrut	avouch	banian	batter	behave
arrear	astute	avowal	banish	battle	behead
arrect	aswarm	avower	banker	battue	behest
arrest	asylum	awaken	banner	bauble	behind
arride	ataxia	awakes	bantam	bawble	behold
arrive	atomic	aweary	banter	bawdry	behoof
arroba	atoned	aweigh	banyan	bayard	behove
arrowy	atonic	awhile	baobab	bay-rum	beiram
artery	atrial	awning	barbed	bazaar	belace
artful	atrium	axilla	barbel	beacon	belate
artist	attach	aye-aye	barber	beaded	belaud
ascend	attain	azalea	barbet	beadle	beldam

belfry	bibber	blight	botany	breton	bugler
belial	biceps	blithe	botchy	brevet	bulbed
belief	bicker	blonde	botfly	brewer	bulbel
belike	bicorn	bloody	bother	briary	bulbul
belled	bidder	bloomy	bothie	briber	bulimy
bellow	bidery	blotch	bottle	bribes	bullet
belong	biffin	blouse	bottom	bricky	bum-bag
belted	bifold	blower	bought	bridal	bumper
beluga	biform	blowze	bougie	bridge	bunchy
bemire	bigamy	blowzy	bounce	bridle	bundle
bemoan	biggin	bluffy	bounty	briery	bungle
benign	bijoux	bluish	bourne	bright	bunion
benumb	bikini	bobbin	bourse	briony	bunker
berate	billed	bobcat	bovine	briton	bunkum
berber	billet	bob-wig	bowery	broach	bunyon
bereft	billon	bodice	bowler	brogue	burbot
berlin	billow	bodied	bowman	broken	burden
beseem	bimana	bodily	bow-saw	broker	bureau
beside	binary	bodkin	bowyer	bromic	burgee
besmut	binate	boggle	boxing	bronze	burgle
bespot	binder	boiler	boyish	brooch	burgoo
bestir	bionic	bolary	brains	broody	burial
bestow	biotic	boldly	braise	broomy	buried
bestud	bireme	bolero	braize	browse	burlap
betake	bisect	bolide	branch	bruise	burner
betide	bishop	bolter	brandy	brumal	burnet
betony	bisque	bomber	branks	brushy	burrow
betook	bisson	bonbon	branny	brutal	bursar
betray	bistre	bonded	brassy	bryony	burton
better	bistro	bonder	bravos	bubble	bushel
bettor	biting	bonito	brawny	bubbly	busily
bewail	bitter	bon-mot	brayer	buboes	buskin
beware	bladed	bonnet	brazen	buccal	bussed
beweep	blamer	bon-ton	brazil	bucker	bustle
bewray	blanch	booted	breach	buckle	butler
beyond	blazer	bootes	breast	buckra	butter
bezant	blazon	borage	breath	buddle	button
bezoar	bleach	borate	breech	budget	buyout
biased	blench	border	breeks	budlet	buzzer
biases	blende	boreal	breeze	buffer	by-blow
biaxal	blenny	borrow	breezy	buffet	bye-bye

bye-law	calkin	capful	casual	centre	chigre
bygone	caller	capias	catena	cerate	childe
bylane	callet	caplin	catgut	cereal	chilli
byline	callid	capote	cathay	cereus	chilly
by-name	callow	capped	catkin	ceriph	chinch
bypass	callus	capric	cat-lap	cerise	chined
bypath	calmer	captor	catnap	cerite	chinky
by-play	calmly	carack	catnip	cerium	chintz
byroad	calmuc	carafe	catsup	ceroon	chippy
byssus	calque	carbon	cattle	certes	chisel
by-view	calves	carboy	caucus	ceruse	chitin
byword	calxes	carder	caudal	cestus	chiton
cabala	camber	careen	caudex	cesura	choice
cabman	camera	career	caudle	chabuk	choler
cachet	camlet	caress	caught	chacma	choose
cachou	canaan	caries	cauker	chafer	chopin
cackle	canard	carina	caulis	chaffy	choppy
cacoon	canary	carman	causal	chaise	choral
cactus	cancan	carmen	causer	chalet	chorea
caddie	cancel	carnal	causey	chalky	choree
caddis	cancer	carpal	cautel	chance	choric
cadent	candid	carpel	cavass	change	chorus
cadger	candle	carpet	caveat	chapel	chosen
caecal	candor	carpus	cavern	chappy	chough
caecum	canine	carrot	caviar	charge	chouse
caesar	caning	cartel	cavity	charry	chowry
cafard	canker	carter	cawass	chaser	chrism
caffre	cannie	carton	cayman	chaste	christ
caiman	cannon	carvel	cedara	chatty	chrome
caique	cannot	carver	cedran	cheery	chromo
cairus	canopy	casein	celery	cheese	chubby
cajole	cantab	casern	cellar	cheesy	chuffy
calash	canter	cashew	celled	chelae	church
calcar	canthi	casing	celtic	chemic	cicada
calces	cantle	casino	cement	cheque	cicely
calcic	canton	casket	censer	cherry	cicola
calefy	cantor	casque	censor	cherty	cicuta
calice	cantos	cassia	census	cherub	cierge
calico	canute	caster	cental	chetah	cinder
caliph	canvas	castle	center	chevin	cinema
calker	canyon	castor	centos	chigoe	cinque

cipher	clotty	collet	copeck	cotter	creeky
cippus	cloudy	collie	copier	cotton	creepy
circle	clough	collop	coping	cotyle	creese
circus	cloven	colony	copper	cougar	cremor
cirque	clover	colour	coptic	coulee	creole
cirrus	clumpy	colter	copula	coulis	cressy
cistus	clumsy	column	copyer	counts	cresta
cither	clutch	colure	coquet	county	cretin
citric	coaita	combat	corbel	couple	crewel
citron	coarse	combed	corbie	coupon	crinal
citrus	coatee	comber	corcle	course	cringe
civics	coaxal	comedo	corded	cousin	crises
civism	coaxer	comedy	cordon	covert	crisis
clammy	cobalt	comely	corium	coving	crispy
clamor	cobble	comfit	corked	coward	critic
claque	coburg	comfry	cornea	cowboy	croaky
claret	cobweb	coming	corned	cowled	crocus
clause	coccyx	comity	cornel	coyote	croppy
clawed	cocker	commit	corner	coypou	crosse
clayey	cocket	commix	cornet	cozily	crotch
cleans	cockle	common	corona	cradle	croton
cleave	cocoon	compel	corpse	crafty	crouch
clench	codded	comply	corpus	craggy	cruise
clergy	coddle	concur	corrie	crambo	cruive
cleric	codify	condom	corset	cranch	crumby
clever	codlin	condor	cortes	cranky	crummy
clich,	coerce	confab	cortex	cranny	crunch
client	coeval	confer	corvee	crasis	crural
cliffy	coffee	congee	corymb	crater	cruset
climax	coffer	conger	coryza	cravat	crusts
clinch	coffin	congou	cosher	craven	crusty
clingy	cogent	conics	cosily	craver	crutch
clinic	cognac	conoid	cosine	crayon	crying
clique	coheir	consul	cosmic	crazed	cubage
cloaca	cohere	convex	cosmos	creaky	cuboid
cloddy	cohort	convey	corral	creamy	cuckoo
cloggy	coifed	convoy	cosset	crease	cuddle
clonic	coiled	cooler	costal	creasy	cudgel
closer	coiner	coolie	coster	create	cuisse
closet	coldly	coolly	costly	crŠche	cuiter
clothe	collar	cooper	cottar	credit	culdee

culler	cutter	dapple	decker	dentil	dewlap
cullet	cuttle	daring	decoct	denude	dexter
cullis	cyanic	darken	decode	deodar	dhurra
culmen	cyclic	darkle	decree	depart	diadem
cultch	cyclop	darkly	deduce	depend	diaper
cultus	cygnet	darnel	deepen	depict	diatom
culver	cymbal	darner	deeply	deploy	dibber
cumber	cymose	darter	deface	depone	dibble
cummin	cymous	dartre	defame	deport	dicast
cumuli	cymric	darwin	defeat	depose	dicing
cuneal	cypher	dasher	defect	depute	dicker
cupful	cyprus	dative	defend	deputy	dickey
cupola	cystic	dauber	defier	deride	dictum
cupric	dabber	dawdle	defile	derive	diddle
cupula	dabble	day-bed	define	dermal	dieter
cupule	da-capo	dayboy	deform	dermic	differ
curacy	dacoit	dayfly	defray	dermis	digest
curare	dactyl	day-glo	defyer	dervis	digger
curari	daedal	dazzle	degree	descry	dilate
curate	daemon	deacon	dehort	desert	dilute
curdle	dagger	deaden	deific	design	dimity
curfew	daggle	deadly	deject	desire	dimple
curios	dagoba	deafen	delate	desist	dimply
curled	dahlia	deafly	delete	desman	dingey
curler	daimio	dealer	delian	despot	dinghy
curlew	dainty	dearly	delude	detach	dingle
cursed	dakoit	dearth	deluge	detail	dinner
curser	damage	debark	de-luxe	detain	diodon
curtal	damask	debase	delver	detect	diplex
curtly	dammar	debate	demain	detent	diploe
curtsy	damned	debile	demand	detest	dipnoi
curule	dampen	deblai	demean	detour	dipper
curved	damper	debris	dement	deuced	direct
curvet	damsel	debtor	demise	devest	disarm
cuscus	damson	decade	demure	device	disbar
cushat	dancer	decamp	denary	devise	disbud
custom	dandle	decant	dengue	devoid	discal
custos	danger	deceit	denial	devoir	discus
cutler	dangle	decent	denier	devote	dishes
cutlet	danish	decern	denote	devour	dismal
cut-off	dapper	decide	dental	devout	dismay

disown	dotard	dunlin	egesta	empire	entr,e
dispel	doting	dunner	egg-cup	employ	envier
distal	double	dupery	eggery	enable	enwrap
distil	doubly	duplex	eggler	enamel	eocene
disuse	douche	durbar	egg-nog	encage	eolian
ditone	doughy	duress	egoism	encamp	eozoic
divers	dowlas	durian	egoist	encase	eparch
divert	drachm	during	egress	encave	epaule
divest	draffy	durion	eighth	encore	epizoa
divide	dragon	duster	eighty	encyst	epodic
divine	draper	dynamo	either	endear	eponym
diving	drawee	dynast	elapse	ending	epopee
djerid	drawer	dysury	elated	endive	equate
docile	dreamt	eaglet	elater	endure	equery
docket	dreamy	earing	eldest	energy	equine
doctor	dreary	earthy	elects	enfold	equity
dodder	dredge	earwax	elench	engage	eraser
dodgem	dreggy	earwig	eleven	engine	erbium
dodger	drench	easily	elfish	engird	erebus
dogate	dressy	easter	elicit	engore	erenow
dog-day	drifty	eatage	elijah	engulf	eringo
dogged	drivel	eating	elisha	enigma	ermine
dogger	driver	,cart,	elixir	enjoin	erotic
doings	dropsy	echoes	elohim	enlace	errand
dolent	drosky	eclair	eltchi	enlist	errant
dollar	drossy	ectype	elvish	ennuye	errata
dolman	drouth	eczema	elytra	enough	eryngo
dolmen	drover	eddish	embalm	enrage	escape
dolour	drowse	edenic	embank	enrich	escarp
domain	drowsy	edging	embark	enrobe	eschar
domino	drudge	edible	emblem	enrole	eschew
donate	dry-rot	editor	embody	enroot	escort
donjon	ducker	efface	emboss	ensign	escudo
donkey	duello	effect	embrue	ensile	eskimo
doomed	duenna	effete	embryo	ensure	espial
dorian	duetto	effigy	emerge	entail	espied
dormer	duffel	efflux	emetic	entice	espier
dorsal	dugong	effort	,meute	entire	esprit
dosage	dulcet	effuse	,migr,	entity	essene
dossil	dumbly	efreet	empale	entomb	estate
dotage	dunder	egence	empery	entrap	esteem

esther	expose	farina	ferial	finial	flinch
estray	expugn	farmer	ferine	fining	flinty
etcher	extant	far-off	ferity	finish	flitch
ethics	extasy	far-out	ferret	finite	flocky
ethnic	extend	farrow	ferric	finned	floppy
etymic	extent	fasces	ferule	finner	floral
etymon	extern	fascia	fervid	fin-ray	floret
etypic	extort	fasten	fervor	fiorin	florid
euchre	extras	faster	fescue	firing	florin
euclid	ex-voto	fastly	festal	firkin	flossy
eulogy	eyelet	father	fester	firman	floury
eunuch	eyelid	fathom	fetich	firmly	flower
eureka	fabian	fatten	fetish	fiscal	fluent
eutaxy	fabled	fauces	fetter	fisher	fluffy
evenly	fabric	faucet	fettle	fishes	flunky
evicts	fa‡ade	faulty	feudal	fistic	flurry
evince	facete	faunal	fiacre	fitful	fluted
evolve	facial	favose	fianc,	fitter	flying
exarch	facile	favour	fiasco	fixity	fodder
excamb	facing	fawner	fibber	fizgig	foeman
exceed	factor	fealty	fibril	fizzle	foemen
except	facula	fecula	fibrin	flabby	foetal
excess	fading	fecund	fibula	flaggy	foetus
excise	faecal	feeble	fickle	flagon	fogeys
excite	faeces	feebly	fiddle	flamen	fogies
excuse	fagend	feeder	fidget	flange	foible
exempt	faggot	feeler	fierce	flashy	foiler
exhale	faille	feline	figure	flatly	foison
exhort	fairly	fellah	filial	flaunt	folder
exhume	fakeer	feller	filing	flavor	foliar
exocet	falcon	felloe	filler	flaxen	follow
exodus	fallow	fellow	fillet	flayer	foment
exogen	falter	felony	fillip	fleche	fondle
exotic	family	female	filose	fledge	fondly
expand	famine	fenced	filter	fleece	fontal
expect	famish	fencer	filthy	fleecy	footed
expend	famous	fender	finale	flense	forage
expert	fanged	fenian	finder	fleshy	forbid
expire	fanner	fennec	finely	flexor	forcat
expiry	fantom	fennel	finery	flight	forced
export	fardel	feodal	finger	flimsy	forcer

forego	frouzy	gaggle	gas-jet	girder	gomuti
forest	frowzy	gaiety	gasket	girdle	goodly
forger	frozen	gainer	gas-tar	glacis	gopher
forget	frugal	gainly	gather	gladly	gorget
forgot	fruity	'gainst	gaucho	glaive	gorgon
forked	frusta	gaited	gauger	glance	gospel
formal	frying	gaiter	gayety	glassy	gossip
former	fucoid	galaxy	gazing	glazer	gothic
formic	fuddle	galena	gazump	gleamy	gotten
forted	fulcra	galiot	gemini	glibly	govern
fossae	fulfil	galley	gemmae	glitch	grainy
fossil	fulgid	gallic	gender	glitzy	graith
foster	fuller	gallon	genera	gloomy	grakle
fother	fulmar	gallop	geneva	gloria	gramme
fought	fumble	galore	genial	glossy	grange
foully	fungal	galosh	genius	gloved	grassy
fourth	fungus	gambir	gentes	glover	grater
fowler	funnel	gambit	gentle	glowed	gratis
fox-bat	furfur	gamble	gently	glumly	gravel
fracas	furies	gambol	gentry	gluten	graver
fraise	furore	gaming	george	gnarly	graves
framer	furred	gammer	german	gnawer	gravid
freaky	furrow	gammon	germen	gneiss	grayly
freely	fusile	gander	gerund	gnomic	grazer
freeze	fusion	ganger	gestic	gnomon	grease
french	fusted	gangue	gewgaw	gnosis	greasy
frenzy	fustet	gannet	geyser	gobbet	greave
fresco	fustic	ganoid	ghetto	gobble	greedy
fretty	futile	gaoler	gibber	gobies	greeny
friday	future	garble	gibbet	goblet	grieve
friend	fylfot	garden	gibbon	goblin	grille
frieze	gabble	gargle	gibcat	go-cart	grilse
fright	gabies	garish	giblet	godson	grimly
frigid	gabion	garlic	gifted	godwit	grippe
fringe	gables	garner	giggle	goffer	grisly
fringy	gablet	garnet	giglet	goggle	gritty
frisky	gadder	garret	giglot	goiter	groats
frizzy	gadfly	garrot	gilder	goitre	grocer
frolic	gadoid	garter	gillie	golden	groggy
frosty	gaelic	gascon	gimlet	golfer	groove
frothy	gaffer	gasify	ginger	golosh	groped

grotto	hacker	hatted	hereat	holily	howdah
ground	hackle	hatter	hereby	holism	howler
grouse	hadjee	hauler	herein	holloa!	howlet
grovel	haemal	haunch	hereof	hollow	hoyden
grower	hagbut	havana	hereon	holpen	hubbub
growth	hagged	having	heresy	homage	huckle
groyne	haggis	havock	hereto	homely	huddle
grudge	haggle	haw-haw	heriot	homily	hugely
grumpy	haired	hawker	herman	homing	humane
grunge	halite	hawser	hermit	hominy	humble
grungy	halloh!	haybox	hernia	honcho	humbly
gueber	halloo!	hazard	heroes	honest	humbug
guebre	hallow	headed	heroic	honour	humeri
guffaw	hallux	header	herpes	hooded	hummer
guggle	halter	healer	heyday	hoofed	humour
guidon	halves	health	hiatus	hookah	humous
guilty	hamate	heaper	hibrid	hooked	humped
guinea	hamite	hearse	hiccup	hooker	hunger
guiser	hamlet	hearth	hickup	hooped	hungry
guitar	hammer	hearty	hidden	hooper	hunter
gulden	hamose	heater	hiding	hoopoe	hurdle
gullet	hamous	heathy	hiemal	hoopoo	hurler
gum-lac	hamper	heaven	higgle	hoover	hurrah
gunman	handed	heaver	higher	hooves	hurtle
gunnel	handle	hebrew	highly	hopper	husked
gunner	hanger	heckle	hilted	hopple	hussar
gun-wad	hang-up	hectic	hinder	horary	hussif
gurgle	hanker	hector	hindoo	horned	hustle
gurkha	hansom	heddle	hipped	horner	hyades
gurnet	happen	hedger	hippie	hornet	hyaena
gusher	harass	hegira	hispid	horrid	hybrid
gusset	harbor	heifer	hi-tech	horror	hyemal
guttae	harden	height	hither	horsey	hyetal
gutter	hardly	hejira	hitter	hosier	hymnal
guttle	harken	helmed	hoarse	hostel	hymnic
guzzle	harlot	helmet	hobble	hot-dog	hyphen
gymnic	harper	helper	hobnob	hotbed	hyssop
gypsum	harrow	hempen	hockey	houdah	iambic
gyrate	hassle	heptad	hodman	hourly	iambus
gyrose	hasten	herald	hoiden	housel	iatric
hackee	hatred	herbal	holder	houses	ibises

ice-saw	incult	innate	iritis	jewish	kamala
icicle	incuse	inning	ironer	jigger	kaolin
idiocy	indeed	inroad	isabel	jingal	karate
idolon	indent	inrush	island	jingle	karroo
ignite	indian	insane	isobar	jinnee	kavass
ignore	indict	insect	isopod	jobber	kawass
iguana	indigo	insert	issued	jockey	keblah
illude	indite	inside	italic	jocose	kecksy
illume	indium	insist	itself	jocund	keeled
imbibe	indoor	inspan	jabber	jogger	keenly
imbody	induce	instep	jacana	joggle	keeper
imbrue	induct	instil	jackal	joiner	kelpie
immesh	infamy	insult	jacket	jojoba	kelson
immune	infant	insure	jadish	joseph	keltic
immure	infect	intact	jagged	jostle	kennel
impact	infelt	intake	jaguar	jotter	kermes
impair	infest	intend	jailer	jovial	kermis
impale	infirm	intent	jailor	joyful	kernel
impark	inflow	intern	jangle	joyous	kersey
impart	influx	intone	jargon	jubate	kettle
impawn	infold	intuit	jarool	judaic	keypad
impede	inform	invade	jarrah	jugate	kibble
impend	infula	invent	jasper	juggle	kiblah
impish	infuse	invert	jaunty	jujube	kicker
implex	ingest	invest	jeerer	julian	kidnap
import	ingulf	invite	jejune	jumble	kidney
impose	inhale	invoke	jennet	jumper	killer
impost	inhere	inwall	jerboa	jungle	kilted
impugn	inhume	inward	jereed	jungly	kimono
impure	inject	inworn	jerked	junior	kincob
impute	in-joke	inwrap	jerkin	junker	kindle
inarch	injure	iodide	jersey	junket	kindly
inborn	injury	iodine	jessed	juries	kingly
inbred	ink-bag	iodism	jester	jurist	kipper
incage	inking	iodize	jesuit	justle	kirtle
incase	inkjet	iolite	jet-lag	justly	kismet
incest	ink-sac	ionian	jetsam	kaffir	kitbag
incise	inlaid	ireful	jet-set	kaftan	kit-cat
incite	inland	iridal	jetson	kaiser	kitten
income	inmate	irised	jewels	kalium	knaggy
incubi	inmost	irises	jewess	kalmuk	knight

knives	lankly	leased	lictor	lively	lovely
knobby	lanner	leaved	lidded	livery	loving
knotty	lapdog	leaven	lifter	living	lowery
knower	lapper	leaves	lights	lizard	lowest
kobold	lappet	lecher	lignum	llanos	lowing
koodoo	lapsed	ledger	ligula	lloyd's	lubber
kosher	laptop	leeway	ligule	loaded	lucent
kosmos	larder	legacy	ligure	loader	lucern
kraken	lariat	legate	likely	loafer	lugger
kroner	larvae	legato	liking	loathe	lumbar
kumara	larval	legend	lilies	loaves	lumber
kumiss	larynx	legged	limbed	lobate	lumper
kummel	lascar	legion	limber	lobule	lunacy
kung-fu	lasher	legist	limner	locale	lunate
laager	lassie	legume	limous	locate	lunged
labial	lastly	lender	limpet	locker	lunula
labium	lateen	length	limpid	locket	lunule
labour	lately	lenity	linden	lock-up	lupine
labret	latent	lenses	lineal	loculi	lurdan
labrum	lathen	lenten	linear	locust	lurker
laches	lather	lentil	lingam	lodger	lustra
lacing	latish	lentor	linger	loggat	lustre
lacker	latten	l'envoi	linhay	log-hut	lutine
lackey	latter	l'envoy	lining	loggia	lutist
lacmus	launch	lesion	linnet	loggie	luxate
lactic	laurel	lessee	lintel	loiter	luxury
lacuna	lavish	lessen	lionel	loment	lyceum
ladder	lawful	lesser	lionet	lonely	lydian
lading	lawyer	lesson	liplet	looker	lyrate
ladies	laxity	lessor	lipped	loosen	lyrist
lagoon	layman	lethal	liquid	lopper	macron
lagune	lazily	letter	liquor	lorate	macula
lamely	lazuli	levant	lisper	lorcha	madcap
lament	leaded	levier	lissom	lordly	madden
lamina	leaden	levite	listen	lorica	madder
lammas	leader	levies	litany	lorrie	madman
lanate	leafed	levity	lithia	losing	maenad
lancer	league	lewdly	lithic	lotion	maggot
lancet	leanly	liable	litmus	loudly	magian
landau	lean-to	libyan	litter	lounge	magilp
landed	leaper	lichen	little	louvre	magnet

magnum	marble	mayhem	merino	minnow	monism
magpie	marbly	maying	merlin	minter	monist
magyar	marcid	mazard	merlon	minuet	monkey
mahout	margin	mazily	merman	minute	monody
maiden	marina	meadow	mesial	mirage	moonie
maigre	marine	meagre	metage	mirror	moorya
mainly	marish	meanly	meteor	misery	mopish
make-up	marked	measly	method	misfit	mopsey
making	markee	meatus	methyl	mishap	morale
malady	marker	meddle	metope	mislay	morass
malaga	market	medial	metric	missal	morbid
malice	marmot	median	mettle	missee	moreen
malign	maroon	medica	miasma	mister	morgue
mallee	marque	medici	mickle	misuse	morion
mallet	marrow	medium	micron	mitral	mormon
mallow	marshy	medlar	midair	mitred	morose
maltha	marten	medley	midday	mitten	morris
mammae	martin	medusa	midden	mizzen	morrow
mammal	martyr	meekly	middle	mizzle	morsel
mammee	marvel	meetly	mid-leg	mobcap	mortal
mammon	mascle	megilp	midway	mobile	mortar
manage	mascot	megohm	mighty	mob-law	morula
manana	masher	megrim	mikado	mocker	mosaic
manchu	masked	mellay	milden	modern	moslem
manege	masker	melley	mildew	modest	mosque
manful	masque	mellow	mildly	modify	mostly
manger	masted	melody	milker	modish	motett
mangle	master	melter	milled	module	mother
maniac	mastic	member	miller	mohair	motile
manila	matrix	memoir	millet	moiety	motion
manioc	matron	memory	milter	molder	motive
manito	matted	menace	mimosa	molest	motley
manner	matter	menage	minced	mollah	motory
mantel	mature	mender	minder	moloch	mottle
mantis	maugre	menhir	mingle	molten	mottos
mantle	maundy	menial	minify	moment	mouldy
mantua	maybug	menses	minima	monday	mouser
manual	mayday	mental	mining	moneys	mouths
manure	may-dew	mentor	minion	monger	moving
maoris	mayfly	mercer	minish	mongol	mowing
maraud	mayhap	merely	minium	monied	mucose

mucous	namely	nibble	nuance	odious	orders
muddle	nankin	nicely	nubile	oedema	ordure
muesli	napery	nicene	nuchal	off-day	oregon
muffin	napkin	nicety	nuclei	offend	orgasm
muffle	narial	niched	nudely	office	orgeat
muftee	narrow	nickel	nudged	offing	orgies
mulish	narwal	nidify	nudity	offset	orient
mullen	naseby	niello	nugget	ogress	origin
mullet	nasute	nigger	nullah	oidium	oriole
mumble	natant	nilgau	number	oilery	orison
mummer	nation	nimble	nuncio	oil-gas	ormolu
mumper	native	nimbly	nursed	oldish	ornate
murder	natron	nimbus	nutant	omasum	oroide
murmur	nature	ninety	nutmeg	omelet	orphan
murrey	naught	nipper	nutria	omened	orphic
muscat	nausea	nipple	nuzzle	onager	orrery
muscle	neaped	nitric	nylgau	onrush	osiery
museum	nearly	nobody	oafish	onward	osmium
musing	neaten	noddle	obelus	ooidal	osmose
musket	neatly	nodose	obeyer	oolite	ospray
musk-ox	nebula	nodule	object	oology	osprey
muslim	necked	noetic	oblate	oomiak	ossein
muslin	nectar	noggin	oblige	opaque	ossify
mussel	needed	nomade	oblong	opened	ostler
muster	needle	nonage	oboist	opener	oswald
mutely	needly	non-ego	obolus	openly	otalgy
mutiny	negate	noodle	obsess	ophite	otiose
mutter	nephew	normal	obtain	opiate	otitis
mutton	nereid	norman	obtest	oppose	ouster
mutual	neroli	notary	obtuse	oppugn	outbid
muzzle	nerved	notice	occult	optics	outcry
myopia	nestle	notify	occupy	option	outfit
myosis	nether	notion	ocelli	orache	outing
myotic	netted	nougat	ocelot	oracle	outlaw
myriad	nettle	nought	ochrea	orally	outlay
myrtle	neural	nounal	octant	orange	outlet
myself	neuter	novena	octave	orator	output
mystic	new-age	novice	octavo	orchid	outrun
mythic	newark	noways	octroi	orchis	outset
naevus	newish	nowise	ocular	ordain	outsit
nailer	new-man	nozzle	oddity	ordeal	outvie

outwit	pander	patois	penmen	picket	pitier
ovally	pandit	patrol	penner	pickle	pitman
overdo	pantry	patron	pennon	picnic	pit-saw
ovisac	papacy	patten	penult	picric	pitted
owlery	papery	patter	penury	piddle	placer
owlish	papist	paunch	people	piecer	placid
oxalic	pappus	pauper	peplus	pierce	plague
ox-eyed	papula	paving	pepper	pigeon	plaice
ox-gall	papyri	pavior	pepsin	piggin	plaint
oxgang	parade	pavise	peptic	piglet	planet
oxygen	paraph	pawner	perdue	pignut	plaque
oxymel	parcel	paxwax	period	pigsty	plashy
oyster	pardon	payday	perish	pileus	plasma
pacify	parent	paynim	permit	pilfer	platan
packer	parget	peachy	perron	piling	platen
packet	pariah	peaked	person	pillar	plater
padder	parian	pea-nut	pertly	pillau	player
paddle	paring	pearly	peruke	pillaw	pleach
pagoda	parish	pebble	peruse	pillow	please
paigle	parity	pebbly	peseta	pilule	pledge
pakeha	parley	pecker	pester	pimple	pleiad
palace	parlor	pecten	pestle	pimply	plenty
palate	parody	pectic	petard	pineal	plenum
paleae	parole	pedant	petite	pinery	pleura
palely	parrot	pedate	petrel	pinion	plexus
paling	parsee	peddle	petrol	pinked	pliant
palish	parson	pedlar	pewter	pinnae	pliers
pallah	partly	pedler	pharos	pintle	plight
pallet	parvis	peeler	phases	pinyin	plinth
pallia	passee	peeper	phasis	piping	plough
pallid	passer	peewee	phlegm	pipkin	plover
pallor	passim	peewit	phloem	pippin	plucky
palmar	pastel	pegged	pholas	piquet	plumed
palmed	pastil	peg-top	phonic	piracy	plummy
palmer	pastor	pelage	phrase	pirate	plumpy
palpus	pastry	pellet	phylum	pisces	plunge
palter	patchy	peltry	physic	pisgah	plural
paltry	patent	pelvic	pianos	pistil	poachy
pampas	patera	pelvis	piazza	pistol	pocket
pamper	pathos	pencil	picked	piston	podded
panary	patina	penman	picker	pitchy	podium

poetic	portly	profit	purity	rachis	rapids
poetry	posset	proleg	purple	racial	rapier
poiser	postal	prolix	purser	racily	rapine
poison	poster	prompt	pursue	racing	rappee
police	pot-ale	propel	purvey	racker	rapper
policy	potash	proper	putlog	racket	rarefy
polish	potato	proser	putrid	racoon	rarely
polish	potboy	proven	putter	raddle	rarity
polite	poteen	prover	puzzle	radial	rascal
polity	potent	pruner	pygarg	radish	rasher
pollan	pother	prying	python	radium	rashly
polled	potion	pseudo	quagga	radius	rasper
pollen	potman	psyche	quaggy	raffia	rasure
pollex	potter	public	quaint	raffle	rather
polony	pottle	pucker	quaker	rafter	ratify
polype	pounce	puddle	quango	ragged	rating
polypi	pouter	puddly	quarry	ragman	ration
pomace	powder	puffer	quarte	ragout	ratios
pomade	praise	puffin	quarto	raider	ratite
pommel	prance	pug-dog	quartz	railer	ratlin
poncho	prater	puisne	quasar	raiser	rat-pit
ponder	praxis	puling	quaver	raisin	rattan
pongee	prayer	pulkha	queasy	raking	ratten
ponies	preach	pullet	quench	rakish	ratter
poodle	precis	pulley	quince	ramble	rattle
poonac	prefer	pulpit	quinoa	ramify	ravage
pooper	prefix	pumice	quinsy	ramjet	ravine
poorly	prepay	pummel	quirky	rammer	raving
pop-art	presto	pumper	quitch	ramose	ravish
popery	pretor	punchy	quiver	ramous	rawish
popgun	pretty	pundit	quorum	ramrod	razzia
poplar	priced	punish	quoter	ramson	reader
poplin	priest	punkah	quotha!	ranche	really
popper	primal	punter	qwerty	rancho	realty
poppet	primer	puppet	rabbet	rancid	reaper
porgie	primly	purely	rabbin	random	reason
porism	primus	purfle	rabbis	ranger	reaver
porker	prince	purger	rabbit	rankle	rebate
porous	priory	purify	rabble	rankly	rebeck
portal	prison	purism	rabies	ransom	rebuff
porter	privet	purist	raceme	ranter	rebuke

recall	regain	renter	revert	roamer	rueful
recant	regale	reopen	review	roarer	ruffle
recast	regard	repaid	revile	robber	rufous
recede	regent	repair	revise	robust	rugate
recent	reggae	repand	revive	rochet	rugged
recess	regime	repass	revoke	rocker	rugose
recipe	regina	repast	revolt	rocket	rugous
recite	region	repeal	reward	rococo	ruiner
reckon	regius	repeat	rexine	rodent	ruling
recoil	reglet	repent	rhesus	roller	rumble
record	regnal	repine	rheumy	romaic	rummer
recoup	regret	report	rhinal	romish	rumour
rector	rehash	repose	rhymer	rondel	rumple
rectum	rehear	repute	rhythm	ronion	rumpus
re-echo	reject	rescue	rialto	ronyon	runlet
redact	rejoin	reseat	riancy	roofer	runnel
redcar	relate	resect	ribald	rooted	runner
redden	relent	resent	ribbed	ropery	runnet
reddle	relict	reship	ribbon	ropily	runrig
redeem	relief	reside	riches	rosary	rushes
red-eye	relier	resign	richly	rosery	ruskin
red-hot	relish	resile	riddle	rosiny	russet
redial	relive	resiny	riding	roster	rustic
redout	relume	resist	rifely	rostra	rustle
redraw	remain	resorb	rifler	rotary	sachem
reduce	remake	resort	rigger	rotate	sachet
reechy	remand	result	rigour	rotten	sacker
reeded	remark	resume	rillet	rotund	sacque
reefer	re-mark	retail	rimple	rouble	sacral
refill	remedy	retain	ringed	rouche	sacred
refine	remind	retake	ringer	rubber	sacrum
reflex	remiss	retard	rinser	rubble	sadden
reflux	remora	retina	rioter	rubied	saddle
refold	remote	retire	ripely	rubies	safari
reform	remove	retort	ripple	rubigo	safely
re-form	rename	return	riprap	rubine	safety
refuel	renard	retuse	rising	rubric	sagely
refuge	render	revamp	risker	rudder	sagger
refund	rennet	reveal	ritual	ruddle	sailer
refuse	renown	revels	rivage	ruddoc	sailor
refute	rental	revere	rivery	rudely	sakieh

salaam	savant	script	seemer	server	shelve
salami	savine	scroll	seemly	sesame	shelvy
salary	saving	scummy	seesaw	sestet	sherry
salify	savory	scurfy	seethe	set-off	shewed
salina	savour	scurry	seggar	setose	shield
saline	sawfly	scurvy	seiner	settee	shifty
saliva	saw-pit	scutch	seizer	setter	shi'ite
sallow	sawyer	scutum	seizin	settle	shiner
salmis	saying	scythe	sejant	set-up	shinty
salmon	scabby	sea-cat	seldom	severe	shiver
saloon	scaled	sea-cow	select	severn	shoaly
saloop	scaler	sea-dog	seller	sŠvres	shoddy
salter	scanty	sea-ear	selves	sewage	shoppy
saltly	scapus	sea-eel	semite	sewing	shored
salute	scarab	sea-egg	semola	sexism	should
salver	scarce	sea-fir	senary	sexist	shovel
salvor	scarfs	sea-fox	senate	sexton	shower
samara	scarry	sea-god	sendal	sexual	shrewd
samian	scathe	sealer	sender	shabby	shriek
samite	scenic	seaman	send-up	shadow	shrift
samlet	scheik	seamer	seneca	shaggy	shrike
samosa	scheme	sea-mew	senega	shaken	shrill
sampan	schism	seance	senile	shaker	shrimp
sample	schist	searce	senior	shalli	shrine
sandal	scilla	search	sennit	shaman	shrink
sandix	sconce	seared	senora	shammy	shrive
sandyx	scorch	season	sentry	shamoy	shroud
sanies	scorer	seaway	septet	shanny	sicken
sanity	scoria	secant	septic	shanty	sickle
sanjak	scotch	secede	septum	shaper	sickly
santon	scoter	secern	sequal	sharer	siding
sapper	scotia	second	sequin	shaver	sienna
sarong	scrape	secret	seraph	sheafy	sierra
sasine	scrawl	sector	serene	shears	siesta
sateen	screak	secund	serial	sheath	sifter
satiny	scream	secure	series	sheave	signal
satire	screed	sedate	seriph	sheeny	signer
satrap	screen	seduce	sermon	sheers	signet
saturn	screes	seeded	seroon	shekel	signor
saucer	scribe	seeing	serous	shelfy	silage
savage	scrimp	seeker	serval	shelly	silent

silica	skurry	smugly	sordid	sponge	stamen
silken	slabby	smutch	sorely	spongy	stanch
silure	slaggy	smutty	sorrel	spooky	stanza
silvan	slangy	snaggy	sorrow	spoony	stapes
silver	slated	snappy	sorter	sporan	staple
simian	slater	snarer	sortie	spotty	starch
simile	slaver	snatch	souled	spouse	stared
simmer	slavic	sneaky	source	sprain	starer
simnel	slayer	snivel	sourly	sprang	starry
simony	sleave	snobby	sovran	sprawl	starve
simoom	sleaze	snooze	sowans	spread	stated
simoon	sleazy	snorer	sowens	spring	static
simous	sledge	snouty	spadix	sprint	statue
simper	sleeky	snuffy	sparry	sprite	status
simple	sleepy	snugly	sparse	sprout	staves
simply	sleety	soaked	sparta	spruce	stayer
sinaic	sleeve	soaker	spathe	sprung	steady
sinewy	sleezy	socage	spavin	spunge	steamy
sinful	sleigh	social	specie	spurge	steely
singer	slicer	socket	speech	sputum	steepy
single	slider	sodden	speedy	squall	steeve
singly	slight	sodium	spence	squama	stelae
sinker	sliver	sodomy	sphere	square	stench
sinner	slogan	soever	sphery	squash	steppe
sinter	sloppy	soffit	sphinx	squawk	stereo
siphon	slouch	soften	spider	squeak	sticky
sippet	slough	softly	spigot	squeal	stifle
sirdar	sloven	soiree	spilth	squill	stigma
sirius	slowly	solace	spinal	squint	stilly
sirrah	sludge	solder	spined	squire	stingo
siskin	sludgy	solely	spinel	squirm	stingy
sister	sluice	solemn	spinet	squirt	stipes
sitcom	sluicy	soleus	spinny	stable	stitch
sitter	slushy	solver	spiral	stably	stithy
sizing	smiler	sombre	spired	stacte	stiver
skater	smirch	somite	spirit	staffs	stodge
skerry	smiter	sonant	splash	stager	stodgy
sketch	smithy	sonata	spleen	stagey	stocks
skewer	smoker	sonnet	splice	stairs	stoker
skinny	smooth	soothe	splint	staith	stolen
skiver	smudge	sophie	spoken	stalky	stolid

stolon	stumpy	sunset	tackle	tartar
stoned	stupid	superb	tactic	tarter
stoner	stupor	supine	taenia	tartly
stones	sturdy	supper	tag-rag	tasker
stooge	stylar	supple	t'ai-chi	tassel
stop-go	stylet	supply	tailed	taster
storax	stylus	surely	tailor	tatter
storer	stymie	surety	taking	tattle
storey	suable	surtax	talcky	tattoo
stormy	subdue	survey	talent	taurus
strain	sublet	sutile	talion	tautog
strait	submit	sutler	talker	tavern
strake	suborn	suttee	tallow	tawdry
strand	subset	suture	talmud	tawery
strass	subtle	swampy	tamely	t-cloth
strata	subtly	swardy	tamine	teacup
strath	suburb	swarth	taminy	teapot
strawy	subway	swathe	tamper	teapoy
streak	succor	sweaty	tam-tam	tearer
stream	sucker	sweepy	tan-bed	teasel
street	suckle	swerve	tandem	teaser
stress	sudden	swinge	tangle	tea-set
striae	suffer	swipes	tangly	teated
strict	suffix	switch	tanist	tea-urn
stride	sugary	swivel	tanner	tedder
strife	suitor	sylvan	tannic	tedium
strike	sulcus	symbol	tannin	teemer
string	sullen	syndic	tan-pit	teethe
stripe	sultan	syntax	tanrec	teller
strive	sultry	syphon	tan-vat	telson
stroke	sumach	syriac	tappet	temper
stroll	summer	syrian	target	temple
strong	summit	syrinx	targum	tenant
strove	summon	syrupy	tariff	tender
struck	sunbow	system	tarpan	tendon
struma	sunday	syzygy	tarpon	tennis
strung	sunder	tabard	tarpum	tenrec
stubby	sundew	tablet	tarsal	tensor
stucco	sundry	tabour	tarsia	tented
studio	sunken	tabret	tarsus	tenter
stuffy	sunlit	tabula	tartan	tenure

tepefy	threat	timous	tonsor	trepan
teraph	threne	tinder	tooter	tressy
tercel	thresh	tinges	toothy	tribal
teredo	thrice	tingle	topper	tricky
terete	thrift	tinker	topple	trifid
tergal	thrill	tinkle	tories	trifle
termly	thrips	tinman	torpid	trigon
terror	thrive	tinner	torpor	trigyn
tester	throat	tinsel	torque	trilby
tetchy	throne	tipcat	torrid	trimly
tether	throng	tippet	tosser	trinal
tetrad	throve	tipple	toss-up	triple
tetter	thrown	tiptoe	tother	triply
teuton	thrush	tiptop	totter	tripod
thaler	thrust	tirade	toucan	tripos
thanks	thwack	tiring	touchy	triton
thatch	thwart	tissue	toupee	triune
thebes	thymol	titbit	toupet	trivet
thecal	thymus	tither	tousle	triune
theine	thyrse	titled	touter	trocar
theism	thyrsi	titter	towage	troche
theist	tibial	tittle	toward	trogon
thence	ticket	tmesis	towery	trojan
theory	tickle	tocsin	toyman	trolly
theses	tidbit	toddle	tracer	troops
thesis	tidily	toffee	traces	trophi
thetis	tie-dye	toggle	trader	trophy
thewed	tiepin	toiler	tragic	tropic
thieve	tierce	toilet	trance	trough
thinly	tie-rod	toller	tranny	troupe
thirst	tie-wig	tomato	trapan	trover
thirty	tiffin	tomaun	trapes	trowel
thisbe	tights	tombac	trashy	truant
thorax	tilery	tombak	travel	trudge
thorny	tiling	tomboy	travis	truism
thorpe	tiller	tom-cat	treaty	trumps
though	tilter	tomtit	treble	trusty
thowel	timber	tom-tom	trebly	trying
thrall	timbre	tongue	tremor	tsetse
thrash	timely	tonite	trench	t-shirt
thread	timist	tonsil	trendy	tubful

tubing	tyrant	unhurt	unship	upside
tubule	tyrian	unhusk	unshod	upsoar
tucker	ubiety	uniped	unsold	upward
tucket	uglily	unique	unstop	uranic
tufted	ullage	unisex	unsung	uranus
tugger	ulster	unison	untidy	urbane
tulwar	ultimo	united	untold	urchin
tumble	umbles	uniter	untrod	uremia
tumefy	umlaut	unjust	untrue	ureter
tumour	umpire	unkind	untune	urgent
tumult	unable	unknit	unused	urinal
tundra	unbend	unlace	unveil	ursine
tuning	unbias	unlade	unwary	usable
tunnel	unbind	unless	unwell	usance
turban	unbolt	unlike	unwept	useful
turbid	unborn	unlink	unwind	usurer
turbot	uncase	unload	unwise	uterus
tureen	uncial	unlock	unworn	utmost
turfen	uncoil	unmake	unwrap	utopia
turgid	uncord	unmask	unyoke	uvular
turkey	uncork	unmeet	upbear	vacant
turner	uncurl	unmixt	upbind	vacate
turnip	undine	unmoor	upcast	vacuum
turret	undoer	unpack	upcoil	vagary
turtle	undone	unpaid	upcurl	vagina
turves	unduly	unread	update	vainly
tuscan	uneasy	unreal	uphill	valise
tusked	uneven	unrest	uphold	vallar
tusker	unfair	unripe	upkeep	valley
tussle	unfelt	unrobe	upland	valour
tuyŠre	unfold	unroll	uplift	valuer
twelve	unfree	unroof	up-line	valved
twenty	unfurl	unroot	uplink	vamper
twiggy	ungird	unruly	upmost	vandal
twinge	unglue	unsafe	uppish	vanish
twitch	ungual	unsaid	uprear	vanity
two-ply	unhand	unseal	uprise	vapour
tympan	unholy	unseat	uproar	varied
typhus	unhood	unseen	uproot	varlet
typify	unhook	unsent	uprush	vassal
typist	unhung	unshed	upshot	vastly

vatful	vilely	wadmal	wealth	wieldy
vaward	vilify	waffle	weapon	wifely
veined	vinery	wafter	wearer	wigeon
velcro	vinous	waggle	weasel	wigged
vellum	vinose	waggon	weaver	wigwam
velvet	violas	waiter	weazen	wilder
vendee	violet	wainer	webbed	wildly
vender	violin	walker	web-eye	wilful
vendor	virago	waller	wedded	wilily
vendue	virgin	wallet	weeder	willow
veneer	virile	wallop	weekly	wimble
venery	virose	wallow	weeper	wimple
venial	virtue	walnut	weever	wincer
venose	visage	walrus	weevil	wincey
venous	viscid	wampum	weight	winder
venter	viscum	wander	welder	window
verbal	visier	wanion	welkin	wind-up
verger	vision	wanter	welter	winery
verify	visual	wanton	wether	winged
verily	vitals	wapiti	whaler	winker
verity	vitric	warble	whammy	winkle
vermin	vittae	war-cry	wharfs	winner
vernal	vivace	warden	wheeze	winnow
versed	vivify	warder	wheezy	winsey
versus	vizier	warily	whence	winter
vertex	voiced	warmer	wherry	wintry
vesper	voider	warmly	wheyey	wisdom
vessel	volant	warmth	whilom	wisely
vestal	volley	warner	whilst	wisher
vested	volume	warped	whimsy	withal
vestry	volute	warper	whiner	wither
vetchy	voodoo	warren	whinny	within
viable	vortex	washer	whisky	witted
vibrio	votary	waster	whiten	wivern
victim	votive	watery	whites	wizard
victor	vox-pop	wattle	wholly	wobble
vicuna	voyage	wax-end	whoops!	wobbly
vielle	vulcan	waylay	wicked	woeful
viewer	vulgar	way-out	wicker	wolves
vigour	wabble	weaken	wicket	wombat
viking	waddle	weakly	widely	wonder

wonted	wreath	yarrow	yuppie	zigzag
wooded	wrench	yclept	zaffre	zincky
wooden	wrests	yearly	zander	zipper
wooing	wretch	yeasty	zareba	zircon
woolly	wright	yellow	zealot	zither
worker	writer	yeoman	zebeck	zodiac
wormed	writhe	yeomen	zechin	zonary
worrit	wrongs	yester	zenana	zonate
worsen	wyvern	yields	zenith	zonule
worser	xyloid	yoicks!	zephry	zouave
worthy	xystus	yonder	zereba	zounds!
wraith	yankee	yttria	zeugma	zygoma

7-Letter Words

aaronic
abalone
abandon
abattis
abaxial
abdomen
abetter
abiding
abietic
abigail
ability
abluent
abolish
abreast
abridge
abroach
abscess
abscind
abscond
absence
absolve
abstain
abusive
abysmal
abyssal
academy
acantha
acclaim
accompt
account
accurse
accused
accuser
acerous
acetate
acetify
acetous

achaean
achieve
acicula
acidify
acidity
acolyte
aconite
acquire
acreage
acrobat
acrogen
actable
actinia
actinic
actress
actuary
actuate
acutely
acyclic
adagial
adamant
adamite
adapter
addable
addible
address
adducer
adenoid
adherer
adhibit
adipose
adjourn
adjudge
adjunct
adjurer
admiral
admirer

adopter
adulate
advance
adverse
advised
adviser
aeolian
aerator
aerobic
aerosol
affable
affably
affixal
afflict
affront
afghani
african
against
agatine
agatize
aggress
agilely
agility
agitate
agnomen
agonist
agonize
agraffe
aground
aidless
ailment
aimless
air-bath
air-cell
air-cool
airhead
airless

air-miss
airplay
airport
air-pump
air-raid
airtime
ajutage
alameda
alamode
...-la-
   mode
alarmed
albumen
alcalde
alcazar
alchemy
alcohol
alcoran
al-dente
alecost
alembic
alewife
alfalfa
algebra
aliform
aliment
alimony
aliquot
alkanet
alkoran
allegro
all-hail
allower
all-time
almanac
almoner
almonry

almsman
aloetic
already
alumina
alumnus
amalgam
amateur
amative
amatory
amazing
ambatch
ambient
amender
amenity
amentia
amiable
amiably
amianth
ammonia
amnesia
amnesty
amorino
amorous
amphora
amplify
ampulla
amusing
amusive
amylene
amyloid
anaemia
anaemic
anagoge
anagram
analect
analogy
analyse

analyst
anapest
anarchy
anatomy
anberry
anchovy
ancient
andante
andiron
anemone
aneroid
angelic
angelus
angevin
anglify
angling
angrily
anguish
angular
aniline
animate
animism
animist
aniseed
annates
annatto
annelid
annotto
annoyer
annuent
annuity
annular
annulet
annulus
anodyne
anomaly
anorexy

60

anosmia
another
antacid
ant-bear
ant-bird
antenna
ant-hill
anthine
anthrax
antique
antlion
antonym
anurous
anxiety
anxious
anybody
anywise
apanage
apatite
apepsia
aphasia
aphemia
aphesis
aphetic
aphonia
aphthae
apishly
apocope
apology
apostle
apparel
appease
applaud
appoint
apprise
approve
appulse
apricot
a priori
apropos
apsidal

apteryx
aptness
aquatic
aqueous
arabian
arachis
aramaic
aramean
araneid
arapaho
arbiter
arblast
arbutus
arcaded
arcanum
archaic
archery
archive
archway
arcuate
ardency
arduous
areolar
argyria
arietta
aridity
armhole
armiger
armilla
armoric
armoury
arnotto
arraign
arrange
arrival
arsenal
arsenic
artisan
artiste
artless
art-rock

aruspex
ascetic
ascites
ascribe
asexual
ashamed
asiatic
asinine
askance
asperse
asphalt
aspirer
asquint
assagai
assault
assayer
assegai
assizer
assuage
assumer
assured
assurer
astatic
asteria
astound
astrict
astride
asunder
atavism
atelier
atheism
atheist
atheous
athlete
athwart
atomism
atomist
atomize
atropal
atrophy
atropin

attach,
attaint
attempt
attract
auction
audible
audibly
auditor
augitic
augment
augural
aurated
aurelia
aureola
auricle
aurochs
auroral
auspice
austere
austral
autocar
avarice
avenger
average
averter
aviator
avidity
awarder
awfully
awkward
axially
axillar
axolotl
azimuth
azotise
azurite
azygous
baalism
baalite
babbler
babyish

babyism
baby-sit
baccate
bacchic
backing
baddish
badness
baffler
bagasse
baggage
bagging
bag-lady
bagpipe
bailiff
balance
balanus
balcony
baleful
ballade
ballast
balloon
bandage
bandana
bandbox
bandeau
bandlet
bandore
bandrol
bandsaw
baneful
banking
banquet
banshee
baptise
baptism
baptist
barbour
bar-code
bar-iron
bar-shot
barbule

bargain	bedevil	bespeak	biscuit	blucher	botcher
barilla	bedight	bestead	bismuth	blue-cap	bottine
bark-bed	bedizen	bestial	bistort	blue-gum	boudoir
barmaid	bedouin	bestrew	bittern	blueing	bouilli
barn-owl	bedroom	bethink	bitters	blunder	boulder
baronet	bedtime	betimes	bitumen	bluntly	bouncer
baroque	beechen	betoken	bivalve	bluster	bounded
barrack	beef-tea	betroth	bivouac	boarded	bounden
barrage	beehive	between	bizarre	boarder	bouquet
barrier	beeline	betwixt	blabber	boarish	bourdon
barwood	bee-moth	bewitch	blacken	boaster	bow-hand
barytes	beestie	bezetta	blackly	boat-fly	bowhead
barytic	beeswax	bezique	bladder	boatman	bowline
bascule	beggary	bibasic	blanket	bobtail	bowling
bashful	beghard	bicycle	blankly	bobstay	bowshot
basilar	begonia	bidding	blarney	bodeful	box-tree
bassoon	beguile	bifilar	blaster	body-bag	boxwood
bastard	beguine	big-bang	blatant	boggler	boycott
bastion	belgian	bigfoot	bleakly	boiling	boyhood
battery	believe	biggish	bleater	boletus	brabble
battish	bellman	bighorn	bleeper	bollard	bracing
bay-salt	bellied	bigness	blemish	bolster	bracken
bay-wood	bellite	bigoted	blesbok	bombard	bracket
bayonet	bellows	bigotry	blessed	bombast	bradawl
beached	beloved	biliary	blewits	bonanza	bragget
beaming	beltane	bilious	blinded	bondage	brahman
beanbag	belting	billion	blinder	bondman	brahmin
bearded	bemused	billman	blindly	bone-ash	braided
bearing	bencher	billowy	blinker	bonfire	brained
bearish	beneath	binacle	blister	bookman	bramble
beastly	benefit	bindery	bloated	bookish	brambly
beatify	benight	binding	bloater	booklet	bran-new
beating	benison	binocle	blossom	boorish	branchy
beauish	benzene	biogeny	blotchy	bootleg	branded
bebeeru	benzoin	biology	blotter	boracic	brander
because	bequest	biomass	bloused	boredom	brangle
becloud	bereave	biotaxy	blow-dry	borough	brasier
bed-post	berried	biplane	blowfly	boscage	brattle
bed-tick	beseech	bipolar	blowgun	boskage	bravado
bedding	besiege	birchen	blowzed	botanic	bravely
bedegar	besmear	biretta	blubber	botargo	bravery

bravura	broking	burgage	caesura	canakin
brawler	bromate	burgeon	cafe-bar	candent
brazier	bromide	burgess	caffein	candied
breadth	bromine	burghal	cahoots	candour
breaker	bronzed	burgher	caisson	canella
break-up	brothel	burglar	caitiff	cannery
breathe	brother	burmese	cajeput	cannula
breccia	brought	burning	cajoler	canonry
breeder	brownie	burnish	cajuput	cantata
brevier	bruiser	burrock	calamus	canteen
brevity	brusque	bursary	calcify	canthus
brewage	brutify	burthen	calcine	canting
brewery	brutish	bush-cat	calcite	cantlet
brewing	bryozoa	bushman	calcium	canvass
bribery	buckeye	bustard	caldron	canzone
bricole	buckish	bustler	calends	capable
bridoon	buckler	butcher	calibre	cap-a-pie
briefly	buckram	butient	calipee	caperer
brigand	bucolic	buttery	caliper	capital
brigate	budding	buttock	callboy	capitol
brimful	buffalo	butyric	calling	caprice
brimmer	buffoon	buxomly	callous	caprine
brinded	bugbear	buzzard	calmuck	capsize
brindle	bugloss	by-gones	calomel	capstan
bringer	builder	byssine	caloric	capsule
brinish	bulbous	cabaret	calotte	captain
brisket	bulimia	cabbage	caloyer	caption
briskly	bulldog	cabbala	caltrop	captive
bristle	bullace	cabined	calumba	capture
bristly	bullate	cabinet	calumet	caracal
british	bullion	caboose	calumny	caramel
brittle	bullock	cachexy	calvary	caravan
broaden	bulrush	cacique	calycle	caravel
broadly	bulwark	cackler	camaieu	caraway
brocade	bumpkin	cacolet	cambist	carbide
brocage	bungler	caddice	cambium	carbine
brocard	bunk-bed	cadence	cambric	carcass
brocket	bunting	cadenza	camelry	cardiac
broider	buoyage	cadmean	camphor	cardoon
broiler	buoyant	cadmium	campion	careful
brokage	burdock	caesium	camwood	cariboo

caribou	caterer	chablis	cheapen	cholera	clap-net
cariole	cat-fish	chabouk	cheaply	chooser	clapper
carious	cat-head	chaffer	cheater	chopine	clarion
carline	cathode	chagrin	checker	chopper	clarity
carlist	cathood	chaldee	cheddar	chorion	clasper
carlock	catling	chalice	cheerer	chorist	classic
carmine	catmint	chamade	cheerio	choroid	clatter
carnage	cat's-eye	chamber	cheerly	chrisom	clavate
carnify	cat's-paw	chamfer	cheetah	chromic	clavier
caroche	caudate	chamois	chemise	chronic	clay-pit
carolus	cauline	champac	chemist	chuckle	cleaner
carotid	caustic	chancel	chequer	chutney	cleanly
carouse	cautery	chancer	cherish	chylify	cleanse
carping	caution	chancre	cheroot	chylous	clearer
carrack	cavalry	changer	chervil	chymify	clearly
carrier	caveson	channel	chesnut	chymous	cleaver
carrion	caviare	chanter	chessel	ciliary	clement
carroty	cayenne	chantry	chested	cimbric	clerisy
cartage	cazique	chaotic	cheviot	cimeter	clerkly
cartoon	cedilla	chaplet	chevron	cindery	clicker
cart-way	cedrate	chapman	chiasma	cipolin	climate
carving	ceiling	chapped	chicane	circean	climber
cascade	celadon	chapter	chicken	circled	clinger
caseous	cellule	charade	chicory	circler	clinker
cashier	censure	charger	chiefly	circlet	clipper
cassada	centage	charily	chiffon	circuit	clivers
cassava	centaur	chariot	chignon	cirrose	cloacal
cassock	centime	charity	chikara	cissoid	closely
casting	centner	charmed	chiliad	cistern	closing
castled	central	charmer	chimera	citable	closure
cast-off	centric	charnel	chimere	citadel	clothes
casuist	century	charpie	chimney	cithara	clouded
catalan	ceramic	charpoy	chinese	cithern	clouted
catarrh	cereous	charqui	chinned	citizen	clovery
catawba	certain	charter	chipper	citrine	cloying
catbird	certify	chasmed	chirper	civilly	club-law
catcall	cerumen	chassis	chirrup	clachan	cluster
catcher	cervine	chasten	chisleu	clacker	clutter
catchup	cession	chateau	chlamys	clamant	clyster
catechu	cestoid	chattel	chloral	clamber	coagent
cateran	cetacea	chatter	chloric	clamour	coal-bed

coal-gas	colonel	concert	consort	corrupt
coal-pit	coloury	concise	consult	corsage
coal-tar	coltish	concoct	consume	corsair
coaming	columba	concord	contact	cortege
coaster	combine	concuss	contain	corvine
coating	combing	condemn	contemn	cosaque
coaxial	comfort	condign	contend	cosmism
cobbler	comfrey	condole	content	cossack
cocaine	comical	condone	contest	costard
cochlea	comique	conduce	context	costate
cockade	comitia	conduct	contort	costive
cockney	command	conduit	contour	costrel
cockpit	commend	condyle	control	costume
coconut	comment	confect	contuse	coterie
coctile	commode	confess	convene	cothurn
coction	commove	confest	convent	cotidal
codicil	commune	confide	convert	cottage
codilla	commute	confine	convict	cottier
codling	compact	confirm	convoke	cottony
coehorn	company	conflux	cookery	couchee
coeliac	compare	conform	coolish	coucher
coequal	compart	confuse	copaiba	cougher
coexist	compass	confute	copyist	couloir
cogency	compeer	congeal	copious	coulomb
cognate	compend	congest	coppery	coulter
cognize	compete	conical	coppice	council
cohabit	compile	conifer	coracle	counsel
cohibit	complex	conjoin	corcule	counter
coinage	complot	conjure	cordage	country
coition	comport	conjury	cordate	coupler
cojuror	compose	connate	cordial	couplet
coldish	compost	connect	cordite	coupure
colibri	compute	conning	cornice	courage
colicky	comrade	connive	cornish	courier
collate	conacre	connote	corolla	courser
collect	concave	conquer	coronal	courter
college	conceal	consent	coroner	courtly
collide	concede	consign	coronet	couvade
collier	conceit	consist	corpora	coverer
colloid	concept	console	correct	coveter
collude	concern	consols	corrode	cowbane

cowbell	crested	crumbly	cursing	dasyure	decorum
cow-calf	crevice	crumpet	cursive	daunter	decreer
cowhage	cribble	crumple	cursory	dauphin	decreet
cow-heel	cricket	crupper	curstly	dawdler	decrial
cowherb	cricoid	crusade	curtail	dawning	decrier
cowherd	crimper	crusado	curtain	daybook	decuman
cowhide	crimple	crusher	curvity	daycare	decuple
cowitch	crimson	cryptal	cushion	daylong	deedful
cowlick	cringer	cryptic	custard	daysman	deep-sea
cowling	cringle	crystal	custody	daystar	defacer
cowslip	crinite	ctenoid	cutaway	daytime	defamer
cow-tree	crinkle	cubhood	cuticle	daywork	default
coxcomb	crinoid	cubical	cutlass	dazzler	defence
coyness	cripple	cubicle	cutlery	deadeye	defiant
cozener	crisper	cubital	cutting	deadpan	deficit
crabbed	crispin	cuckold	cyanean	dead-pay	defiler
crab-oil	crisply	cudbear	cranium	dead-set	defined
cracked	crizzle	cudweed	cyclist	dealing	definer
cracker	croaker	cuirass	cycloid	deanery	deflect
crackle	crochet	cuisine	cyclone	deathly	deforce
cragged	crocket	cullion	cyclops	debacle	defraud
crammer	crofter	culprit	cynical	debased	defunct
cramped	crooked	culturf	cypress	debaser	degrade
crampon	cropper	culvert	cyprian	debater	degauss
cranage	croquet	cumerey	czarina	debauch	dehisce
cranial	crosier	cumshaw	dabbler	debouch	deicide
cranium	crossed	cumulus	dacoity	decadal	deictic
crankle	crossly	cuneate	daisied	decagon	deiform
crannog	crowbar	cunning	dakoity	decagyn	deistic
craunch	crowded	cupping	dallier	decanal	delaine
craving	crowned	cuprous	damnify	decapod	delayer
crawler	crozier	cuprite	damning	decease	delight
crazily	crucial	curable	dampish	deceive	deliver
creatin	crucify	curacao	dandify	decency	delphic
creator	crudely	curator	dangler	decided	deltaic
credent	crudity	curious	dappled	decider	deltoid
creeper	cruelly	curling	darkish	decidua	deluder
cremate	cruelty	currant	darling	decimal	demerit
cremona	cruiser	current	dashing	declaim	demesne
crenate	cruisie	currier	dashpot	declare	demigod
cresset	crumble	currish	dastard	decline	demirep

demonic	develop	dilator	disobey	dog's-ear
demotic	deviate	dilemma	dispark	dog-sick
denizen	devilry	diluent	dispart	dogskin
densely	devious	dimeter	display	dogtrot
density	devisee	dimmish	dispone	dogwood
dentate	deviser	dimness	disport	dolabra
dentine	devisor	dimpled	dispose	doleful
dentist	devolve	dimyary	dispute	dolphin
deodand	devoted	dinette	disrobe	doltish
deplete	devotee	diocese	disroot	domical
deplore	dewclaw	diorama	disrupt	dominie
deplume	dewdrop	diorite	dissect	donnish
deposer	dewfall	dioxide	dissent	doorway
deposit	dextral	diploma	distaff	dor-hawk
deprave	diabase	diplopy	distain	dormant
depress	diagram	dipolar	distant	doublet
deprive	dialect	diptych	distend	doubter
derange	dialist	direful	distich	douceur
derider	dialyse	dirt-bed	distort	doughty
deriver	diamond	dirtily	disturb	dovecot
dermoid	diapasm	dirt-pye	disyoke	dovelet
derrick	diarchy	disable	ditcher	dowager
dervish	diarian	disavow	dittany	dowered
descant	diarist	disband	diurnal	drachma
descend	dibbler	discage	diverge	draggle
descent	dice-box	discard	diverse	dragnet
deserve	dickens	discern	divider	dragoon
desirer	dictate	discoid	diviner	drainer
desktop	diction	discord	divisor	drapery
despair	dietary	discous	divorce	drastic
despise	dietist	discuss	divulge	draught
despoil	difform	disdain	dizzily	drawing
despond	diffuse	disease	djereed	drayage
dessert	digamma	disgust	dockage	drayman
destine	digging	dishing	doeskin	dreamer
destiny	digital	disjoin	dogcart	dredger
destroy	dignify	dislike	dogfish	dresser
detente	dignity	dislink	doggish	dribble
deterge	digraph	dismask	doggone	driblet
detract	digress	dismast	dog-hole	drifter
detrude	dilater	dismiss	dog-rose	drinker

drizzle
drizzly
dromond
dronish
droplet
dropper
drought
drouthy
drugget
druidic
drummer
drunken
dryness
dry-shod
dualism
dualist
duality
dubiety
dubious
ducally
duchess
ductile
dudgeon
dukedom
dulcify
dullard
dullish
dulness
dumpish
duncery
dungeon
dunnage
dunnish
dupable
durable
durably
duramen
durance
durmast
duskily
duskish

dustman
duteous
dutiful
duumvir
dweller
dwindle
dyewood
dye-work
dyingly
dynamic
dynasty
dyslogy
dysuria
dysuric
eagerly
eanling
earache
eardrop
eardrum
ear-hole
earldom
earless
earmark
earnest
earning
ear-pick
earring
earshot
earthen
earthly
easeful
eastern
easting
eatable
ebb-tide
ebonite
ebonize
ebriety
ecbatic
ecbolic
ecdysis

echelon
echidna
echinus
eclipse
eclogue
economy
ecstasy
ectopia
ectozoa
ectypal
edacity
edictal
edifice
edition
educate
eel-buck
eel-pout
effable
effendi
effulge
egg-bird
egg-flip
egotism
egotist
egotize
ego-trip
ejector
elastic
elation
elderly
elector
electro
elegant
elegiac
elegist
elegize
element
elevate
elf-bolt
elfland
elflock

elision
elixate
ellagic
ellipse
elogium
elohist
elusion
elusive
elusory
elysian
elysium
elytron
elytrum
elzevir
emanant
emanate
embargo
embassy
emblaze
embosom
embowel
embower
embrace
embroil
embrown
embryos
emerald
emerods
eminent
emotion
emperor
empiric
empower
empress
emprise
emptier
empyema
emulate
emulous
enactor
enamour

encenia
enchain
enchant
enchase
enclasp
enclave
enclose
encrust
endemic
endless
endlong
endmost
endogen
endorse
endower
end-user
endwise
energic
enfeoff
enforce
engaged
engorge
engraft
engrail
engrain
engrave
engross
enhance
enjoyer
enlarge
enliven
ennoble
enounce
enquire
enslave
ensnare
entasis
entente
enteric
enthral

enticer
entitle
entomic
entonic
entrail
entrain
entrant
entreat
entrust
entwine
entwist
e-number
envelop
envious
envenom
environ
epacrid
epacris
eparchy
epaulet
epergne
epicarp
epicene
epicure
epiderm
epidote
epigene
epigram
episode
epistle
epitaph
epithet
epitome
epizoan
epizoon
epochal
equable
equably
equally
equator
equerry

equinox	eupnoea	extatic	fancied	felting
erasion	evangel	extinct	fancier	fencing
erasure	evanish	extract	fancies	feodary
erecter	evasion	extreme	fanfare	feoffee
erector	evasive	extrude	fan-palm	feoffer
erectly	evening	exuviae	fantail	feoffor
erelong	evictor	exuvial	fantasm	ferment
eremite	evident	eyeball	faradic	fernery
ergoted	evolver	eyebrow	farceur	fern-owl
ericoid	exacter	eyelash	farcing	ferrugo
eristic	exactor	eyeless	fardage	ferrule
ermined	exalter	eyeshot	farming	fertile
erodent	examine	eyesore	farmost	fervent
erosion	example	eyewash	farness	fervour
erosive	excerpt	fabliau	farrago	festive
erratic	exciter	facette	farrier	festoon
errhine	exclaim	faction	farther	fetlock
erudite	exclude	factoid	fascine	feudary
escaper	excreta	factory	fashion	fewness
escheat	excrete	facular	fast-day	fianc,e
escuage	excuser	faculty	fatally	fiascos
esparto	execute	faddist	fateful	fibster
espouse	exegete	faddish	fatigue	fibrine
esquire	exergue	fadedly	fatling	fibroid
essayer	exhaust	faecula	fatness	fibrous
essence	exhibit	faience	fatuity	fictile
esthete	exigent	failing	fatuous	fiction
estival	exogamy	failure	faunist	fictive
estrade	expanse	faintly	faux-pas	fidgety
estreat	expense	fairily	fearful	fielder
estuary	expiate	fairing	feaster	fierily
etagŠre	explain	fairish	feather	fifteen
etching	explode	falcate	feature	fifthly
eternal	exploit	fallacy	febrile	fighter
etesian	explore	fallout	federal	figment
ethical	exposed	falsely	feeding	figural
ethmoid	exposer	falsify	feeling	figured
eugenic	expound	falsism	feigned	filbert
eulogic	express	falsity	feigner	filcher
eupepsy	expunge	famulus	felsite	filemot
euphony	exscind	fanatic	felspar	filiate

filibeg	flanker	flutist	forging	fritter	fuscous
filical	flannel	flutter	forgive	frizzle	fusible
filings	flapper	fluvial	forgoer	frizzly	fussily
filling	flaring	fluxion	forlorn	frocked	fustian
finable	flatten	flyover	formula	frogged	gabbler
finally	flatter	flypast	forsake	frontal	gabelle
finance	flaunty	foggage	fortify	fronted	gadwell
finback	flavour	fogyism	fortlet	frounce	gainful
finding	fleeced	foggily	fortune	froward	gaining
finesse	fleecer	foliage	forward	frustum	gainsay
finical	fleerer	foliate	fossick	fuchsia	gairish
finikin	fleetly	foliole	foulard	fuddler	galanga
finless	fleming	foolery	foumart	fuguist	galeate
finnish	flemish	foolish	founder	fulcrum	galenic
firearm	fleshed	footing	foundry	fulgent	galilee
firebox	flesher	footman	fourgon	fulling	galipot
firedog	fleshly	footpad	foveate	fulmine	gallant
firefly	fleuret	footway	fractal	fulness	galleon
fireman	flexile	fopling	fragile	fulsome	gallery
fire-new	flexion	foppery	frailty	fulvous	galling
firepan	flexure	foppish	framing	fumbler	galliot
fire-pot	flicker	forager	frankly	fumette	gallium
firstly	flighty	foramen	frantic	funeral	galloon
fishery	flipper	forayer	fraught	fungoid	gallows
fish-fag	flitter	forbade	freckle	fungous	galumph
fishgig	floater	forbear	freckly	funicle	gambier
fishing	flogger	forbore	freedom	funnily	gambler
fissile	floorer	forceps	freeman	furbish	gamboge
fission	florist	forcing	freight	furcate	gambrel
fissure	flotsam	forearm	freshen	furcula	gangway
fistula	flounce	foreign	freshet	furioso	gantlet
fitchet	flouter	foreleg	freshly	furious	garbage
fitchew	flowage	foreman	fretful	furlong	garbler
fitness	flowery	forerun	fretted	furmity	garboil
fitting	flowing	foresee	friable	furnace	gardant
fixable	fluency	foretop	fribble	furnish	garfish
fixedly	flunkey	forever	friezed	furrier	gargoil
fixture	fluoric	forfeit	frigate	furring	garland
flaccid	fluster	forfend	fringed	furrowy	garment
flaming	flutina	forgave	frisian	further	garnish
flaneur	fluting	forgery	frisket	furtive	garotte

garrots	ghastly	glottal	gradual	griskin
gaseity	gherkin	glottic	grafter	grisled
gaseous	ghostly	glottis	grained	gristle
gastric	giantly	glowing	gramary	gristly
gateway	giantry	glucina	grammar	grizzle
gaudily	gibbose	glucose	grampus	grizzly
gauffer	gibbous	gluteal	granary	grocery
gaulish	giddily	glutton	grandam	grogram
gauntly	giggler	glyphic	grandee	grogran
gavotte	gilding	glyptic	grandly	groined
gayness	gimbals	gnarled	granger	grooved
gazelle	gimblet	gnathic	granite	grossly
gazette	gingham	gnostic	grantee	grottos
gearing	ginseng	goatish	granter	groupie
gehenna	gipsies	gobbler	grantor	growler
gelatin	giraffe	goddess	granule	grubber
gelding	girlish	godhead	grapery	grudger
gelidly	gittern	godless	graphic	gruffly
gemmate	gizzard	godlike	grapnel	grumble
gemmule	glacial	godlily	grapple	grumous
general	glacier	godsend	grasper	grunter
generic	gladden	godship	gratify	gruyŠre
genesis	glamour	godward	grating	guanaco
genette	glaring	goitred	gravely	guarded
genetic	glazier	golfing	gravity	gudgeon
genevan	gleaner	gondola	grayish	guerdon
genipap	glebous	gonidia	grazier	guesser
genital	gleeful	goosery	grazing	guilder
genitor	gleeman	gordian	greatly	guildry
genteel	glimmer	gorilla	greaves	guipure
gentian	glimpse	gormand	grecian	gumming
gentile	glisten	goshawk	gremlin	gummous
genuine	glister	gosling	grenade	gunnery
genuses	glitter	gossipy	griddle	gunshot
geodesy	globate	gouache	griffin	gunwale
geogeny	globose	gourmet	griffon	gurnard
geogony	globous	goutily	grimace	gushing
geology	globule	grabber	grimily	guttate
georgic	glorify	gracile	grinder	guttler
germane	glosser	grackle	griping	guzzler
gesture	glossic	gradate	gripper	gymnast

habitat	harshly	heirdom	history	humoral	imbosom
habited	harvest	heiress	hoarder	hundred	imbowel
habitu,	hashish	helical	hobnail	hunting	imbower
hachure	hassock	helices	hoggish	hurried	imbrown
hackbut	hastate	hellish	holding	hurtful	imitant
hacking	hastily	helotry	holibut	husband	imitate
hackler	hatable	helpful	holiday	huskily	immense
hackney	hatchel	hemlock	holland	hussite	immerge
hacksaw	hatcher	henbane	holster	huswife	immerse
haddock	hatchet	hennery	homeric	hyaline	immoral
haggard	hateful	henotic	homonym	hyalite	impanel
haggish	hauberk	hepatic	honesty	hyaloid	impasse
haggler	haughty	herbage	hopeful	hydatid	impaste
halberd	haulage	herbose	hoplite	hydrant	impasto
halcyon	haunted	heretic	horizon	hydrate	impeach
halibut	haunter	hernial	hornlet	hydride	impearl
halidom	hautboy	heroine	horrent	hydrous	imperil
halyard	hauteur	heroism	hosanna	hygeian	impetus
hamitic	hawking	heroize	hoseman	hygiene	impiety
hammock	hazelly	heronry	hosiery	hymnody	impinge
hamster	headily	herring	hospice	iambize	impious
hanaper	heading	herself	hostage	iberian	implant
handful	headway	hessian	hostess	iceberg	implead
handily	healing	hetaera	hostile	icefoot	implore
handsel	healthy	hetaira	hostler	ichnite	impound
hands-on	hearing	hexagon	hot-line	iciness	impress
hanging	hearken	hexapla	hotness	ideally	imprest
hangman	hearsay	hexapod	hotspur	identic	imprint
hapless	hearted	hickory	housing	idiotic	improve
happily	hearten	hidalgo	howbeit	idolize	impulse
harbour	heathen	hideous	however	idyllic	imputer
hardily	heather	higgler	howling	igneous	inanity
hardish	heating	highway	hueless	ignoble	inboard
harelip	heavily	hilding	huffish	ignobly	inbreak
haricot	hebraic	hillock	hulking	illapse	inbreed
harmful	heckler	hilltop	humanly	illegal	incense
harmony	hectare	himself	humdrum	illicit	incisor
harness	hedging	hippish	humeral	illness	incivil
harpist	hedonic	hipster	humerus	imagery	incline
harpoon	heedful	hircine	humidly	imagine	inclose
harrier	heinous	hirsute	hummock	imbiber	include

incomer	initial	iricism	jollity	kirtled
incrust	injurer	iridian	jonquil	kitchen
incubus	inkhorn	iridium	jotting	knacker
incurve	inkling	irksome	journal	knagged
indexes	inlayer	ischium	journey	knarred
indexer	innerve	isolate	jouster	knarled
indices	inquest	isonomy	joyless	knavery
inditer	inquire	isthmus	jubilee	knavish
indoors	inquiry	italian	judaism	kneeler
indorse	inshore	iterate	judaize	knitter
inducer	insight	jacinth	judases	knobbed
indulge	insipid	jackass	jugated	knocker
indusia	insnare	jackdaw	juggler	knotted
indwell	inspect	jacobin	jugular	knowing
ineptly	inspire	jacobus	jump-jet	knuckle
inertia	install	jaconet	juniper	koumiss
inertly	instant	jaggery	jupiter	kreuzer
inexact	instate	jaghire	juryman	kursaal
infancy	instead	janitor	jussive	kyanize
infanta	insular	january	justice	labiate
infante	insurer	jargoon	justify	laconic
infeoff	integer	jasmine	kainite	lacquer
infidel	intense	jaspery	kalmuck	lacteal
inflame	interim	javelin	karaoke	lactine
inflate	intitle	jealous	katydid	lactose
inflect	intrant	jehovah	keelson	lacunae
inflict	introit	jejunum	keeping	lacunar
infulae	intrude	jellies	keramic	ladanum
ingesta	intrust	jemadar	kestrel	laggard
ingoing	intwine	jemidar	ketchup	laicize
ingraft	intwist	jeopard	khaliff	lakelet
ingrail	invader	jetties	khanate	lambent
ingrain	invalid	jewelry	khedive	lambkin
ingrate	inveigh	jobbery	killing	lamella
ingress	inverse	jocular	kindred	laminae
inhabit	inviter	jogging	kinetic	laminar
inhaler	invoice	joinery	kingdom	lampion
inherit	involve	joining	kinglet	lampoon
inhibit	inwards	jointed	kinless	lamprey
in-house	inweave	jointly	kinsman	landing
inhuman	iranian	jollily	kinsmen	languid

languor	legging	lignify	logical	lustral	mandate
laniary	leghorn	lignine	logwood	lustrum	mandrel
lantern	legible	lignite	lollard	lycopod	mandril
lanyard	legibly	limited	lombard	lyingly	mangler
lapelle	legitim	limiter	longing	lyrated	manhole
lapilli	legless	limosis	longish	lyrical	manhood
lapwing	leister	lineage	loosely	machete	manihot
larceny	leisure	lineate	lopping	machine	manikin
largely	lemming	lingual	lorgnon	maculae	manilla
largess	lengthy	lingula	lottery	madding	maniple
lashing	lenient	linkage	lounger	madeira	manitou
lasting	lentoid	linnean	loutish	madness	mankind
latchet	lentigo	linseed	lovable	madonna	manlike
latency	leonine	lioness	lowland	maestro	mannish
lateral	leopard	lionism	lowness	magenta	mannite
lathing	leprose	lionize	low-rise	maggoty	mansion
latrine	leprosy	liquate	loyally	magical	mantlet
lattice	leprous	liquefy	loyalty	magnate	manumit
laugher	lesbian	liqueur	lozenge	magnify	marabou
laundry	lethean	lissome	lucarne	mahatma	mariner
lawless	lettuce	literal	lucency	majesty	marital
lawsuit	leucoma	lithium	lucerne	malaise	marline
laxness	levator	lithoid	lucidly	malaria	marplot
lazaret	levelly	litotes	lucifer	malayan	marquee
leading	leveret	lituate	luckily	malefic	marquis
leafage	levitic	liturgy	luggage	malison	married
leaflet	lexical	livered	lugworm	mallard	marrowy
leagued	lexicon	loading	lullaby	malleus	marsala
leaguer	liaison	loather	lumbago	malmsey	marshal
leakage	liassic	loathly	lumping	maltese	martial
learned	liberal	lobated	lumpish	malting	martlet
learner	liberty	lobelet	lunated	maltman	masonic
leasing	library	lobelia	lunatic	mamelon	masonry
leather	librate	lobiped	lunette	mammary	massage
lechery	licence	lobster	lunular	mammoth	masseur
lectern	license	lobular	lunulet	manacle	massive
lection	licitly	lobworm	lupulin	manager	mastery
lecture	lidless	locally	lurcher	manakin	mastich
leeward	lighten	lockage	lurdane	manatee	mastiff
legally	lighter	lodging	lustful	manchet	mastoid
legatee	lightly	loftily	lustily	manchoo	matador

matelot	menisci	mindful	modicum	mortise
matin,e	menthol	mind-set	modiste	moselle
matrass	mention	mineral	modular	mothery
mattery	mercery	miniate	modulus	mottled
matting	mercies	minicab	moidore	mottoes
mattock	mercury	minicar	moisten	mouflon
maudlin	mermaid	minikin	mollify	moulder
maunder	merrily	minimum	mollusc	mounted
mawkish	mersion	miniver	mollusk	mourner
mawworm	meseems	minster	momenta	mousing
maxilla	message	mintage	monadic	mouthed
maximal	messiah	minuend	monarch	mouther
maximum	mestizo	miocene	moneyed	movable
mayoral	metayer	miracle	moneyer	movably
mazurka	metonym	mirific	mongrel	mowburn
mazzard	mettled	miscall	monitor	mucific
meadowy	miasmal	misdate	monkeys	muddily
mealies	microbe	misdeed	monkish	mueddin
meander	microhm	misdeem	monocle	muezzin
meaning	midland	misdoer	monodic	muffled
measled	midlent	miserly	monogyn	muffler
measles	midmost	misgive	monsoon	muggish
measure	midnoon	mislead	monster	mugwort
mechlin	midriff	mislike	montero	mulatto
meconic	midship	misname	monthly	mullein
medalet	midwife	misrule	moonish	mullion
meddler	migrant	missile	moorage	multure
mediate	migrate	missing	mooring	mumbler
medical	mileage	mission	moorish	mummery
mediums	milfoil	missive	moraine	mummify
medulla	miliary	mistake	morally	mumpish
medusae	militia	mistily	morassy	muncher
meeting	milkman	mistime	morceau	mundane
meiosis	milksop	mixable	mordant	muraena
melange	milling	mixedly	morisco	murices
melanic	million	mixture	morning	muriate
melilot	milreis	moanful	morocco	murkily
melissa	mimetic	mobbish	morphia	murrain
melodic	mimicry	mockery	morrice	murther
melting	minaret	modally	mortice	muscled
memento	mincing	modesty	mortify	muscoid

musical	needily	nomadic	obliger	olympic	organic
musrole	neglect	nomarch	obligor	omentum	organon
mustang	negress	nominal	oblique	omental	organum
mustard	negroes	nominee	obloquy	ominous	organza
mustily	negroid	nonagon	obovate	omnibus	orifice
mutable	neither	nonplus	obscene	oneness	orleans
mutably	nelumbo	nonsuit	obscure	onerary	orogeny
myalgia	nemesis	noology	observe	onerous	orology
mycelia	nemoral	noonday	obtrude	oneself	orotund
myeloid	neology	nooning	obverse	ongoing	orphean
mylodon	neptune	nosegay	obviate	onicolo	ortolan
myology	nervous	nostril	obvious	onwards	osculum
myotomy	nervure	nostrum	ocarina	oolitic	osiered
myrrhic	netball	notable	occiput	ootheca	osmanli
mystery	netting	notably	occlude	opacity	osmotic
mystify	network	nothing	oceanic	opacous	osseine
nacelle	neutral	nourish	ocellus	opaline	osselet
nailery	neutron	novella	octagon	opalize	osseous
naively	newness	novelty	octavos	opening	ossicle
naivete	newsman	nowhere	october	operant	ossific
nakedly	news-peg	noxious	octopod	operate	ossuary
namable	new-wave	nucleus	octopus	operose	ostiole
nankeen	nibbler	nullify	octuple	opinion	ostitis
naphtha	niblick	nullity	oculate	opossum	ostrich
napless	nictate	numbles	oculist	oppidan	otalgia
nardine	niggard	numeral	odalisk	opposed	otaries
narrate	nightly	nummary	oddment	opposer	otocyst
narthex	nilotic	nunnery	oddness	oppress	otolite
narwhal	ninthly	nunnish	odorous	optical	otolith
nasally	niobium	nuptial	oestrus	optimal	otology
nascent	nippers	nursery	offbeat	opulent	ottoman
nastily	nitrate	nurture	offence	opuntia	ourself
nattily	nitrify	nutcase	offense	opuscle	outcast
natural	nitrous	oakling	offerer	oration	outcome
naughty	niveous	oarsman	officer	oratory	outcrop
navvies	nocturn	obconic	off-road	orbital	outdare
nebulae	nodated	obelisk	ogreish	orchard	outdoor
nebular	nodding	obelize	oldness	orderer	outface
necklet	nodular	obesity	oldster	orderly	outfall
nectary	noisily	obliged	olitory	ordinal	outflow
needful	noisome	obligee	olivine	oregano	outgrow

outlast	overtop	pancake	parvise	peerage
outlier	oviduct	pandean	paschal	peeress
outline	oviform	pandect	pasquil	peevish
outlive	ovoidal	pandore	pasquin	pelagic
outlook	own-goal	panicle	passage	pelecan
outmost	oxidate	pannier	passant	pelican
outpost	oxidize	panoply	passing	pelisse
outpour	oxonian	pansies	passion	peloria
outrage	oxytone	panther	passive	peloric
outride	ozonize	pantile	pastern	peltate
outroot	pabular	pantler	pastime	penally
outrush	pabulum	papally	pasture	penalty
outsail	pacable	papilla	patcher	penance
outside	pacific	papulae	patella	penates
outspan	package	papular	paterae	pendant
outstay	packing	papyrus	pathway	pendent
outtalk	paction	parable	patient	pending
outvote	padding	paradox	patrial	penfold
outwalk	paddler	paragon	patriot	penguin
outward	paddock	parapet	patrist	pennant
outwear	padella	parasol	pattern	pennies
outwork	padlock	parboil	patties	pensile
ovarian	pageant	pareira	paucity	pension
ovarial	pailful	parerga	pauline	pensive
ovation	painful	paresis	paunchy	pentile
overact	painter	paretic	paviour	peonage
overawe	paktong	parlour	payable	peonism
overbid	paladin	parodic	payload	peppery
overdue	palatal	paronym	payment	pepsine
overeat	palaver	parotid	peacock	peptics
overjoy	paletot	parquet	pearled	percher
overlap	palette	parsley	peasant	percuss
overlay	palfrey	parsnip	peascod	perdure
overlie	pallial	partake	pebbled	perfect
overpay	pallium	partial	peccant	perfidy
overrun	palmary	parting	peccary	perform
oversea	palmate	partlet	pectose	perfume
oversee	paludal	partner	peddler	perhaps
overset	pampean	partook	pedicel	periapt
overtax	panacea	parties	pedlary	peridot
overtly	panache	parvenu	pedlery	perigee

periwig	pianino	pinners	plating	poetize	posture
perjure	pianist	pinnula	platoon	pointed	potable
perjury	piaster	pinnule	platter	pointer	potassa
permian	piastre	pintail	plaudit	poitrel	potency
permute	pibroch	pioneer	playful	polacca	pottage
perpend	picador	piously	pleader	polemic	pottery
perplex	piccolo	pipette	pleaser	polenta	pouched
persian	piceous	piquant	pledgee	politic	poultry
persist	pickaxe	piragua	pledger	pollack	pounced
pertain	picking	piratic	pledget	pollard	pounder
perturb	picotee	pirogue	pleiads	poll-tax	poverty
pertuse	picquet	piscina	plenary	pollute	powdery
perusal	picture	piscine	plenish	polygon	praetor
peruser	piddock	pismire	pleurae	polygyn	prairie
pervade	piebald	pistole	pleural	polypus	praiser
pervert	pierage	pitcher	pliable	polyzoa	prancer
pessary	piercer	piteous	pliably	pomatum	prating
petaled	pietism	pitfall	pliancy	pompion	prattle
petiole	pietist	pithily	plicate	pompous	pravity
petrify	piggery	pitiful	plodder	poniard	praying
petrine	piggish	pivotal	plotter	pontage	prebend
petrous	pigment	pivoted	plucker	pontiff	precede
pettily	pikeman	placard	plugger	pontoon	precept
pettish	pileate	placate	plumage	popedom	precise
petunia	pilgrim	placket	plumber	poppied	predate
pewtery	pillage	placoid	plumbic	popular	predial
phaeton	pillion	plaguer	plumery	porcine	predict
phalanx	pillory	plaided	plummet	porifer	predoom
phallic	pillowy	plainly	plumose	porrigo	preface
phantom	pilular	plaited	plumous	portage	prefect
pharynx	pimento	plaiter	plumped	portend	prelacy
philter	pimenta	planish	plumper	portent	prelate
philtre	pimpled	planner	plumule	portico	prelect
phloeum	pincase	plantar	plunder	portion	prelude
phoebus	pincers	planter	plunger	portray	premier
phoenix	pincher	plasmic	pluvial	possess	premise
phone-in	pinetum	plaster	poacher	postage	premiss
phonics	pinfold	plastic	pochard	postboy	premium
phrenic	pinhole	platane	podagra	postern	prepaid
physics	pinnace	plateau	poetess	postfix	prepare
phytoid	pinnate	platina	poetics	postman	prepuce

presage
present
preside
presume
pretend
pretext
prevail
prevent
previse
pricker
pricket
prickle
prickly
pridian
primacy
primage
primary
primate
primely
priming
printer
prithee
privacy
private
privily
privity
probang
probate
probity
problem
proceed
process
proctor
procure
prodigy
produce
product
profane
profess
proffer
profile

profuse
progeny
program
project
prolate
prolong
promise
promote
pronely
pronged
pronoun
propane
prophet
propose
prosaic
prosody
prosper
protean
protect
prot,g,
proteid
protein
protend
protest
proudly
proverb
provide
proviso
provoke
provost
prowess
prowler
proximo
prudent
prudery
prudish
prurigo
psalter
psychic
ptarmic
puberty

publish
puckery
pudding
puddler
pudency
pudenda
puerile
puffery
pulleys
pulsate
pumpion
pumpkin
puncher
pungent
punning
punster
puppies
purging
puritan
purlieu
purloin
purples
purport
purpose
purpura
pursuer
pursuit
purview
pushing
pustule
put-down
putrefy
puttock
puzzler
pyaemia
pyaemic
pygmean
pygmies
pyjamas
pylorus
pyloric

pyramid
pyretic
pyrexia
pyrites
pyritic
pyrosis
pyrrhic
pythian
quadrat
quaffer
qualify
quality
quantum
quarrel
quartan
quarter
quartet
quartzy
quassia
quayage
queenly
queerly
queller
queries
querist
quester
questor
quibble
quicken
quickly
quieten
quietly
quietus
quilled
quinary
quinine
quintal
quintan
quintet
quondam
rabidly

raccoon
radiant
radiate
radical
radicle
raffish
ragwort
railing
railway
raiment
rainbow
ramadan
rambler
rammish
rampage
rampant
rampart
rampion
ramsons
rancour
ransack
rapidly
rapport
rapture
rarebit
rasores
ratable
ratably
ratafia
ratchet
ratline
rat-pack
ratteen
raucous
ravager
ravelin
rawness
rayless
reacher
readily
reading

79

readmit
read-out
reagent
realgar
realism
realist
reality
realize
reannex
reargue
rebound
rebuild
rebuker
receipt
receive
recency
recense
recital
reciter
reclaim
recline
recluse
recount
recover
recruit
rectify
rectory
recurve
recycle
redcoat
reddish
redness
redoubt
redound
redpoll
redraft
redress
redskin
redtail
retread
reducer

redwing
redwood
referee
refined
refiner
reflect
reforge
refound
refract
refrain
refresh
refugee
refusal
refuser
refuter
regaler
regalia
regally
regatta
regency
regimen
regnant
regorge
regrant
regrate
regreet
regress
regular
regulus
reinter
reissue
rejoice
rejudge
relapse
related
relater
relator
release
reliant
relieve
relievo

relight
remarry
remnant
remodel
remorse
remould
remount
removal
removed
remover
renewal
renewer
rentier
renuent
repaint
repiner
replace
replant
replete
replevy
replica
replier
reposal
reposer
reposit
repress
reprint
reproof
reprove
reptant
reptile
repulse
request
requiem
require
requite
reredos
rescind
rescuer
resieze
reserve

residue
resolve
resound
respect
respell
respire
respite
respond
restful
restiff
restive
restore
retiary
retinal
retinue
retiral
retired
retouch
retrace
retract
retreat
reunion
reunite
revelry
revenge
revenue
reverer
reverie
reverse
reviler
revisal
reviser
revisit
revival
reviver
revolve
rewrite
reynard
rhenish
rhizoid
rhizoma

rhizome
rhodium
rhombic
rhombus
rhubarb
ribbing
rickets
rickety
rigging
righter
rightly
rigidly
rilievo
ringent
ringlet
riotous
riposte
risible
risibly
rissole
rivalry
riveted
riveter
rivulet
roadway
roaring
roaster
robbery
rockery
roebuck
roguery
roguish
roister
rolfing
rollick
rolling
rollock
romance
romanic
romaunt
rommany

rompish
rondeau
roofing
rookery
roomful
roomily
rooster
rootlet
rorqual
roseate
roseola
rosette
rosolio
rostral
rostrum
rotator
rotifer
rotunda
roughen
roughly
roulade
rouleau
roundel
rounder
roundly
rousing
routier
routine
rowlock
royally
royalty
rubasse
rubbing
rubbish
rubella
rubeola
rubific
rucking
ruddily
ruddock
ruffian

ruffled	saltish	saviour	scoriae	sective
ruffler	saluter	savoury	scorify	secular
ruinate	salvage	sawdust	scorner	securer
ruinous	samovar	sawmill	scorpio	sedilia
rulable	sampler	scabbed	scourer	seducer
rummage	sanable	scabies	scourge	seedily
runaway	sanctum	scabrid	scraggy	seeming
rundlet	sanctus	scaldic	scraper	seepage
running	sangria	scalene	scrappy	segment
rupture	sanicle	scalled	scratch	seismal
rurally	sanious	scallop	screech	seismic
russian	sapajou	scalpel	screwer	seizure
rustily	sapient	scamper	scribal	sejeant
ruthful	sapless	scandal	scrotal	selenic
ruttish	sapling	scantly	scrotum	selfish
sabaoth	sapphic	scapula	scrubby	selvage
sabbath	saracen	scarves	scrunch	seminal
saccule	sarcasm	scarfed	scruple	semitic
sackage	sarcode	scarify	scudder	senator
sackbut	sarcoid	scarlet	scuffle	senatus
sacking	sarcoma	scarped	sculler	sensory
sacring	sarcous	scarper	sculpin	sensual
sacrist	sardine	scatter	scumble	sequela
saddler	sardius	scenery	scummer	sequent
sadness	satanic	scepter	scupper	sequoia
safe-sex	satchel	sceptic	scutage	seraphs
saffron	satiate	sceptre	scutate	seredom
sailing	satiety	schemer	scuttle	seriate
sainted	satinet	scherzo	scythed	serious
saintly	satiric	schnaps	seagull	serpent
salable	satisfy	scholar	sealing	serpigo
salicin	satrapy	scholia	seaport	serrate
salient	satyric	schorly	seaward	serried
salique	saucily	sciatic	sebacic	servant
sallies	saunter	science	seceder	service
salmiac	saurian	scissel	seclude	servile
salsify	sauroid	scissil	secrecy	sessile
saltant	sausage	scoffer	secrete	session
saltern	savable	scolder	sectary	setting
saltier	savanna	scollop	sectile	settled
saltire	saveloy	scooper	section	settler

seventh	shifter	signior	skinner	smoking	soprano
seventy	shimmer	signora	skipper	smolder	sorcery
several	shiness	silence	skirret	smother	sorghum
sex-shop	shingle	silicic	skulker	smuggle	sororal
sextain	shingly	silicle	skulpin	snaffle	sorosis
sextant	shining	silicon	skylark	snakish	sorrily
shackle	shipper	siliqua	skyward	snapper	sottish
shadily	shippon	silique	slabber	snarler	souffl,
shading	shipper	sillery	slacken	sneerer	soundly
shadoof	shirker	sillily	slackly	snigger	sourish
shadowy	shivery	silurus	slander	snipper	soutane
shafted	shoebox	silvern	slangey	snippet	spacial
shallop	shooter	silvery	slantly	snorter	spangle
shallot	shopman	silimar	slashed	snouted	spangly
shallow	shorten	simious	slating	snowish	spaniel
shamble	shortly	simitar	slavery	snuffer	spanish
shammer	shotten	sincere	slavish	snuffle	spanker
shampoo	shouter	sinewed	sleekly	snuggle	spanner
shandry	showery	sinking	sleeper	soakage	sparely
shanked	showily	sinless	sleeved	soaking	sparing
shapely	showing	sinople	sleight	soberly	sparkle
sharded	showman	sinuate	slender	soccage	sparrer
sharpen	shreddy	sinuous	sliding	society	sparrow
sharper	shrilly	sirenia	sliness	softish	spartan
sharply	shrivel	sirloin	slinger	sojourn	spastic
shaster	shrubby	sirocco	slipper	soldier	spathal
shastra	shudder	sistrum	slitter	solicit	spathed
shatter	shuffle	sitting	slobber	solidly	spathic
shaving	shutter	situate	sloughy	soliped	spatial
sheaves	shuttle	sixfold	slubber	soloist	spatter
shearer	shyness	six-pack	slumber	soluble	spattle
sheathy	siamang	sixteen	slyness	solvent	spatula
shebeen	siamese	sixthly	smarten	somatic	spawner
shedder	siccate	sizable	smartly	somehow	speaker
shellac	siccity	skeptic	smasher	sonance	special
shelled	sickbag	sketchy	smatter	sonless	species
shelter	sickish	skilful	smeller	sonship	specify
shelves	sighted	skilled	smelter	soother	speckle
sherbet	sightly	skillet	smiling	sophism	specter
sheriff	sigmoid	skimmer	smitten	sophist	spectre
shiatsu	signify	skinful	smokily	soprani	spectra

specula	spriggy	staring	stiffen	stubbed
speller	spright	starkly	stiffly	stubble
spelter	springe	starlit	stigmas	stubbly
spencer	springy	starred	stiller	studded
spender	spurner	starter	stilted	student
spheral	spurred	startle	stilton	studied
spheric	spurner	start-up	stimuli	studier
spicate	spurney	stately	stinter	studies
spicery	sputnik	statics	stipend	stuffer
spicily	sputter	station	stipple	stumble
spicula	squabby	statist	stipule	stumper
spicule	squalid	statued	stir-fry	stun-gun
spiller	squally	stature	stirrer	stunner
spinach	squalor	statute	stirrup	stunted
spindle	squamae	staunch	stoical	stupefy
spinner	squashy	stealer	stomach	stutter
spinney	squeeze	stealth	stomata	stygian
spin-off	squelch	steamer	stonily	stylish
spinose	squinch	stearic	stopper	stylist
spinous	stabber	stearin	stopple	stylite
spiraea	stabler	steepen	storage	styloid
spirant	staddle	steeper	storied	styptic
spirits	stadium	steeple	stories	suasion
spitter	stagger	steeply	stoutly	suasive
spittle	staging	steerer	stowage	suavely
splashy	staidly	stellar	strange	suavity
spleeny	stainer	stencil	stratum	subacid
splenic	stalked	stepper	stratus	subdean
splotch	stalker	stepson	strayer	subdual
splurge	stamina	sterile	streaky	subduce
spoiler	stammer	sterlet	streamy	subduct
spondee	stamper	sternal	stretch	subdued
sponger	stand-by	sterned	striate	subduer
sponsor	stander	sternly	strigil	suberic
spooney	stand-up	sternum	striker	subject
sporran	staniel	steward	stringy	subjoin
sporule	stannic	sthenic	striped	sublime
spotted	stanzas	stibial	striver	subside
spousal	stapler	stichic	stroker	subsidy
spouter	starchy	sticker	strophe	subsist
sprayey	stardom	stickle	strumae	subsoil

subsume	surfing	syncope	tangent	tendril	thereof
subtend	surgeon	synergy	tanghin	tenfold	thereon
subtext	surgery	synodal	tankard	tenioid	thereto
subtile	surlily	synodic	tank-top	tensely	thermae
subvene	surloin	synonym	tanling	tensile	thermal
subvert	surmise	synovia	tannage	tension	thermic
succeed	surname	syringa	tannery	tensity	theurgy
success	surpass	syringe	tanning	tenthly	thicken
succory	surplus	systole	tantivy	tenuity	thicket
succour	surtout	tabaret	tantrum	tenuous	thickly
succumb	survive	tabbies	tapioca	terbium	thieves
sucking	suspect	tabetic	tapping	termini	thimble
sucrose	suspend	tabinet	tapster	termite	thinker
suction	sustain	tableau	tardily	ternary	thirdly
suffice	sutling	tabloid	tarnish	ternate	thirsty
suffuse	sutural	taborer	tartish	terrace	thistle
suggest	sutured	taboret	tastily	terrene	thistly
suicide	swabber	tabulae	tatting	terrier	thither
sulcate	swaddle	tabular	tattler	terrify	thorium
sulkily	swagger	tacitly	taunter	tersely	thought
sullens	swallow	tactics	taurine	tertian	thready
sulphur	swarthy	tactile	taxable	tessera	thrifty
sultana	swearer	taction	taxicab	testacy	thriver
sumless	sweater	tactual	teacher	testate	throaty
summary	swedish	tadpole	teach-in	testify	through
summons	sweeper	taffeta	tearful	tetanic	thrower
sumpter	sweeten	taffety	teasing	tetanus	thrummy
sunbeam	sweetly	talcose	tea-tree	textile	thuggee
sunbelt	swelter	talcous	techily	textual	thumbed
sundown	sweltry	taliped	technic	texture	thumper
sunfish	swiftly	talipes	tedious	thalami	thunder
sunless	swiller	talipot	teeming	thallus	thyroid
sunrise	swimmer	talking	tegular	thanage	thyrsus
sunward	swindle	tallage	telling	theater	thyself
support	swingle	tallier	tempera	theatre	tiaraed
suppose	swinish	tallowy	tempest	theorbo	ticking
supreme	switzer	tallies	templar	theorem	tickler
surbase	swollen	tamable	templet	therapy	tidings
surcoat	sycosis	tambour	tempter	thereat	tiercel
surface	syenite	tampion	tenable	thereby	tiffany
surfeit	sylphid	tanager	tenancy	therein	tighten

tightly
tigress
tigrine
tigrish
tillage
timbrel
timeous
timidly
tindery
tinning
tinting
tinware
tippler
tipsily
titanic
tithing
titlark
titling
titmice
titrate
titular
toadies
toaster
tobacco
tobogan
toddler
togated
toilful
tollage
tollman
tombola
tomfool
tompion
tongued
tonnage
tonsile
tonsure
tontine
tooling
toothed
topiary

topical
topless
topmast
topmost
topping
torment
tormina
tornado
torpedo
torpefy
torrefy
torrent
torsion
tortile
tortive
torture
toryism
totally
totemic
tottery
toucher
toughen
toughly
tourism
tourist
tourney
towards
towered
toxical
toyshop
tracery
trachea
tracing
tracker
trading
traduce
traffic
tragedy
trailer
trained
trainer

traipse
traitor
trammel
tramper
trample
tramway
trannie
transit
transom
trapeze
trapper
travail
trawler
treacle
treader
treadle
treason
treater
treddle
trefoil
trekkie
trellis
tremble
tremolo
trenail
trental
trepang
tressed
tressel
trestle
triable
triadic
tribune
tribute
tricker
trickle
tricksy
tricorn
trident
trifler
triform

trigamy
trigger
trigram
trilith
trilogy
trimmer
tringle
trinity
trinket
triolet
tripang
tripery
triplet
tripoli
tripper
trireme
trisect
trismus
tritely
triumph
trivial
trochar
trochee
trodden
troller
trolley
trollop
trooper
tropism
tropist
trotter
trouble
trounce
truancy
trucker
truckle
truffle
trumpet
trundle
trunked
trussed

trustee
truster
tryable
tubbing
tubbish
tubular
tuesday
tuition
tumbler
tumbrel
tumbril
tumidly
tumular
tumulus
tunable
tunably
tuneful
tunnage
tunnies
turbine
turgent
turkish
turkois
turmoil
turnery
turning
turn-off
turnkey
turnsol
tussock
tutelar
twaddle
twaddly
twangle
twattle
twelfth
twibill
twiddle
twining
twinkle
twinned

twin-tub
twister
twitter
twofold
twosome
two-step
two-time
two-tone
tympana
tympani
typeset
typhoid
typhoon
typhous
typical
tyranny
tzarina
ulcered
ululate
umbilic
umbrage
unacted
unaided
unarmed
unasked
unaware
unbegot
unblest
unbosom
unbound
unbrace
unburnt
uncanny
uncared
unchain
uncivil
unclasp
unclean
uncloak
unclose
uncouth

uncover
uncrown
unction
undated
underdo
undergo
undoing
undress
undying
unearth
unequal
unfitly
unfrock
unglove
ungodly
unguent
unhandy
unhappy
unhardy
unheard
unhinge
unhitch
unhoped
unhorse
unhouse
unicorn
unideal
uniform
unitary
unities
unitive
unkempt
unknown
unlatch
unlearn
unleash
unloose
unlucky
unmanly
unmixed
unmoved

unnamed
unnerve
unnoted
unowned
unpaved
unquiet
unravel
unready
unscrew
unshorn
unsized
unsling
unsound
unspent
unswept
unsworn
untamed
untaxed
unteach
untried
untruly
untruth
untwine
untwist
unusual
unwaged
unweave
unwooed
unwrung
upbraid
upbreak
upfront
upheave
upraise
upright
uprouse
upscale
upstart
upthrow
uptight
upwards

uraemia
uranium
urethra
urgency
urinary
urinate
urodela
urodele
useless
usually
usurper
utensil
uterine
utility
utilize
utopian
utricle
utterer
utterly
uxorial
vacancy
vaccine
vacuity
vacuole
vacuous
vacuums
vaginae
vaginal
vagrant
vaguely
valance
valence
valency
valiant
validly
vallary
valleys
valonia
valvate
valvule
vampire

vanilla
vantage
vapidly
vapoury
variant
variety
variola
various
varices
varnish
vascula
vatican
vaulted
vaulter
vaunter
vavasor
vedette
veering
vegetal
vehicle
veining
veinlet
velamen
velvety
vendace
venison
ventage
ventral
venture
veranda
verbena
verbose
verdant
verdict
verdure
vermeil
vernier
versant
versify
version
vertigo

vervain
vesical
vesicle
vestige
vesture
veteran
vexilla
viaduct
vibrant
vibrate
vibrios
viceroy
vicious
victory
victual
vicugna
vidette
vidimus
viduity
village
villain
villein
villose
villous
vincula
vinegar
vintage
vintner
violate
violent
violist
virelay
virgate
virtual
visaged
viscera
viscous
visible
visibly
visitor
visored

vitally	wallaby	weevily	whistle	witness	wryneck
vitiate	walling	weigher	whither	wittily	wryness
vitrify	walloon	weighty	whiting	wizened	wysiwyg
vitriol	waltzer	welcome	whitish	wofully	xanthic
vivaria	wanness	welfare	whitlow	wolfish	xanthin
vividly	wannish	wencher	whitsun	wolfkin	xerasia
vivific	warbler	wergild	whittle	wolfram	xerotes
vixenly	warfare	werwolf	whoever	womanly	xiphoid
vocable	warlike	western	whopper	woodman	ycleped
vocalic	warning	westing	whorish	woollen	yelling
vocally	warrant	wet-look	whorled	woorali	yielder
volapuk	warring	wetness	widgeon	wordily	youngly
volcano	warrior	wettish	widower	wording	younker
volleys	washing	whaling	wielder	working	yttrium
voltaic	waspish	wharves	wiggery	workman	zanyism
volubly	wassail	wheaten	wigging	worldly	zealous
volumed	wastage	wheedle	wigless	worrier	zedoary
voluted	wasting	wheeled	wilding	worship	zeolite
voucher	watcher	wheeler	wildish	worsted	zetetic
voyager	watered	whene'er	wileful	wounder	zincode
vulgate	wattled	whereas	willing	wourali	zincoid
vulpine	wavelet	whereat	willowy	wrangle	zincous
vulture	waverer	whereby	windage	wrapper	zip-code
wadding	wayside	where'er	winding	wreathe	zonular
waddler	wayward	wherein	windrow	wreathy	zoogamy
waddles	wayworn	whereof	wine-bar	wrecker	zoogony
wadmoll	wealden	whereon	winglet	wrester	zoogeny
waftage	wealthy	whereto	winning	wrestle	zoolite
wagerer	wearily	whether	winsome	wriggle	zoology
waggery	wearing	whetter	wintery	wringer	zoonomy
waggish	weasand	whiffle	wishful	wrinkle	zootomy
wagoner	weazand	whimper	wistful	wrinkly	zymogen
wagtail	weather	whimsey	wistiti	write-in	zymosis
wailing	weaving	whipper	withers	writing	zymotic
wakeful	webbing	whirler	without	written	zymurgy
wakener	wedding	whisker	withies	wronger	
walking	wedlock	whiskey	witless	wrongly	
walkman	weeping	whisper	witling	wrought	

8-Letter Words

aardvark
aardwolf
abattoir
abbatial
abdicant
abdicate
abducent
abductor
aberrant
abetment
abeyance
abhorrer
abjectly
ablation
ablative
ablepsia
ablution
abnegate
abnormal
abomasus
abortion
abortive
abradant
abrasion
abrogate
abruptly
abscissa
absentee
absently
absinthe
absolute
absolver
absonant
absterge
abstract
abstruse
absurdly

abundant
abutment
academic
acanthus
acaridan
acarpous
acauline
acaulous
accadian
accentor
accepter
accident
accolade
accoutre
accredit
accresce
accuracy
accurate
accursed
accustom
acentric
acerbity
acervate
acescent
achiever
acicular
acidific
acid rain
acierage
aconitic
aconitin
acorn cup
acosmism
acoustic
acquaint
acquirer
acreable

acridity
acrimony
acritude
acrolith
acromion
acrostic
acrotism
actinism
actioner
actively
activity
actually
aculeate
adamitic
addendum
addition
additive
adducent
adductor
adenitis
adequacy
adequate
adherent
adhesion
adhesive
adiantum
adjacent
adjuster
adjutant
admonish
adoption
adoptive
adorable
adorably
adroitly
adscript
adulator

adultery
aduncous
advancer
advisory
advocacy
advocate
advowson
aeration
aerially
aeriform
aerobics
aerocyst
aerolite
aerology
aeronaut
aerostat
aesthete
aestival
affected
afferent
affiance
affinity
affirmer
afflatus
affluent
afforest
affright
affusion
agar-agar
agastric
aggrieve
agiotage
agitated
agitator
aglitter
agnostic
agnusdei

agraphia
agrarian
agrestic
agrimony
agronomy
ague-cake
aiguille
ailantus
air-borne
air-brake
air-built
air-drain
airiness
air-plant
air-shaft
airtight
alacrity
alarmgun
alarming
alarmist
albacore
albinism
alburnum
alchemic
aldehyde
alderman
aleatory
ale-berry
alehouse
algerian
algidity
alguazil
alienage
alienate
alienism
alienist
alkalify

alkaline	ambrosia	annually	apparent	armament
alkalize	ambulant	annulata	appendix	armature
alkaloid	amenable	annulate	appetent	armenian
alkarsin	amenably	annulose	appetite	arminian
allegory	american	anointer	appetize	armorial
all-fours	amethyst	anorexia	applause	armourer
alliance	amicable	anserine	apple-pie	army list
all-in-one	amicably	answerer	apposite	army worm
allocate	ammoniac	antalgic	appraise	aromatic
allodial	ammonite	ant-eater	approach	arpeggio
allodium	ammonium	antecede	approval	arquebus
allopath	amoebean	antedate	approver	arranger
alloyage	amoretti	antelope	apterous	arrester
allspice	amortize	antepast	aptitude	arrogant
alluring	amphibia	anterior	apyretic	arrogate
allusion	amphipod	anteroom	aquarium	arterial
allusive	amphoral	antidote	aquarius	artesian
alluvial	amputate	antilogy	aquatint	artfully
alluvion	anabasis	antimask	aqueduct	art-house
alluvium	anaconda	antimony	aquiform	artifice
almighty	anaglyph	antiphon	aquiline	artistic
alms-deed	analogue	antipode	arbalist	aruspicy
alopecia	analysis	antipope	arborial	asbestos
alphabet	analytic	antitype	arborist	ascidian
alpinery	anaphora	antlered	arboured	ascidium
alsatian	anarchic	anything	arcadian	asperity
altarage	anasarca	anywhere	archaean	asphodel
alterant	anathema	aoristic	archaism	asphyxia
although	ancestor	aperient	archduke	aspirant
altitude	ancestry	aperture	archness	aspirate
altruism	anchoret	aphelion	archwise	aspiring
aluminum	anecdote	aphorism	arc-light	asporous
alum-root	aneurism	apiarist	arcturus	assailer
alveolar	angelica	apodosis	ardently	assassin
alveolus	anglican	apologue	argental	assaying
amadavat	animated	apoplexy	argonaut	assemble
amaranth	anisette	apostasy	arguable	assembly
amazedly	ankylose	apostate	argument	assenter
ambeotic	annalist	aposteme	arhizous	assertor
ambition	annotate	apothegm	arianism	assessor
amblygon	announce	appanage	armagnac	assignee

assigner	austrian	baldness	barretor	becoming
assonant	autocrat	baldrick	barterer	bedabble
assorted	autonomy	balefire	bartizan	bedesman
assuager	autopsia	ballcock	barytone	bedrench
assuming	autotype	ballista	basaltic	bedstead
assyrian	autumnal	ball-park	basanite	bedstraw
asterisk	ave-maria	balsamic	bascinet	beefwood
asterism	averment	baluster	baseball	beeswing
asteroid	aversion	bandelet	baseborn	beetling
asthenia	aviation	band-fish	baseless	beetroot
asthenic	avifauna	banisher	baseline	befriend
astonish	avoucher	banister	basement	begetter
astragal	avowable	banjoist	baseness	beggarly
astucity	avowedly	bankable	basicity	beginner
astutely	avulsion	banknote	basilica	begrudge
atheling	aweather	bankrupt	basilisk	beguiler
athenian	baby-boom	bannered	bass-clef	behemoth
atheroma	babyhood	banneret	bassinet	beholden
athletic	baccarat	banterer	bass-viol	beholder
atlantes	bacchant	bantling	bastardy	belabour
atlantic	bachelor	banxring	batavian	believer
atmology	bacillar	baptiser	bat-horse	belittle
atomizer	bacsllus	barracan	bayadere	bell-pull
atonable	backbite	barbaric	bayberry	bell-rope
atrocity	backbone	barbecue	bdellium	bemoaner
attacker	back-door	barberry	beaconed	bendable
attemper	backhand	barbette	bead-roll	benedick
attender	backlash	barbican	beads-man	benefice
attester	backmost	bardling	beam-ends	bengalee
atticist	backside	barefoot	beamless	benignly
attitude	backstay	bareness	bean-king	benjamin
attorney	backward	bargeman	bean-tree	bepraise
aucipial	baconian	baritone	bearable	bequeath
audacity	baculite	barnacle	bearably	bergamot
audience	badigeon	barnyard	bearskin	bergmehl
auditory	badinage	baronage	bearward	berthage
augurial	bailable	baroness	beatific	besieger
augustan	bailment	baronial	beautify	beslaver
augustly	bakshish	barouche	beavered	besotted
auricula	balancer	barrator	bechamel	bespread
auriform	bald-erne	barratry	bechance	besprent

bestiary
bestowal
bestower
bestride
betel-nut
betrayal
betrayer
beverage
bewailer
bewilder
bezonian
biblical
bibulous
biconvex
bicuspid
biddable
bidental
biennial
bigamist
bignonia
bilander
bilberry
bill-hook
billy-boy
bilobate
bimanous
bimensal
bind-weed
binnacle
binomial
biologic
biometry
bioplasm
biparous
biramous
bird-bolt
bird-call
bird-lime
bird's-eye
birthday
biserial

bisexual
bistoury
bitheism
biting-in
bitingly
bitnoben
bittacle
bitterly
biweekly
black-box
black-cap
blacking
blackish
black-leg
black-tin
black-wad
bladdery
blamable
blamably
blameful
blandish
blastula
blazoner
blazonry
bleacher
bleeding
blenheim
blesbuck
blessing
blindage
blinding
blinkard
blissful
blistery
blithely
blizzard
blockade
blockish
block-tin
bloodily
bloomery

blooming
blossomy
blow-hole
blowpipe
bludgeon
bluebell
bluebird
blue-book
blueness
blue-pill
bluntish
blushing
boarding
boastful
boat-bill
boathook
boatrace
bobbinet
bobolink
bock-beer
bodement
bodiless
bog-earth
boggling
bohemian
boldness
bolt-head
bolt-rope
bombazet
bonafide
bondmaid
bone-dust
bone-lace
bone-mill
boniface
bonneted
boobyish
book-debt
book-oath
book-post
book-worm

bookworm
boothook
boot-hose
boot-jack
boot-lace
bootless
boot-rack
boot-tree
boot-last
borachio
boracite
borderer
borecole
borrower
bostangi
botanist
botanize
botchery
botherer
botryoid
bottomed
bottomry
bouffant
bouncing
boundary
bourgeon
bow-drill
bowsprit
boyishly
bracelet
brachial
brackish
bradypod
braggart
braiding
brainish
brakeman
brake-van
branched
brandied
brandish

brand-new
brat-pack
brattice
brawling
brazenly
breadnut
breakage
breasted
breather
breeched
breeches
breeding
brethren
brettice
breviary
breviate
breviped
brewster
bribable
brickbat
brick-tea
brighten
brightly
brimless
brimming
brindled
brine-pan
brine-pit
bristled
britzska
broacher
brocaded
brocatel
broccoli
brochure
broidery
brokenly
bromelia
bronchia
bronchus
bronzite

brooklet	busy-body	call-note	capsular	caryatid
brougham	butchery	calmness	captious	cascabel
browbeat	buttress	calotype	capuchin	casemate
browning	buzzword	calycine	capybara	casement
brownish	by-corner	calycoid	carabine	case-shot
brunette	bystreet	calyptra	caracara	case-worm
brutally	caballer	cambrian	caracole	cash-book
bryology	cabin-boy	cameleon	carapace	cashmere
buckshot	cabriole	cameline	carap-oil	cassette
buckskin	cachalot	camellia	carbolic	castanet
buddhism	cachucha	camisade	carbonic	castaway
buddhist	cacodyle	camisole	carburet	cast-iron
bufonite	cacology	camomile	carcajou	castling
building	cadastre	campaign	carcanet	castrate
bukshish	caducean	camphine	cardamom	casually
bulk-head	caduceus	canadian	card-case	casualty
bull-calf	caducous	canaille	cardigan	catacomb
bulletin	caesural	canalize	cardinal	catapult
bull-frog	caffeine	canaster	carditis	cataract
bull-head	cageling	cancelli	careless	catchfly
bull's-eye	caimacam	cancroid	care-worn	catching
bulrushy	cajolery	candidly	cariacou	category
buncombe	calabash	cane-mill	cariatid	catenary
bungalow	calamary	canister	carillon	cateress
bung-hole	calamine	cannibal	carinate	cathedra
bungling	calamint	cannikin	carnally	catheter
buntline	calamite	canoeist	carnauba	catonian
buoyancy	calamity	canoness	carneous	cat's-tail
burgamot	calciner	canonist	carnival	caudicle
burganet	calc-spar	canonize	caroline	cauldron
burgeois	calc-tuff	canopied	carousal	caulicle
burglary	calcular	canorous	carousel	causable
burgrave	calcwlus	canticle	carouser	causally
burgundy	calendar	cantonal	car-phone	causeway
burletta	calender	canzonet	carriage	cautious
burnable	calf-love	capacity	carriole	cavalier
burnoose	califate	capeline	carroche	cavatina
burnt-ear	calipash	capitate	cart-load	cave-bear
burrower	calipers	capriole	cartouch	caverned
business	calisaya	capsicum	carucate	cavicorn
buskined	call-bird	capsizal	caruncle	caviller

celerity
celibacy
celibate
cellarer
cellaret
cellular
cemetery
cenobite
cenotaph
centuary
centoist
centuple
cephalic
cerastes
ceratose
cerberus
cerebral
cerebrin
cerebrum
ceremony
cerulean
cerulein
cerusite
cervical
cesarean
cesspool
cetacean
cetology
chainsaw
chairman
chaldaic
chaldron
chamfron
champion
chancery
chandler
chantage
chap-book
chaperon
chapiter
chaplain

chaptrel
charcoal
charisma
charlock
charming
chartism
chartist
chasseur
chastely
chastise
chastity
chasuble
chatline
chat show
chauffer
cheatery
cheating
cheerful
cheerily
chefring
chemical
chenille
cherubic
chessman
chestnut
chetvert
chicaner
chick-pea
chiefdom
chiefery
chiefess
childbed
childing
childish
children
chiliasm
chilling
chimaera
china-ink
chinaman
chinless

chipmunk
chipping
chiragra
chit-chat
chivalry
chloasma
chloride
chlorine
chlorite
choicely
choleric
chopping
choragus
chorally
choultry
chrismal
christen
chromate
chromium
chromite
chuffily
churlish
chyluria
chymical
ciborium
cicatrix
cicerone
ciderkin
ci-devant
ciliated
cimolite
cinchona
cincture
cinerary
cinnabar
cinnamon
circular
cirriped
ciselure
cistella
citation

citatory
civet-cat
civilian
civilist
civility
civilize
claimant
clamance
clamancy
clangour
clannish
clanship
clansman
clap-sill
claptrap
claqueur
clarence
classify
classist
clavecin
clavicle
claviger
clawback
clay-cold
clay-marl
clay-mill
claymore
cleanser
clearing
cleavage
cleavers
clematis
clemency
clencher
clerical
cleverly
clew-line
cliental
climatic
climbing
clincher

clinical
clipping
cliquish
cliquism
cloak-bag
cloddish
clodpoll
cloister
clothier
clothing
cloudily
cloudlet
clovered
clownish
clubbist
club-foot
club-moss
club-room
clumsily
clypeate
coach-box
coach-dog
coachman
coactive
coagency
coagulum
coalesce
coal-fish
coal-mine
coal-work
coarsely
coasting
cobaltic
co-bishop
cobwebby
cocculus
cockaded
cockatoo
cockboat
cockcrow
cockerel

cock-loft
cocksure
cocktail
codifier
coercion
coercive
coextend
coffered
cogently
cogitate
cognomen
cogwheel
coherent
cohesion
cohesive
cohobate
coiffure
coincide
colander
coldness
cole-seed
colewort
colicked
collapse
collaret
collator
colliery
colloquy
colonial
colonist
colonize
colophon
colorize
colossal
colossus
coloured
columnar
columned
comatose
combined
combiner

comedian
cometary
comitial
commence
commerce
commoner
commonly
communal
compiler
complain
complect
complete
complice
complier
compline
composed
composer
compound
compress
comprise
computer
conceder
conceive
concerto
conchoid
conclave
conclude
concrete
condense
conferee
conferva
conflate
conflict
confound
confrere
confront
confused
congener
conglobe
congress
congreve

conicity
coniform
conjoint
conjugal
conjunct
conjurer
conniver
conquest
conserve
consider
consoler
conspire
constant
construe
consular
consumer
consumpt
contango
contempt
continue
contract
contrary
contrast
contrite
contrive
convener
converge
converse
convexly
conveyal
conveyer
convince
convolve
convulse
cony-wool
cookware
coolness
copperas
copulate
copybook
copyhold

coquetry
coquette
coracoid
coral-rag
corbeile
cordovan
corduroy
cordwain
coregent
coreless
cormogen
corneous
cornered
cornetcy
corn-flag
corn laws
corn-mill
corn-pipe
corn-rose
corn-rent
cornuted
coronach
coronary
coronoid
corporal
corridor
corrival
corselet
cortical
corundum
corvette
corybant
coryphee
cosecant
cosenage
cosmetic
cost-free
costless
costmary
costumed
co-surety

cotenant
cotquean
cottager
cotyloid
couchant
coulisse
countess
coupling
coursing
court-day
courtesy
courtier
cousinly
covenant
covering
coverlet
coverlid
covertly
covetous
covinous
cowardly
cowberry
coworker
coxswain
cozenage
crab-tree
crabwood
cracknel
craftily
cragsmen
crane-fly
crankily
crannied
crawfish
crayfish
creamery
creasote
creation
creative
creature
credence

credible
credibly
creditor
cremator
crenelle
creosote
crescent
cretonne
creutzer
crevasse
cribbage
cribrate
crimeful
criminal
crimping
crispate
cristate
critical
critique
croaking
crockery
cromlech
cromorne
crop-full
crop-sick
crossbow
crosscut
cross-eye
crossing
crosslet
crossway
crotched
crotchet
croupier
crowfoot
crowning
crownlet
crown-saw
crucible
crucifer
crucifix

crumpled
crusader
crush-hat
crushing
crustily
crutched
cryolite
cryonics
cubature
cube-root
cubiform
cucumber
cucurbit
cul-de-sac
culinary
culpable
culpably
cultrate
cultural
cultured
culverin
cumbrian
cumbrous
cumulate
cupboard
cupidity
cupreous
curassou
curative
curatrix
curbable
curb-roof
curculio
cureless
currency
curricle
cursedly
cursores
curtness
cushiony
cuspidor

customer
cutpurse
cutwater
cyanogen
cyanosis
cybernet
cyclamen
cyclonic
cyclopic
cyclopes
cylinder
cynanche
cynicism
cynosure
cyrenaic
cyrillic
cystitis
czarevna
dabchick
dacryoma
dactylic
daffodil
dahabieh
daintily
dairying
dairyman
dalesman
dalmatic
dal segno
damassin
damnable
damnably
dampness
dandruff
dandyish
dandyism
danseuse
daringly
darkling
darkness
darksome

dastardy
database
dateless
date-palm
date-tree
date-plum
daturine
daughter
davy-lamp
daybreak
day-dream
daylight
dazzling
dead-beat
dead-born
deadfall
dead-duck
deadhead
dead-heat
deadlock
dead-meat
deadness
deadwood
deaf-mute
deafness
deal-fish
deanship
dearness
death-bed
deathful
debasing
debility
debonair
debutant
decadent
decagram
decanter
deceased
deceiver
december
decemvir

decently
decimate
decipher
decision
decisive
deck-load
deck-hand
declared
declarer
declinal
decolour
decorate
decorous
decrease
decrepit
decretal
decurion
dedicate
deedless
deemster
deep-laid
deepness
deer-hair
defecate
defendee
defender
deferent
deferrer
defiance
defilade
definite
deflower
defluent
deformed
deformer
defrayal
deftness
degraded
dejected
dejeuner
delation

95

delegate	deranged	diaconal	dilution	disguise
deletion	derelict	diadelph	diluvial	dishevel
delicacy	derision	diademed	diluvian	dishorse
delicate	derisive	diaglyph	diluvion	disinter
delirium	dermatic	diagnose	diluvium	disjoint
delivery	derogate	diagonal	dimerous	disjunct
delphian	describe	diallage	diminish	dislodge
delusion	descrier	dialling	dingdong	disloyal
delusive	deselect	dialogue	dinornis	dismally
delusory	deserter	dialyser	dinosaur	disorder
demander	deserver	dialysis	diocesan	dispatch
demented	designer	diameter	dioecian	dispeace
dementia	desirous	diapason	diopside	dissever
demijohn	desolate	diastase	dioptase	dissolve
demi-lune	despatch	diastema	dioptric	dissuade
demiurge	despiser	diastole	dioramic	distally
demivolt	despotic	diatomic	diplomat	distance
demi-wolf	detached	diatonic	diplopia	distaste
democrat	detailed	diatribe	dipteral	distinct
demolish	detailer	dichroic	directly	distract
demoniac	detainer	diclinic	director	distrain
demonism	detector	dictator	disabuse	distrait
demonist	detester	didactic	disagree	distress
demonize	dethrone	didapper	disannex	district
demurely	detonate	didymium	disannul	distrust
demurrer	detonize	didymous	disarray	disunion
denarius	detrital	dieresis	disaster	disunite
dendrite	detritus	dietetic	disburse	disusage
dendroid	deucedly	diffract	disciple	ditheism
deniable	devilish	diffuser	disclaim	ditheist
denounce	devonian	digester	disclose	diuretic
denticle	devotion	diggable	discount	dividend
departed	devoutly	digitate	discount	divi-divi
depender	dewberry	dignian	discover	dividual
depilate	dewiness	dignynous	discreet	divinely
deplorer	dewpoint	dihedral	discrete	divinity
deponent	dextrine	dihedron	discrown	division
depraved	dextrose	dilation	diseased	divisive
depraver	diabetes	dilative	disendow	divorcee
depriver	diabetic	dilatory	disgorge	divorcer
depurate	diabolic	diligent	disgrace	docility

docimasy	doubling	druidism	easterly	eggplant
dockyard	doubloon	drumhead	eastward	eggshell
doctoral	doubtful	drunkard	eaudevie	egg-slice
doctrine	doughnut	dry-nurse	eburnean	egg-spoon
document	dovetail	dry-point	eburnine	egoistic
doddered	downcast	dubitate	ecaudate	egressor
dog-cheap	down-come	ducatoon	echinate	egyptian
dog-eared	downfall	duck-bill	echinite	eight-day
doggedly	downhill	duckling	echinold	eighteen
doggerel	down-line	duck-mole	eclectic	eighthly
dog-grass	downpour	duck-weed	ecliptic	ejection
dog-latin	downside	duelling	economic	elapsion
dogmatic	downsize	duellist	ecostate	elatedly
dogs-bane	downward	dulcimer	ecraseur	eldorado
dog-sleep	doxology	dullness	ecstatic	election
dog-tooth	draconic	dumb-bell	ecumenic	elective
dog-watch	dragoman	dumbness	edacious	electric
doldrums	dragonet	dumpling	edentata	electron
dolerite	drainage	dung-fork	edentate	elegance
dolomite	dramatic	dunghill	edge-bone	elegancy
dolorous	dram-shop	duodenum	edgeless	elegiast
domainal	draughty	duologue	edge-tool	elenchus
domestic	drawable	duration	edgeways	elephant
domicile	drawback	dust-ball	edgewise	elevator
dominant	draw-well	dust-cart	edifying	eleventh
dominate	dreadful	dutiable	editress	elf-arrow
domineer	dreamily	dwarfish	educable	eligible
dominion	drearily	dwelling	educator	eligibly
dominoes	dressing	dye-house	educible	ellipsis
donation	drift-net	dye-stuff	eel-spear	elliptic
donative	drilling	dynamics	eeriness	elongate
doomsday	dripping	dynamite	effecter	eloquent
doomsman	drollery	dynastic	effector	eludible
doornail	dropping	dyspnoea	efferent	elvishly
doorpost	dropsied	eagle-owl	efficacy	emaciate
doorstep	dropwort	ear-shell	effluent	embalmer
dormancy	droughty	earth-hog	effusion	embattle
dormouse	drowsily	earthnut	effusive	embezzle
dotation	drubbing	earth-pig	egestion	embitter
dotingly	drudgery	easement	egg-apple	emblazon
dotterel	druggist	easiness	egg-glass	embolden

embolism
embracer
embrasor
emergent
emeritus
emersion
emigrant
emigrate
eminence
emissary
emission
emissive
emissory
empannel
emphasis
emphatic
employee
employer
empoison
emporium
empurple
empyreal
empyrean
emulator
emulgent
emulsify
emulsion
emulsive
enactive
enallage
enceinte
enchoric
encircle
enclitic
encomium
encrinal
encrinic
encroach
encumber
encyclic
endamage

endanger
endermic
endocarp
endogamy
endomose
endorser
enduring
energize
enervate
enfeeble
enfilade
enforest
engender
engineer
engorged
engraver
enhancer
enkindle
enlarged
enlarger
enneagon
enormity
enormous
enroller
ensample
ensconce
ensemble
enshrine
ensiform
ensilage
enslaver
entailer
entangle
entellus
enthrall
enthrone
enticing
entirely
entirety
entomoid
entozoal

entozoic
entozoon
entracte
entrance
entreaty
entrench
entrepot
entresol
enuresis
envelope
enviable
enviably
environs
envisage
enzootic
eolipile
ephemera
ephesian
epicalyx
epicycle
epidemic
epigeous
epigraph
epilepsy
epilogic
epilogue
epinasty
epiphany
epiphyte
epiploic
epiploon
episodic
episperm
epistler
eponymic
epulotic
epyornis
equality
equalize
equation
equipage

equitant
equivoke
erastian
erectile
erection
erective
eremitic
erethism
ergotine
ergotism
erotetic
errantry
errorist
eructate
eruption
eruptive
erythema
escalade
escallop
escapade
eschalot
esculent
esoteric
espalier
especial
espousal
espouser
esquimau
essayist
esthetic
estimate
estoppel
estovers
estrange
esurient
eternity
eternize
etheling
ethereal
etherify
etherism

etherize
ethicist
ethiopic
ethnical
ethology
ethylene
etiolate
etiology
etruscan
etypical
eucalypt
eugenics
eulogist
eulogium
eulogize
eupepsia
eupfptic
euphonic
euphrasy
euphuism
euphuist
eurasian
european
eurostar
evacuant
evacuate
evadable
evadible
evaluate
evanesce
evenness
eventful
eventide
eventual
evermore
eversion
everyday
everyone
eviction
evidence
evildoer

evilness
evulsion
exacting
exaction
examinee
examiner
excavate
exchange
excision
excitant
exciting
excursus
execrate
executed
executor
exegesis
exegetic
exemplar
exequial
exercise
exertion
exhalant
exhalent
exhorter
exigence
exigency
exigible
exiguity
exiguous
existent
exorable
exorcise
exorcism
exorcist
exorcize
exordial
exordium
exosmose
exoteric
expecter
expedite

expeller
expertly
expiable
expiator
explicit
explorer
exponent
exporter
exposure
exserted
extender
extensor
exterior
extfrnal
extoller
extrados
extrorse
exultant
exuviate
eyeglass
eyepiece
eyesight
eyetooth
eye-water
fabulist
fabulous
face-ache
facetiae
facially
facility
factious
factotum
fadeless
fadingly
fail-safe
fairness
faithful
falcated
falchion
falconer
falconet

falconry
fallible
fallibly
fall-trap
falsetto
fameless
familiar
famously
fanciful
fandango
fanfaron
fan-light
fantasia
farcical
farcy-bud
farewell
farmable
farmyard
farriery
farthest
farthing
fasciate
fascicle
fashious
fastback
fast-food
fastener
fastness
fatalism
fatalist
fatality
fatherly
fattener
faultily
fauteuil
favonian
favoured
favourer
fearless
feasible
feasibly

feathery
featured
february
feckless
feculent
federate
feedback
feed-pipe
feed-pump
feldspar
felicity
fellness
felo-de-se
felstone
feme-sole
fencible
feracity
feretory
feringee
fern-seed
ferocity
ferreous
ferreter
ferriage
ferryman
fervency
fervidly
festally
festival
fetation
feticide
feudally
feverfew
feverish
fibrilla
fibrosis
fidelity
fiducial
field-day
field-gun
fiendish

fiercely
fiftieth
fighting
figuline
figurant
figurate
figurine
figuring
filament
filatory
filature
file-fish
filially
filicoid
filiform
filigree
fillibeg
filthily
filtrate
finality
finedraw
fineness
finespun
fingered
finisher
finitely
finitude
fireball
fire-clay
firedamp
firelock
fireplug
fire-ship
fireside
firewood
firmness
firmware
fishcake
fish-hook
fishwife
fistular

fitfully	floscule	foredoom	foundery	frosting
fivefold	flotilla	forefend	fountain	frothily
fixation	flounder	foregoer	fourfold	fructify
fixative	flourish	foregone	fourteen	fructose
flabbily	flowered	forehand	fourthly	frugally
flabella	floweret	forehead	foxglove	fruitage
flagella	fluently	foreknow	fraction	fruitery
flagging	fluidity	foreland	fracture	fruitful
flagrant	flummery	forelock	fragment	fruition
flagship	fluorite	foremast	fragrant	frumenty
flambeau	fluxible	foremost	frampold	frumpish
flamingo	fly-drive	forenoon	frankish	frustule
flashily	focalize	forensic	franklin	frustums
flatting	fogeyism	forepart	fraudful	fugacity
flatlong	foliated	forepeak	freakish	fugitive
flatness	follicle	foresaid	freckled	fugleman
flattery	follower	foresail	freeborn	fulcrate
flatting	fomenter	foreshew	freedman	fulcrums
flatwise	fondling	foreshow	freehand	fulgency
flaunter	fondness	foreside	freehold	fullness
flautist	fontanel	foreskin	freeness	full-time
flawless	foodless	forestal	freezing	fulminic
fleabite	foolscap	forester	frenetic	fumarole
flection	football	forestry	frenzied	fumeless
fleeting	footfall	foretell	frequent	fumigate
fleshpot	footgear	forewarn	frescoes	fumitory
flexible	foothold	foreward	frescoed	function
flexibly	footmark	formalin	freshman	fundable
flextime	footpath	formally	fretwork	funereal
flexuose	footstep	formerly	fribbler	funguses
flexuous	foramina	formless	friction	furbelow
flexibly	forborne	formulae	friendly	furcated
flippant	forcedly	forsaker	frighten	furlough
floatage	forceful	forsooth	frigidly	furmenty
floating	forcible	forswear	frilling	furriery
floccose	forcibly	fortieth	frippery	furthest
flogging	forclose	fortress	friskily	fusarole
flooding	fordable	fortuity	frontage	fusiform
flooring	forebode	forwards	frontier	fusileer
florally	forecast	fosterer	frontlet	futilely
floridly	foredate	foulness	frostily	futility

futurity
gabioned
gadabout
gadhelic
gainless
galactic
galangal
galbanum
galeated
galliard
gallican
gallipot
galloper
galloway
galvanic
gameness
gamesome
gamester
gangliac
ganglion
gangrene
ganister
gantlope
gardener
gardenia
gargoyle
garishly
garlicky
garotter
garrison
garrotte
gasalier
gaselier
gasogene
gastrula
gatherer
gauntlet
gazogene
gazumper
gelatine
gelidity

geminate
geminous
gemmeous
gendarme
generant
generate
generous
genevese
genially
genitals
genitive
geniuses
geodesic
geodetic
geognosy
geolatry
geomancy
geometer
geometry
geoponic
georgian
geranium
germanic
germinal
gestural
giantess
gibingly
gigantic
giggling
glmcrack
gingerly
girasole
girlhood
glabrous
glaciate
gladiate
gladioli
gladness
gladsome
glanders
glandule

glareous
glasnost
glassful
glassily
glaucoma
glaucous
gleesome
glibness
glissade
gloaming
globated
globular
globulet
globulin
gloomily
gloriole
glorious
glossary
glossily
glowworm
gloxinia
glucinum
glumness
gluttony
glyptics
gnatling
gnomical
gnomonic
goatherd
godchild
godwards
goitered
goitrous
golgotha
gonfalon
gonfanon
gonidium
goodness
goodwill
gorgeous
gossamer

gossipry
gourmand
goutwort
goutweed
governor
gownsman
graafian
graceful
gracious
gradient
graduate
graffiti
graffito
graining
gralloch
grandeur
grandson
granitic
granular
graphite
grasping
grateful
gratuity
gravamen
gravelly
gravitas
grayling
grayness
greasily
greedily
greenery
greening
greenish
greeting
gridiron
gridlock
grievous
grillade
grimness
grinding
grisette

grizzled
groining
grosbeak
groschen
grottoes
grouping
growling
grudging
gruesome
grumbler
grumpily
grumpish
grunting
guaiacum
guardian
guerilla
guernsey
guerilla
guicowar
guidable
guidance
guileful
guiltily
guilible
gumption
gunsmith
gurgoyle
guttural
gymnasia
gymnogen
gymnotus
gynander
gynarchy
gypseous
gyration
gyratory
gyroidal
gyrostat
habitant
habitual
habitude

hacienda	hawthorn	helpmate	hireling	hosepipe
haematic	haymaker	helvetic	historic	hospital
haematin	haystack	hematine	hitherto	hostelry
hairless	haziness	hematite	hoarding	hotchpot
haleness	headache	hemipter	hoarsely	howitzer
halliard	headachy	henchman	hogshead	huckster
hamiform	headhunt	henequen	holdfast	hugeness
handbill	headland	hepatite	holiness	huguenot
handbook	headless	hepatize	hollands	humanely
handcuff	headlong	heptagon	hollowly	humanist
handgrip	headmost	heraldic	homeborn	humanist
handicap	headship	heraldry	homefelt	humanity
handline	headsman	herbaria	homeland	humanize
handmaid	healable	herdsman	homeless	humbling
handrail	heartily	heredity	homespun	humidity
handsome	heavenly	hereunto	homeward	humility
hangnail	hebetate	hereupon	homicide	humorist
hangover	hebetude	herewith	homilist	humorous
harangue	hebraism	heritage	homilies	humpback
hardback	hebraist	hermetic	homodont	hungerer
hardball	hebraize	hernshaw	homology	hungrily
hard-copy	hecatomb	heroship	homonymy	huntress
hard-core	hedgehog	herpetic	homopter	huntsman
hard-disk	hedgerow	hesitant	homotype	hurtless
hard-drug	hedonism	hesitate	honestly	hustings
hardened	hedonist	hetarism	honorary	hyacinth
hardness	heedless	hiatuses	honourer	hydrogen
hard-rock	heelball	hibernal	hoodwink	hydromel
hardship	hegelian	hiccough	hopeless	hydropic
hardware	hegemony	hiddenly	horatian	hydrozoa
harebell	heighten	hierarch	hornbeam	hygienic
harlotry	heirloom	hieratic	hornbill	hymeneal
harmless	heirship	highland	hornpipe	hymenean
harmonic	heliacal	highness	hornwork	hymenium
harridan	helicoid	high-rise	horologe	hypnosis
haruspex	hellenic	highroad	horology	hypnotic
hastener	helmeted	high-tech	horrible	hysteria
hatchway	helmsman	hilarity	horribly	hysteric
hautbois	helotism	hinderer	horridly	iambuses
havannah	helpless	hindmost	horrific	iatrical
havildar	helpline	hinduism	horseman	ichorous

idealess	immobile	incubate	inguinal	interior
idealism	immodest	indagate	inhalant	intermit
idealist	immolate	indebted	inhalent	intermix
ideality	immortal	indecent	inherent	internal
idealize	immunity	indented	inhesion	internet
ideation	impanate	indevout	inimical	interval
identify	imparity	indiaman	iniquity	inthrall
identity	imperial	indicant	initiate	intifada
ideogram	impetigo	indicate	injector	intimacy
ideology	impishly	indigene	inkiness	intimate
idiotism	implicit	indigent	inkstand	intonate
idleness	impoison	indirect	inlander	intrados
idocrase	impolicy	indocile	inlaying	intrench
idolater	impolite	indolent	innately	intrepid
idolatry	importer	indurate	innocent	intrigue
idolizer	imposing	indusium	innovate	intromit
ignition	impostor	indusial	innuendo	introrse
ignominy	impotent	industry	inquirer	intruder
ignorant	imprimis	inedited	insanely	inundate
illation	imprison	inequity	insanity	invasion
illative	improper	inexpert	inscribe	invasive
ill-treat	improver	infamous	insecure	inveigle
illumine	impudent	infantry	inserted	inventor
illusion	impugner	infecund	insignia	inverted
illusive	impunity	inferior	insolate	investor
illusory	impurely	infernal	insolent	inviting
imbecile	impurity	infilter	insomnia	invocate
imbitter	impurple	infinite	insomuch	involute
imblazon	inaction	infinity	inspired	inwardly
imbolden	inactive	infirmly	inspirer	iodoform
imborder	inasmuch	inflated	inspirit	irefully
imbution	inceptor	inflatus	instance	irisated
imitable	inchoate	inflexed	instinct	iriscope
imitancy	incident	in-flight	instruct	irishism
imitator	incision	influent	insulate	iriditis
immanate	incisive	informal	intaglio	ironbark
immanent	incisory	informer	integral	ironical
immanuel	incisure	infringe	intended	ironside
immature	inclined	infusion	intently	ironware
imminent	incoming	infusive	interact	irrigate
immingle	increase	infusory	interest	irrision

irritant	jokingly	kinetics	landlady	lavender
irritate	jolthead	kinglike	landless	lavishly
isabella	jovially	kingling	landlord	lawfully
isagogic	joyfully	kingship	landmark	lawgiver
ischuria	joyously	kinkajou	landslip	laxative
islamish	joystick	kinsfolk	landsman	laziness
islamite	jubilant	knapsack	landsmen	leadless
islander	jubilate	knickers	landward	leafless
isocheim	judaical	knightly	landwehr	leanness
isocryme	judgment	knitting	langsyne	learning
isogonic	judicial	knotless	language	leathern
isolated	jugglery	knowable	languish	leathery
isomeric	julienne	kreasote	lankness	leavings
isotherm	jumbo-jet	kreosote	lanneret	lecturer
issuable	jump-suit	kreutzer	lanoline	legalism
iterance	junction	kryolite	lanthorn	legality
jacketed	juncture	labially	lapelled	legalize
jacobean	junk-bond	laboured	lapidary	legatine
jacobite	junk-food	labourer	lapidate	legation
jailbird	junk-mail	laburnum	lapidify	leisured
jalousie	jurassic	lacerate	lappeted	lemonade
janizary	juristic	laconism	lapsable	lengthen
japanner	justness	lacrosse	larboard	lenience
japhetic	juvenile	lacrymal	larcener	leniency
jaundice	kakemono	lacunous	larkspur	lenitive
jauntily	kakodyle	ladyhood	larynges	leporine
jealousy	kalender	ladylike	larynxes	lethargy
jehovist	kangaroo	ladyship	lateness	lettered
jejunely	keelhaul	laically	latently	leucosis
jeopardy	keenness	laid-back	latinism	levanter
jeremiad	keepsake	lamasery	latinist	leveller
jeroboam	kerchief	lamblike	latinity	leverage
jesuitic	kernelly	lambling	latinize	leviable
jesuitry	kerosene	lambskin	latitude	levigate
jettison	keyboard	lamellae	latterly	levirate
jeweller	keystone	lamellar	laudable	levitate
jewishly	kickshaw	lameness	laudably	lewdness
jocosely	kilogram	laminary	laudanum	lewisson
jocosity	kilowatt	laminate	laughter	libation
jocundly	kindling	lancelet	laureate	libatory
jointure	kindness	landfall	lavatory	libeller

liberate	literati	lordling	machismo	mandolin
libretto	literato	lordship	mackerel	mandrake
licensee	litharge	loricate	macropod	mandrill
licenser	litigant	lorikeet	macrural	maneless
lichened	litigate	lothario	maculate	manequin
lichenic	littoral	loudness	madrigal	manfully
licorice	liturgic	loveless	maestoso	manganic
liegeman	liveable	lovingly	magazine	mangonel
lientery	livelily	lowering	magdalen	mangrove
lifeless	livelong	loyalist	magician	maniacal
lifelike	liveried	lubberly	magnesia	manichee
lifelong	lividity	lucernal	magnetic	manicure
lifetime	lixivial	lucidity	magnific	manifest
ligament	lixivium	luckless	magnolia	manifold
ligation	loadstar	luculent	maharani	maniform
ligature	loanable	luggable	mahogany	mannered
ligneous	loathful	lukewarm	maidenly	mannerly
lignitic	loathing	lumberer	maieutic	manorial
ligulate	localism	luminary	mainland	mansuete
likeable	locality	luminous	maintain	mantelet
likeness	localize	lumpfish	majestic	mantilla
likewise	location	lunation	majolica	manually
limitary	locative	luncheon	majorate	manurial
limonite	locution	lungwort	majority	marabout
lincture	lodestar	lunulate	malapert	marasmus
lineally	lodgment	lupuline	malarial	marauder
linearly	logician	luscious	malarian	maravedi
lineated	logistic	lustrate	malignly	marbling
lingerer	logogram	lustring	malinger	marginal
linguist	logotype	lustrous	malodour	margined
liniment	loiterer	lustrums	malstick	margrave
linnaean	lollardy	lutanist	maltreat	marigold
linoleum	lollipop	lutenist	maltster	marinade
linstock	lomentum	lutheran	maltworm	maritime
lipogram	lonesome	luxation	mammalia	marjoram
liquidly	longeval	lycopode	mammifer	markedly
listener	longhand	lymphoid	mammilla	marksman
listeria	longsome	lyricist	manciple	marmoset
listless	longways	macaroni	mandamus	maronite
literary	longwise	macaroon	mandarin	marquess
literate	loophole	macerate	mandible	marquise

marriage	medicine	messmate	minority	modeller
marrying	medieval	messuage	minstrel	moderate
martagon	mediocre	mestizos	minuscle	modestly
martinet	meditate	metalled	minutely	modifier
mascotte	medullar	metallic	minutiae	modishly
massacre	meekness	metamere	miriness	modulate
masseter	meetness	metaphor	mirthful	moisture
masseuse	megapode	meteoric	misapply	molasses
massicot	meiocene	metewand	miscarry	molecule
masterly	melanism	meteyard	mischief	moleskin
masticot	melanite	methinks	miscible	molossus
mastitis	melanoma	methodic	miscount	molybdic
mastless	melasses	methylic	misdoubt	momently
mastodon	melibean	metonymy	misguide	momentum
mateless	melinite	metrical	misheard	monachal
material	melodeon	mezereon	misjudge	monander
maternal	melodics	miasmata	misogamy	monandry
matrices	melodist	microbic	misogyny	monarchy
matronal	melodize	microzoa	misplace	monastic
matronly	meltdown	middling	misprint	monetary
mattress	membered	midnight	misprise	monetize
maturely	membrane	mightily	misprize	mongoose
maturity	memorial	mildness	misquote	monistic
maxillae	memorize	milesian	misshape	monition
maxillar	menhaden	militant	misspeak	monitory
maximize	meninges	military	misspell	monitrix
maximist	meniscus	militate	misspend	monocarp
mayoress	menology	milkmaid	misspent	monocrat
mazarine	menstrua	milleped	misstate	monodist
maziness	mentagra	milliped	mistaken	monogamy
mazourka	mentally	milliard	mistitle	monogram
meagrely	mephitic	milliner	mistress	monolith
meanness	mephitis	milliped	mistrust	monopoly
meantime	merchant	mimicker	mitigant	monotone
measured	merciful	minatory	mitigate	monotony
mechanic	mercuric	mindless	mittimus	monsieur
medalist	meridian	minimize	mnemonic	monticle
medallic	merosome	minimums	mobility	monument
meddling	mesmeric	minister	mobilize	moonbeam
mediator	mesozoic	ministry	moccasin	moonless
medicate	mesquite	minorite	modality	moonshee

moorland	muleteer	nacreous	nectared	nominate
mootable	mulishly	nainsook	needfire	nomology
moralist	multifid	nameable	needless	nonesuch
morality	multiped	nameless	negation	non-event
moralize	multiple	namesake	negative	nonsense
moravian	multiply	napiform	neighbor	noontide
morbidly	mumbling	napoleon	nematode	normally
morbific	mungoose	narcosis	nematoid	norseman
morceaux	muniment	narcotic	neologic	northern
moreover	munition	narghile	neophyte	noseless
morepork	murderer	nargileh	neoteric	nosology
moresque	muriatic	narrator	nepenthe	notarial
moribund	muricate	narrowly	nephrite	notation
morosely	muriform	nasalize	nepotism	notching
morphine	murmurer	nascency	nepotist	notebook
mortally	murrhine	nasicorm	nestling	noteless
mortgage	muscadel	nasiform	neuritis	notional
mortmain	muscatel	natation	neurosis	novelist
mortuary	muscular	natatory	neurotic	november
mosaical	mushroom	national	newscast	novercal
mosquito	musician	natively	newsreel	nowadays
motherly	musingly	nativity	niceness	nuciform
motility	muslinet	naumachy	nickelic	nucleate
motivity	musquash	nauseate	nickname	nucleoli
motorial	musquito	nauseous	nicotian	nudeness
motorway	mustache	nautical	nicotine	nugatory
moufflon	mutation	nautilus	nihilism	nuisance
moulding	mutchkin	navigate	nihilist	numberer
mountain	muteness	nazarean	nihility	numbness
mounting	mutilate	nazarene	ninepins	numerary
mournful	mutineer	nazarite	nineteen	numerate
mourning	mutinous	nearctic	nitrogen	numerous
mouthful	mutterer	nearness	noachian	nummular
moveless	mutually	neatherd	nobility	numskull
movement	mycelium	neatness	nobleman	nuptials
movingly	mycology	nebulose	noblesse	nursling
muchness	myelitis	nebulous	nocturne	nutation
muciform	myriapod	necklace	nodosity	nutrient
mucilage	myrmidon	neckline	noetical	nymphean
mucosity	mystical	necrosis	nomadish	obduracy
mulberry	mythical	necrosed	nomarchy	obdurate

obedient
obeisant
obituary
objector
oblation
obligant
obligate
obligato
obliging
oblivion
obscurer
observer
obsidian
obsolete
obstacle
obstruct
obtainer
obtruder
obturate
obtusely
obvolute
occasion
occident
occultly
occupant
occupier
occelate
ochreous
octopede
octoroon
ocularly
oculated
odiously
odometer
odontoid
oenology
offender
offering
official
offshoot
offshore

ofttimes
oiliness
ointment
oleander
olibanum
oligarch
olympiad
olympian
omission
omissive
omniform
omohyoid
omoplate
omphalic
oncoming
oncotomy
onlooker
ontogeny
ontology
oologist
opaquely
openness
operatic
operator
operetta
ophidian
opopanax
opponent
opposite
optative
optician
optimism
optimist
optimize
optional
opulence
opuscule
oracular
oragious
orangery
oratorio

orbitary
orcadian
orchella
ordainer
ordinand
ordinant
ordinary
ordinate
ordnance
ordurous
organism
organist
organize
orichalc
oriental
original
ornament
ornately
ornithic
orpiment
orthodox
orthoepy
orthogon
oscitant
osculant
osculate
osmanlis
osnaburg
otiosity
otoscope
ouistiti
outargue
outbrave
outbreak
outburst
outdoors
outflank
outgoing
outlawry
outlying
outmarch

outrance
outreach
outrider
outright
outshine
outsider
outskirt
outsmart
outspeak
outstare
outstrip
outswear
outvalue
outwards
outwatch
outweigh
overalls
overarch
overbear
overbold
overbrim
overcast
overcoat
overcome
overdare
overdose
overdraw
overflow
overgrow
overhand
overhang
overhaul
overhead
overhear
overheat
overhung
overkill
overland
overleap
overlive
overload

overlook
overlord
overmuch
overnice
overpass
overplus
override
overripe
overrule
overseas
overseer
overshoe
oversman
overstay
overstep
overtake
overtask
overtime
overtone
overture
overturn
overview
overween
overwind
overwise
overwork
overworn
own-brand
oxidizer
oxymoron
pacifier
packager
packfong
padishah
paduasoy
paganish
paganism
paganize
paginate
painless
painting

pairwise   paradigm   passover   pellucid   peruvian
palatial   paradise   passport   peltated   perverse
palatine   paraffin   pastille   pemmican   pervious
paleness   paragoge   pastoral   penchant   pesterer
palestra   paragram   patagium   pendency   petaline
palimony   parakeet   patchery   pendulum   petaloid
palinode   parallax   patentee   penitent   petiolar
palisade   parallel   paternal   penknife   petioled
palliate   paralyse   pathetic   penology   petition
pallmall   paralyze   pathless   penstock   petitory
palmated   paramere   patience   pentacle   petrific
palmette   paramour   patulous   pentagon   petronel
palmetto   parasang   pauldron   pentagyn   petrosal
palmiped   parasite   pavement   penumbra   pettifog
palmitic   parcener   pavilion   peperine   petulant
palpable   pardoner   pavonine   peperino   pewterer
palpably   parental   pawnshop   perceive   phalange
palstaff   parergon   peaceful   perforce   phantasm
palstave   pargeter   pearlash   perfumer   phantasy
palterer   parhelia   peasecod   periagua   pharisee
paludine   parhelic   peccable   perianth   pharmacy
paludism   parietal   peccancy   pericarp   pheasant
paludose   parisian   pectinal   periderm   phenogam
pamperer   parlance   pectoral   perigean   philabeg
pamphlet   parmesan   peculate   perilous   philibeg
pancreas   parodist   peculiar   perineal   philomel
pandanus   paronymy   pedagogy   perineum   pholades
pandemic   paroxysm   pedantic   periodic   phonetic
pangolin   partaker   pedantry   periplus   phorminx
panicled   parterre   pedestal   perjurer   phormium
pannikin   parthian   pedicure   permeate   photofit
panorama   partible   pedigree   peroneal   phthisic
pantheon   partisan   pedimane   perorate   phthisis
papalist   partizan   pediment   peroxide   phylarch
papalize   part-time   peduncle   perruque   phyletic
papillae   part-work   peerless   persimon   phylloid
papistic   pashalic   pelagian   personal   physalia
papistry   passable   pelasgic   perspire   physical
papulose   passably   pelerine   persuade   physique
papulous   passeres   pellagra   pertness   piacular
parabola   passible   pellicle   pertused   pianette

piassava
picaroon
piciform
pickerel
picklock
piercing
pigeonry
pilaster
pilchard
pileated
pilewort
pilferer
piliform
pillager
pillared
pillowed
pillworm
pilotage
pinafore
pinaster
pindaric
ping-pong
pinnacle
pinnated
pinniped
pinwheel
pipeclay
pipefish
pipeline
pipewort
piquancy
piscator
pisiform
pisolite
pithless
pitiably
pitiless
pittance
pityroid
pizzeria
placable

placeman
placenta
placidly
plagiary
plaguily
planchet
plangent
planless
plantain
plantlet
plastery
plastron
plateaus
plateaux
platform
platinum
platonic
platting
platypus
plausive
playbill
playbook
playgoer
playlist
playmate
pleading
pleasant
pleasing
pleasure
plebeian
plectrum
pleiades
pleonasm
plethora
pleurisy
pliantly
plicated
plighter
pliocene
plodding
plougher

pluckily
plumbago
plumbean
plumbery
plumbery
plumbing
plumelet
plumiped
plurally
plutonic
pluvious
podagral
podagric
podalgia
poetical
poignant
poisoner
polarity
polarize
polemics
policies
polished
polisher
politely
politics
poltroon
polygamy
polyglot
polygram
polygyny
polypary
polypite
polypody
polypous
polyzoon
pomander
pomology
poorness
popinjay
popishly
populace

populate
populous
poriform
poristic
porosity
porously
porphyry
porpoise
porridge
portable
port-fire
port-hole
porticos
portrait
portress
port-wine
position
positive
possibly
postcard
postcode
postdate
post-horn
postmark
post-obit
post-paid
postpone
post-town
posturer
potassic
potation
potatoes
potatory
potently
pot-house
potsherd
poultice
poundage
powdered
powerful
practice

practise
prandial
prankish
prattler
preacher
preamble
precinct
precious
preclude
pre-exist
pregnant
prejudge
prelatic
premolar
premorse
prentice
preparer
prepense
prescind
presence
preserve
pressing
pressman
pressure
prestige
pretence
pretense
preterit
prettily
previous
pricking
prideful
prie-dieu
priestly
priggish
primeval
primness
primrose
princely
princess
printing

print-out	prostate	punisher	queerish	rambling
priorate	prostyle	punitive	quencher	rampancy
prioress	protasis	punitory	question	ranchero
priories	protocol	puparial	quibbler	rancidly
priority	protozoa	pupilage	quickset	rankness
prismoid	protract	pupilary	quiddity	ransomer
prisoner	protrude	puppyish	quidnunc	rapacity
pristine	provable	puppyism	quietism	rape-cake
probable	provably	purblind	quietist	rapeseed
probably	provided	purchase	quietude	rapidity
proceeds	provider	pureness	quilling	raptores
proclaim	province	purifier	quilting	raptured
procuror	proximal	purplish	quincunx	rareness
prodigal	prudence	purseful	quirkish	rascally
producer	prunella	pursenet	quitrent	rashness
proemial	prurient	purslane	quivered	rasorial
profaner	prussian	pursuant	quixotic	rational
profound	psalmist	purulent	quotable	ratsbane
progress	psalmody	purveyor	quotient	ravenous
prohibit	psaltery	pustular	rabbinic	ravingly
prolapse	psychist	putative	racemose	ravisher
prolific	pteropod	pyogenic	rachitic	re-absorb
prologue	ptomaine	pyriform	rachitis	reaction
promiser	ptyalism	pyrology	raciness	reactive
promoter	publican	pyroxene	rack-rent	readable
prompter	publicly	pythonic	radially	readably
promptly	puddling	pyxidium	radiance	readjust
propense	puff-ball	quadrant	radiator	reaffirm
properly	pugilism	quadrate	radicate	realiser
property	pugilist	quadriga	raggedly	realness
prophecy	puissant	quadroon	ragstone	reappear
prophesy	pulingly	quaestor	raillery	rearmost
proplasm	pull-down	quagmire	railroad	rearward
propolis	pulmonic	quaintly	rainband	reasoner
proposal	pumproom	qualmish	raincoat	reassert
proposer	puncheon	quandary	rainfall	reassign
propound	punctate	quantity	rainless	reassume
propylon	punctual	quarrier	raisable	reassure
prorogue	puncture	quartern	raisonne	reattach
prosodic	pungency	quatrain	rakehell	rebuttal
prospect	puniness	queasily	rakishly	rebutter

recanter	regiment	reniform	resigned	revolver
receiver	regional	renneted	resigner	rewarder
recently	register	renounce	resinous	rhapsode
recessed	registry	renovate	resister	rhapsody
reckless	regrater	renowned	resolute	rheostat
reckoner	regrowth	rentable	resolved	rheotome
recommit	regulate	reoccupy	resolver	rhetoric
reconvey	rehearse	reometer	resonant	rhizanth
recorder	reimport	reordain	resorter	rhizogen
recourse	reimpose	repairer	resource	rhizopod
recovery	reinless	repartee	response	rhomboid
recreant	reinsert	repealer	restless	rhonchus
recreate	reinsure	repeater	restorer	rhythmic
recusant	reinvest	repeller	restrain	ribaldry
redactor	rejecter	repenter	restrict	richness
redargue	rejoicer	repeople	resupine	ricochet
redeemer	rekindle	reperuse	retailer	riddance
redolent	relative	repetend	retainer	ridicule
redouble	releaser	replevin	retarder	rifeness
redshank	relegate	reporter	reticent	riffraff
redstart	relevant	repousse	reticule	rifleman
reed-band	reliable	reprieve	retiform	rigadoon
reed-mace	reliably	reprisal	retiring	rightful
reed-pipe	reliance	reproach	retrench	rigidity
re-engage	reliever	reproval	retrieve	rigorous
re-enlist	religion	reprover	retroact	ring-bolt
re-export	relisten	reptilia	retrorse	ring-bone
re-fasten	remanent	republic	returner	ring-dove
referrer	remarker	requital	revealer	ringpull
refinery	remarque	requiter	reveille	ringworm
reflexed	remedial	rereward	reveller	riparial
reflexly	remember	rescript	revenger	ripeness
refluent	reminder	research	reverend	ritually
reforest	remissly	resemble	reverent	riverine
reformed	remittal	resenter	reversal	riveting
reformer	remittee	reserved	reviewal	road-book
refunder	remitter	reserver	reviewer	road-rage
regality	remotely	resetter	revision	roadster
regarder	renderer	resident	revivify	roborant
regather	rendible	residual	revolter	roburite
regicide	renegade	residuum	revolute	rock-cork

rockrose	rubrical	salesman	sapience	scarcely
rock-ruby	rucksack	salicine	saponify	scarcity
rock-salt	rudeness	salience	sapphire	scavenge
rock-soap	rudiment	salivant	saraband	scathing
rock-wood	ruefully	salivate	sarcenet	scenario
rock-work	ruffling	salmonet	sardonic	scenical
rodentia	ruggedly	salt-bush	sardonyx	scentful
roll-call	rugosity	salt-junk	sargasso	sceptred
roly-poly	ruinable	saltless	sarmenta	schedule
romancer	ruleless	salt-lick	sarsenet	scheming
romanism	ruminant	salt-mine	satanist	schemist
romanist	ruminate	saltness	satiable	schiedam
romanize	rummager	salt-work	satirist	schmaltz
romantic	rum-shrub	saltwort	satirize	schnapps
rood-beam	runagate	salutary	saturate	scholium
rood-loft	runology	salvable	saturday	schooner
roofless	ruralise	samaroid	saucebox	sciatica
rooftree	ruralism	sameness	saucepan	scilicet
root-crop	rutabaga	samizdat	savagely	scimitar
rootedly	ruthless	samphire	savagery	sciolism
ropewalk	rye-grass	sanative	savagism	sciolism
ropiness	sabbatic	sanatory	savannah	sciolist
rosarian	sabulous	sanctify	savingly	scioptic
rose-pink	saccular	sanction	savoyard	scirrhus
rosemary	sacredly	sanctity	saw-frame	scission
rosewood	sacristy	sandbank	saxatile	scissors
rosiness	saddlery	sandbath	saxonism	sciurine
rosoglio	sadducee	sand-flea	saxonist	scleroma
rostella	safeness	sand-hill	scabbard	scolding
rostrate	sagacity	sandiver	scabious	scoop-net
rotation	sagamore	sand-mole	scabrous	scornful
rotative	sage-cock	sandwich	scaffold	scorpion
rotatory	sageness	saneness	scalable	scot-free
rotiform	sailless	sangaree	scallion	scotsman
rottenly	sail-loft	sanguine	scammony	scottice
roulette	sainfoin	sanitary	scampish	scottish
rowdyism	salad-oil	sanitize	scandent	scourger
royalism	salaried	sanserif	scansion	scowling
royalist	salaries	sanskrit	scantily	scrabble
rubicund	saleable	sap-green	scaphoid	scragged
rubidium	saleably	sapidity	scapular	scramble

scrannel	seascape	semi-mute	severely	shirting
scraping	seashore	seminary	severity	shocking
scrawler	sea-snake	semitone	sewerage	shoe-horn
screamer	seasonal	semolina	sexangle	shoeless
screechy	seasoner	senility	sextuple	shooting
screw-key	sea-wrack	senorita	sexually	shortage
scribble	secluded	sensible	shabbily	short-rib
scrofula	seconder	sensibly	shabrack	shot-belt
scrolled	secondly	sensific	shaddock	shoulder
scrub-oak	secretly	sensuous	shafting	showroom
scrubber	sectoral	sentence	shagreen	shrapnel
scrupler	securely	sentient	shalloon	shrewdly
scrutiny	security	sentinel	shamanic	shrewish
scuffler	sedately	sentries	shambles	shrimper
scullery	sedation	sepaline	shameful	shrunken
scullion	sedative	sepaloid	shamrock	shuffler
sculptor	sederunt	sepalous	shanties	sibilant
scurrile	sediment	separate	shapable	sibilate
scurvily	sedition	septette	sharp-cut	sick-list
scutcher	sedulity	septicle	sharp-set	sickness
scutella	sedulous	sequelae	shattery	sickroom
scythian	seed-cake	sequence	shealing	side-arms
sea-acorn	seed-corn	seraglio	shearing	side-dish
sea-board	seedling	seraphic	sheathed	sideline
sea-coast	seedsman	seraphim	sheepdog	sidelong
sea-devil	seership	serenade	sheepish	sidereal
sea-eagle	seignior	serenely	sheep-run	siderite
seafarer	seignory	serenity	sheeting	sidesman
seafight	seizable	sergeant	sheiling	sidewalk
seagoing	selector	serially	shelving	sideways
sea-grass	selenite	seriatim	shemitic	side-wind
sea-green	selenium	serjeant	shepherd	sidewise
sea-horse	self-help	serosity	shilling	sigmatic
sea-lemon	self-love	serrated	shin-bone	signable
sea-level	self-made	servitor	shingled	signally
sea-louse	selfsame	sesamoid	shingles	signeted
sealskin	self-will	sess-pool	shipworm	sign-post
seamless	selvedge	sesterce	shipyard	silently
sea-onion	semantic	sestette	shipmate	silicate
searcher	semester	setiform	shipment	silicify
sea-rover	semi-dome	settling	shipping	silicium

silicone	skin-deep	smelling	socratic	sordidly
silicula	skinhead	smeltery	sodomite	soreness
silicule	skinless	smithery	softback	sortable
siliquae	skin-wool	smoke-box	softener	sortment
silk-mill	skipjack	smoothen	softness	souchong
silkworm	skipping	smoothly	soil-pipe	soulless
sillabub	skirmish	smothery	solatium	sounding
silurian	skirrhus	smoulder	solderer	sourness
silverly	skittish	smuggler	soldiery	southern
simoniac	skittles	smugness	solecism	southing
simperer	skua-gull	smut-ball	solecist	souvenir
simplify	skulless	smuttily	solecize	sow-bread
simulate	skylight	snapshot	solemnly	spacelab
sinaitic	slapdash	snappish	soleness	spacious
sinapism	slashing	snarling	solidify	spadeful
sinciput	slattern	snatcher	solidity	spalpeen
sinecure	slaverer	sneaking	solitary	spandrel
sinfully	slavonic	sneezing	solitude	spangled
singsong	sleepily	snivelly	solstice	spaniard
singular	sleeping	snobbery	solution	spanking
sinister	slightly	snobbish	solvable	span-roof
sinology	slime-pit	snobbism	solvency	sparable
siphonal	slimline	softener	somatist	spar-deck
siphonic	slimness	software	sombrely	sparerib
sirenian	slip-dock	snowball	sombrero	sparkish
sisterly	slippery	snowbird	sombrous	sparsely
sitology	slip-shod	snowboot	somebody	spathose
situated	slipslop	snowdrop	somerset	spavined
sitzbath	slobbery	snow-line	some-such	speaking
sixpence	slop-shop	snowshoe	sometime	spearman
sixpenny	slothful	snow-slip	somewhat	specific
sixtieth	slovenly	snub-nose	somnific	specimen
sizeable	slow-worm	snuffbox	song-bird	specious
skean-dhu	slowness	snuffler	songless	speckled
skeletal	sluggard	snuggery	songster	spectral
skeleton	sluggish	snugness	son-in-law	spectrum
skerries	sluttery	sobriety	sonority	specular
sketcher	sluttish	sociable	sonorous	speculum
skew-bald	slyboots	sociably	soothing	speedily
skilless	smacking	socially	sopranos	spelaean
skimming	smallage	socinian	sorcerer	spelling

sperm-oil	sprinkle	starched	stop-cock	stud-book
sphagnum	spritzer	starcher	stoppage	studious
sphenoid	sprucely	starfish	stopping	stuffing
spherics	spurgall	starless	stormful	stultify
spheroid	spur-gear	starlike	stowaway	stumbler
spherule	spurious	starling	straddle	stunning
sphygmic	squabble	statedly	straggle	stupidly
spicular	squadron	statical	straight	stuprate
spikelet	squamate	statuary	strained	stupidly
spike-oil	squamous	steadily	strainer	sturgeon
spinelle	squander	stealing	straiten	subacrid
spinifex	squarely	stealthy	straitly	subacute
spinster	squatter	steam-tug	stramash	subclass
spiricle	squeaker	stearine	stranger	suberose
spirally	squeezer	steatite	strangle	suberous
spirilla	squirrel	stedfast	strapper	sub-genus
spirited	stabling	steeling	strategy	sub-lease
spiteful	stablish	steenbok	stratify	sublunar
spitfire	staccato	steepled	streaker	submerge
spittoon	stagnant	steerage	streamer	submerse
splatter	stagnate	stellary	strength	suborder
splendid	stair-rod	stellate	striated	suborner
splendor	stake-net	stem-leaf	stricken	subovate
splinter	stalking	stemless	strickly	subpoena
splitter	stallage	sterling	strictly	sub-polar
splotchy	stallion	stibnite	strident	subserve
splutter	stalwart	stickler	striking	subtlety
spoliate	stamened	stiletto	stringed	sub-tonic
spondaic	staminal	stimulus	stringer	subtract
sponsion	stamp-act	stingily	stripper	subulate
spontoon	stampede	stinging	strobile	suburban
spookish	stamping	sting-ray	strongly	succinct
spoonful	stancher	stink-pot	strontia	succinic
sporadic	stanchly	stipular	strophic	suchwise
sporidia	standard	stirless	struggle	suckling
sportful	standing	stirring	strumose	sudatory
sporting	standish	stockade	strumous	suddenly
sportive	stanhope	stock-pot	strumpet	sufferer
spotless	stannary	stoicism	strutter	suffrage
sprigged	stanzaic	stomatic	stubbled	suicidal
springer	stapella	stooping	stubborn	suitable

suitably	sweeping	tafferel	tasteful	tendance
sulcated	sweet-bay	tailback	tattered	tendency
sullenly	sweeting	tailless	tattling	tenderly
sulphate	sweetish	tail-race	tattooer	tenement
sulphoid	sweetpea	takeaway	taunting	tenesmic
sulphite	sweet-sop	takingly	taverner	tenesmus
sulphury	swelling	talisman	tawdrily	tenon-saw
sultanic	swimming	talk-show	taxation	tent-wine
summoner	swindler	talliage	tax-break	tentacle
sun-burnt	swinging	tallness	tax-dodge	terminal
sunlight	sword-arm	tallower	tax-exile	terminus
sun-shade	sybarite	tallyman	tax-haven	termless
sunshine	sycamine	talmudic	taxology	terrapin
sunshiny	sycamore	tameable	taxonomy	terrible
superadd	syllabic	tamandua	tea-caddy	terribly
superbly	syllable	taramack	tea-chest	terrific
superior	syllabus	tamarind	teaching	tertiary
superloo	symbolic	tamarisk	teamster	tesserae
superman	symmetry	tameless	tear-drop	testator
superset	sympathy	tameness	tearless	testicle
supinely	symphony	tamperer	teaseler	test-tube
supplant	symposia	tan-balls	technics	tetanoid
supplier	synopsis	tangency	tectonic	tetragon
supposer	synoptic	tangible	teething	tetrapod
suppress	synovial	tangibly	teetotal	tetrarch
surcease	syphilis	tanistry	teetotum	teutonic
surgical	systemic	tannable	tegument	textbook
surmiser	systolic	tantalum	telegram	text-hand
surmount	syzygies	tape-line	teletext	thalamus
surplice	tabbinet	tapestry	telethon	thalline
surround	tabby-cat	tapeworm	tellable	thallium
surveyor	tableaux	tap-house	telltale	thanedom
survival	tabouret	tara-fern	tellural	thankful
survivor	tabulate	tarboosh	telluric	thatcher
suspense	taciturn	targeted	temerity	thearchy
suttling	tackling	tarlatan	tempered	theatric
suzerain	tacksman	tartaric	temporal	theistic
swannery	tactical	tartness	tempting	thematic
swanskin	tactless	tartrate	temulent	theocrat
swap-shop	taenioid	taskwork	tenacity	theodicy
swashing	tafferal	tastable	tenantry	theogony

theology	tide-gate	tolbooth	townward	treasure
theorist	tideless	tolerant	toxicant	treasury
theorize	tidemill	tolerate	tracheal	treating
theories	tide-wave	tollable	trachyte	treatise
therefor	tidiness	tollgate	trackage	treeless
thereout	tie-break	tomahawk	tractate	treenail
thespian	tigerish	tomatoes	traction	trembler
theurgic	tillable	tombless	tractive	trencher
thickish	timbered	tomentum	trade-off	trephine
thickset	time-ball	tom-noddy	traducer	trespass
thievery	time-bill	tomorrow	traffick	triander
thievish	time-fuse	tonality	tragical	triangle
thinking	timeless	toneless	tragopan	triarchy
thinness	time-worn	tonicity	trail-net	triassic
thinnish	timidity	tonsilar	trainers	tribrach
thirster	timorous	tonsured	training	tribunal
thirteen	tincture	toothful	train-oil	trichina
thole-pin	tinkling	top-boots	trampler	trichoma
thoracic	tinplate	top-dress	tram-rail	trichord
thorinum	tinsmith	top-heavy	tram-road	trickery
thorough	tintless	toponomy	tranquil	tricking
thousand	tip-staff	toreador	transact	trickish
thraldom	tiramisu	toreutic	transept	tricycle
thrasher	tiresome	tortious	transfer	trifling
threaten	titanian	tortoise	transfix	triglyph
threnody	titanium	tortuose	tranship	trigonal
thriller	tithable	tortuous	transmit	trigraph
thriving	tithe-pig	torturer	transude	trillion
thrombus	titmouse	totality	trap-ball	trimeter
throstic	titulary	totemism	trapdoor	trimming
throttle	toadfish	totterer	trapezia	trimness
thrummer	toadflax	touchily	trappean	tripping
thumping	toad-spit	touching	trapping	triptote
thundery	toadyism	toughish	trappist	triptych
thurible	to-and-fro	tournure	trashily	tripwire
thurifer	toboggan	towardly	traveled	triumvir
thursday	together	towering	traveler	trivalve
thwarter	toilless	town-hall	traverse	trochaic
thwartly	toilsome	township	travesty	trochoea
tickling	toil-worn	townsman	trawling	trochoid
ticklish	tokenism	town-talk	trawl-net	trolling

trombone	turn-coat	unallied	unfairly	unproved
troopial	turn-cock	unatoned	unfasten	unreason
trophied	turnover	unavowed	unfetter	unrepaid
trophies	turnpike	unawares	unfilial	unriddle
tropical	turnsole	unbelief	unforgot	unsaddle
troubler	turnspit	unbiased	unformed	unsafely
trousers	turreted	unbidden	unfunded	unsealed
troutlet	tutelage	unbolted	ungainly	unseemly
trouvere	tutelary	unbought	ungentle	unsettle
truckage	tutorage	unbroken	ungently	unshaken
truckler	tutoress	unbuckle	unglazed	unshapen
trueblue	tutorial	unbundle	ungulate	unshroud
trueborn	twaddler	unburden	unhanged	unsifted
truebred	tweezers	unburied	unharmed	unslaked
truelove	twilight	unburned	unheeded	unsocial
trueness	twin-born	unbutton	unholily	unsoiled
truffled	twinling	uncalled	uniaxial	unsought
trumpery	twitcher	uncandid	unifilar	unsoured
truncate	two-edged	unchased	unionism	unspoken
trunnion	two-faced	unchurch	unionist	unstable
trussing	twopence	unciform	unipolar	unsteady
trustful	twopenny	uncinate	uniquely	unstring
trustily	tympanic	unclothe	unitedly	unstrung
truthful	tympanum	uncomely	univalve	unsuited
tubercle	typifier	uncommon	universe	unswathe
tuberose	typology	uncouple	univocal	untasted
tuberous	tyrannic	unctuous	unjustly	unthread
tubewell	tyrolese	undecked	unkennel	unthrift
tubiform	ubiquity	underbid	unkindly	untidily
tubulose	udometer	underbuy	unlawful	untimely
tubulous	ugliness	underlay	unlikely	untinged
tumbling	ulcerate	underlie	unlimber	untiring
tumidity	ulcerous	underpin	unlovely	untitled
tuneless	ulterior	undulate	unmeetly	untoward
tungsten	ultimate	unearned	unmuffle	unvalued
tungstic	ultraism	uneasily	unmuzzle	unvaried
tunicate	ultraist	unending	unpathed	unversed
turanian	umbonate	unenvied	unpeople	unvoiced
turbaned	umbrella	unerring	unpitied	unwarily
turgidly	umpirage	unevenly	unpoetic	unwarped
turmeric	unabated	unfading	unpolite	unwashed

unwashen
unwieldy
unwisdom
unwisely
unwished
unwanted
unworthy
upgrowth
upheaval
upholder
uplander
upmarket
uprising
upsetter
upspring
up-stroke
upwardly
urbanity
urethral
urgently
uroscopy
ursuline
urticate
usefully
usufruct
usurious
uxorious
vacation
vagabond
vaginate
vagrancy
vainness
valerian
validate
validity
valorous
valuable
valuator
valvular
vanadium
vandalic

vanguard
vanquish
vaporize
vaporose
vaporous
vapourer
variable
variably
variance
varicose
varietal
variform
variolar
variorum
varletry
vascular
vasculum
vaseline
vasiform
vassalry
vastness
vaulting
vegetate
vehement
veilless
veinless
velarium
velleity
velocity
venality
venation
vendetta
vendible
vendibly
venerate
venereal
venetian
vengeful
venially
venomous
venosity

venturer
veracity
verandah
veratrin
verbally
verbatim
verbiage
verdancy
verderer
verditer
verdured
verifier
verjuice
veronica
versicle
vertexes
vertices
verticle
vertical
vesicant
vesicate
vespiary
vestment
vestured
vesuvian
vexation
vexillar
vexillum
viaticum
vibrator
vicarage
vicarial
vicenary
vicinage
vicinity
victoria
victress
videofit
viennese
viewless
vigilant

vigneron
vignette
vigorous
vileness
vilifier
vilipend
villager
villainy
vincible
vinculum
vine-clad
vineyard
vinosity
vintager
vintnery
violable
violator
violence
viperine
viperish
viperous
virginal
viridity
viaility
virtuoso
virtuous
virulent
visceral
viscount
visigoth
visional
visitant
visiting
vitalism
vitalist
vitality
vitalize
vitellus
vitiator
vitreous
vituline

vivacity
vivarium
vivavoce
vixenish
vocalist
vocality
vocalize
vocation
vocative
voiceful
voidable
voidance
voidness
volatile
volcanic
volition
volitive
voltaism
vomiting
vomitory
voracity
vortices
vorticle
votaress
votarist
votaries
votively
voussoir
vowelism
vowelled
voyageur
volcanic
vulgarly
wagonage
wainscot
waitress
wall-eyed
wallower
wall-tree
wanderer
wanderoo

wantonly	weaponed	whipster	wire-worm	wrangler
war-bride	wearable	whirlwig	wirewove	wrappage
war-crime	weeklies	whirring	wiriness	wrapping
war-dance	weeviled	whistler	wiseacre	wrathful
wardenry	welcomer	whiteboy	wiseness	wreckage
wardrobe	weldable	white-leg	wish-bone	wrestler
ward-room	welladay	whitener	wishlist	wretched
wardship	well-born	white-out	wisteria	wriggler
war-horse	well-bred	whoredom	witch-elm	wrinkled
wariness	well-knit	whoreson	witchery	wristlet
warmness	well-read	wickedly	witching	wrongful
war-paint	well-room	wickered	withdraw	wrongous
warranty	well-to-do	wideness	withhold	xanthoma
warrener	well-worn	wifehood	woefully	xanthous
war-whoop	werewolf	wifelike	womanish	xenogamy
washable	wesleyan	wig-block	wonderer	xylocarp
washroom	westerly	wild-boar	wondrous	yachting
wasteful	westmost	wild-card	woodbine	yataghan
watch-dog	westward	wildfire	woodcock	yeanling
watchful	wet-nurse	wild-fowl	woodenly	year-book
watchman	wharfage	wildness	woodland	yearling
water-dog	whatever	wild-wood	woodlark	yearning
water-gas	wheatear	wilfully	woodruff	yeomanly
water-hen	wheat-eel	wiliness	woodwork	yeomanry
watering	wheat-fly	windfall	woolngly	yielding
waterman	wheedler	windgall	wool-dyed	yokemate
water-pot	wheelman	windlass	wool-mill	youngish
water-pox	whenever	windless	woolpack	yourself
water-ram	wherever	windmill	woolsack	youthful
water-rat	wherries	windowed	woolward	yule-tide
wattling	whey-face	windpipe	wordbook	zamindar
waveless	whiffler	windrose	word-wrap	zealotry
wave-worn	whiggery	windsail	workable	zemindar
wax-cloth	whiggish	windsurf	workaday	zenithal
waxed-end	whimbrel	windward	workrate	zeolitic
waxiness	whimsies	wing-case	workshop	zigzaggy
wax-light	whin-chat	wingless	worm-cast	zodiacal
wayfarer	whip-cord	winnower	wormling	zoetrope
weakling	whip-hand	winterly	wormwood	zoolatry
weakness	whiplash	wire-draw	worrying	zoophile
weanling	whipping	wire-rope	worthily	zoophily

zoophyte   zootomic
zoosperm   zymology
zoospore

9-Letter Words

abandoned
abandoner
abasement
abashment
abatement
abbotship
abdominal
abduction
aberrance
abhorrent
abhorring
abidingly
abjection
abnegator
abolisher
abolition
abominate
aborigine
abrahamic
absconder
absinthic
absorbent
abstainer
abstinent
absurdity
abundance
abusively
acalephae
accentual
accessary
accession
accessory
accidence
accipiter
acclimate
acclivity
acclivous

accompany
accordant
according
accordion
accretion
accretive
accumbent
accusable
acescence
acetifier
acetylene
acidifier
acidulate
acidulent
acidulous
aciniform
acoustics
acquiesce
acquittal
acrobatic
acropolis
acrospire
actualist
actuality
acuminate
acuteness
adaptable
addiction
addressed
addressee
addresser
adducible
adduction
adenotomy
adherence
adipocere
adjacence

adjective
adjoining
adjutancy
admeasure
adminicle
admirable
admirably
admiralty
admission
admixtion
admixture
admonitor
adoptable
adoration
adoringly
adornment
adulation
adulterer
adultness
adumbrant
adumbrate
advantage
adventual
adventure
adverbial
adversary
adversely
advertent
advertise
advisable
advisably
advisedly
advocator
aegophony
aepyornis
aerometer
aerometry

aerophyte
aeroplane
aesthetic
aetiology
affecting
affection
affianced
affidavit
affiliate
affirmant
afflicter
aforehand
aforesaid
aforetime
after-crop
afterdamp
afterglow
afterlife
aftermath
aftermost
afternoon
afterward
aggravate
aggregate
aggressor
agitation
agonistic
agonizing
agony-aunt
agreeable
agreeably
agreement
aimlessly
air-engine
air-jacket
aitchbone
aitiology

alabaster
alack-a-day
alarm-bell
albatross
albescent
albuginea
alburnous
alchemist
alcoholic
ale-conner
alertness
algebraic
alienable
alienator
alignment
alimental
alizarine
allantois
allayment
allegoric
alleluiah
alleviate
all-hallow
alligator
allograph
allopathy
allotment
allotropy
allowable
allowably
allowance
alma mater
almandine
almond-oil
alms-giver
almshouse
aloes-wood

alongside
alpenhorn
altar-tomb
alterable
altercate
alternate
altiscope
aluminium
aluminous
amaryllis
amassment
amaurosis
amaurotic
amazement
amazingly
amazonian
ambergris
ambiguity
ambiguous
ambitious
amblyopia
ambrosial
ambulacra
ambulance
ambuscade
amendable
amendment
amianthus
amidships
amorously
amorphous
ampersand
amphibian
amphibole
amphigory
amphioxus
ampleness
amplified
amplitude
amusement
amusingly

amusively
analectic
analgesia
analogist
analogize
analogous
analytics
anandrous
anapestic
anaplasty
anarchist
anastatic
anatomism
anatomist
anatomize
anatropal
ancestral
anchorage
anchorite
anchylose
anciently
ancillary
anecdotal
angel-cake
angel-dust
angelfish
angle-iron
anglicism
anglicize
angularly
angulated
anhybrite
anhydrous
animalism
animality
animalize
animating
animation
animistic
animosity
ankylosis

annotator
announcer
annoyance
annuitant
annularly
annulment
anomalous
anonymity
anonymous
antalkali
antarctic
ante-choir
antelucan
antemetic
antenatal
anthelion
anthelion
antheroid
anthodium
anthology
anthozoon
anthropic
antichlor
antidotal
antipapal
antipathy
antiphony
antipodal
antipodes
antipyrin
antiquary
antiquity
anti-trade
anxiously
apartment
apathetic
aperitive
apetalous
apheresis
aphyllous
apishness

aplanatic
apocopate
apocrypha
apologist
apologize
apophysis
apostolic
apothecia
appalling
apparatus
apparitor
appellant
appellate
appendage
appendant
appertain
appetence
appetizer
apple-john
appliance
applicant
appointed
apportion
appraiser
apprehend
approbate
aqua-libra
arabesque
arachnida
arachnoid
araucaria
arbitrage
arbitrary
arbitrate
arboreous
arboretum
archangel
archducal
archduchy
archetype
architect

archivist
archstone
arctogeal
arcuation
arduously
areometer
areopagus
argentine
armadillo
armillary
armistice
army-corps
aromatize
arraigner
arrhizous
arriswise
arrogance
arrowroot
arsenical
arsenious
artemisia
arthritic
arthritis
artichoke
articular
artificer
artillery
artlessly
asafetida
asbestine
ascendant
ascension
ascertain
asparagus
aspermous
aspersion
aspersive
asphaltic
asphaltum
asplenium
assailant

assertion	attribute	backslide	barricade	bellicose
assertive	attrition	backstair	barrister	bell-metal
assiduity	audacious	backsword	bashfully	bellpunch
assiduous	audiphone	backwoods	basilicon	bell-tower
assistant	augmenter	bacterium	bas-relief	bellyband
associate	augurship	badminton	bastinado	belonging
assonance	auricular	bagatelle	bastioned	belvedere
assuasive	auriscope	bailiwick	bath-brick	benchmark
assurable	austerely	bakehouse	bath-chair	beneficed
assurance	austerity	balconied	batrachia	benignant
assuredly	authentic	baldachin	battalion	benignity
asthmatic	authoress	bald-eagle	battle-axe	bergamask
astraddle	authorial	bald-faced	bawdiness	berserker
astrakhan	authority	balefully	bay-window	berylline
astrolabe	authorize	balladist	beaconage	beseecher
astrology	autocracy	ballistic	beanfeast	beseeming
astronaut	autograph	ballot-box	bean-goose	besetting
astronomy	automatic	bamboozle	bear-berry	bespangle
astroturf	automaton	banderole	beardless	bespatter
astucious	auxiliary	bandicoot	beatitude	bespeckle
asymmetry	available	bandoleer	beau-ideal	bestially
asymptote	avalanche	bandoline	beaumonde	betrothal
asyndetic	avocation	banefully	beauteous	bevel-gear
asyndeton	avoidable	bank-agent	beautiful	bewitcher
athanasia	avoidance	bank-stock	berberine	biangular
atheistic	avuncular	banqueter	beccafico	bibacious
athenaeum	awakening	banquette	bedlamite	biblicist
athletics	awe-struck	baptismal	bedraggle	bicameral
atmolysis	awfulness	barbarian	bedridden	bicipital
atmometer	awkwardly	barbarist	beech-mast	biconcave
atonement	axiomatic	barbarity	beefeater	bicyclist
atrocious	ayatollah	barbarize	beer-house	biestings
attainder	azedarach	barbarous	beer-money	bifarious
attendant	azimuthal	barefaced	beestings	bifoliate
attention	babirussa	bargainer	befitting	bifurcate
attentive	bacchanal	barnacles	beginning	bigotedly
attenuant	bacchante	barograph	behaviour	bilabiate
attenuate	bacciform	barometer	beleaguer	bilateral
attollent	backbiter	baronetcy	belemnite	bilingual
attracter	backboard	baroscope	believing	biliteral
attractor	backshish	barrelled	bell-glass	billiards

bilocular	blandness	bone-black	break-down	brutishly
bimonthly	blankness	bone-brown	breakfast	bubblegum
bindingly	blaspheme	bone-earth	break-neck	buccaneer
binervate	blasphemy	bon-vivant	breast-pin	bucentaur
binocular	blast-pipe	bookishly	breathing	bucketful
binominal	bleachery	booklouse	breeching	buckhound
binturong	bleakness	bookmaker	breeze-fly	buckshish
biography	blear-eyed	bookplate	bressomer	buckthorn
biologist	blessedly	bookstall	briar-root	bucktooth
biorhythm	blindfold	boomerang	bric-a-brac	buckwheat
bipartite	blindness	boorishly	brick-clay	buff-stick
bipennate	blindworm	boot-maker	brick-kiln	buff-wheel
birch-wine	blockader	bottle-tit	brickwork	bugle-horn
bird-organ	blockhead	boulevard	bridecake	buhrstone
bird's-foot	blond-lace	boundless	bridesman	bulgarian
bird's-nest	blondness	bounteous	bridewell	bulkiness
birthmark	blood-heat	bountiful	briefless	bullfight
birthroot	bloodless	bourgeois	briefness	bull-trout
bisection	bloodshed	bower-bird	brierroot	bumbailif
bisegment	bloodshot	bow-legged	brigadier	bumblebee
bishopric	blossomed	bowstring	brilliant	bumbledom
bismuthal	blue-grass	bow-window	brimstone	bumptious
bisulcate	blue-stone	boxing-day	briquette	buoyantly
bitterish	bluffness	box-keeper	briskness	burlesque
blackball	blunderer	boycotter	britannic	burliness
black-band	bluntness	brachyura	broad-brim	burnisher
blackbird	blush-wine	bracteate	broadcast	bursarial
blackcock	blusterer	brahmanic	broadloom	bursiform
black-fish	boatswain	brainless	broadness	bushiness
black-game	body-clock	brainsick	broadside	bush-metal
black-hole	bodyguard	brambling	broiderer	bussu-palm
black-iron	bog-butter	branchiae	brokerage	butter-bur
blackjack	bold-faced	branchial	bronchial	buttercup
black-lead	boltsprit	branchlet	broom-corn	butterfly
blacklist	bombardon	brand-iron	broom-rape	butterine
blackmail	bombastic	brandling	brotherly	butternut
blackness	bombazine	brass-band	brownness	by-product
bladdered	bomb-ketch	braveness	brushwood	byssolite
blade-bone	bomb proof	brazil-nut	brusquely	bystander
blaeberry	bombshell	bread-corn	brutality	byzantine
blameless	bond-slave	breakable	brutalize	caballine

cabbalism	campanero	carambole	cassocked	cauterize
cabbalist	campanile	carbonado	cassonade	cautioner
cablegram	campanula	carbonate	cassowary	cavalcade
cabriolet	camphoric	carbonize	castalian	cavernous
cachaemia	camp-stool	carbuncle	castelian	ceaseless
cacholong	canaanite	carcinoma	castigate	cebadilla
cacodemon	cancerous	cardboard	castilian	cedarwood
cacoethes	candidate	careenage	castor-oil	celandine
cacophony	candle-nut	carefully	cast-steel	celebrant
cadastral	candlemas	caretaker	casualism	celebrate
cadaveric	candytuft	carmelite	casualist	celebrity
cadetship	cane-brake	carnalist	casuarina	celestial
caesarean	cane-chair	carnality	casuistic	celestine
caesarism	canescent	carnalize	casuistry	cellarage
cainozoic	cane-sugar	carnation	cataclysm	cellarman
cairngorm	canker-fly	carnelian	catalepsy	cellphone
calamanco	cankerous	carnivora	catalogue	celluloid
calandria	cannelure	carnivore	catamaran	cellulose
calcaneum	cannonade	carpenter	catamenia	celticism
calcedony	cannoneer	carpentry	catamount	cenobitic
calculary	canonical	carpetbag	cataplasm	censorial
calculate	cantabile	carpeting	catarrhal	centenary
calculous	canticles	carpet-rod	catchment	centering
calendrer	canvasser	carpingly	catch-poll	centipede
calenture	capacious	carpology	catchword	centrally
calibered	caparison	carrageen	catechism	centre-bit
calibrate	capillary	carronade	catechist	centurial
caliphate	capillose	carron-oil	catechize	centurion
callipers	capitally	carrousel	caterwaul	cephalate
callosity	capitular	cartesian	catharist	cephaloid
callously	capitulum	carthorse	cathartic	ceraceous
calmative	caponiere	cartilage	cathedral	ceratitis
calorific	capriccio	cartridge	catoptric	ceratodus
calvinism	capricorn	cartulary	cat-silver	ceraunite
calvinist	capriform	case-knife	cattle-pen	cerberean
calvities	capsicine	casemated	caucasian	cercarian
camarilla	capsulate	cashew-nut	causality	cerecloth
cambistry	captaincy	cassareep	causation	cerograph
camcorder	captivate	cassation	causative	certainly
camerated	captivity	casserole	causeless	certainty
campagnol	carambola	cassimere	cautelous	certifier

certitude
cespitose
cessation
cetaceous
cevadilla
chafferer
chaffinch
chain-gang
chain-pier
chain-pump
chain-shot
challenge
chalybite
chambered
chamberer
chameleon
chamomile
champagne
champaign
chanceful
chandlery
changeful
character
chariness
charioted
charivari
charlatan
chartered
charterer
charwoman
chastener
chastiser
chatoyant
chatterer
chauffeur
chaw-bacon
cheap-jack
cheapness
cheatable
checkmate
cheekbone

cheerless
cheese-fly
chelonian
chemistry
chemitype
chequered
cherimoya
cherisher
cherry-pit
chevalier
chevelure
chevroned
chibouque
chickling
chickweed
chidingly
chieftain
chilblain
childhood
childless
childlike
chiliarch
chillness
chinaware
china-clay
china-root
china-rose
chinatown
chincapin
chinchona
chincough
chinkapin
chipolata
chirology
chiselled
chivalric
chlorosis
chlorotic
chock-full
chocolate
choke-bore

choke-damp
choke-full
cholaemia
choleraic
chondrify
chop-house
chorister
christian
christmas
chromatic
chronicle
chrysalid
chrysalis
chthonian
chubblock
chub-faced
churching
churchism
churchman
cicatrize
cigarette
cilioform
cimmerian
cinchonic
cinchonin
cinctured
cineraria
cinereous
cingalese
circinate
circulate
cirrhosis
cisalpine
civilized
civilizer
clack-dish
claimable
clamorous
clamourer
clapboard
claret-cup

claret-jug
clarifier
clarionet
classable
classical
classless
classmate
classroom
claustral
clausalar
clavicorn
clay-slate
claystone
cleanness
clearance
clearness
cleavable
clemently
clepsydra
clergyman
clericism
clerkship
cleverish
clientage
clientele
climatize
climbable
clingfilm
cloakroom
clockwork
clog-dance
cloistral
closeness
closetime
cloth-hall
cloth-yard
cloudless
clove-pink
clubbable
clubhouse
coach-hire

coadjutor
coadunate
coagulant
coagulate
coal-black
coal-brass
coalfield
coalition
coal-plant
coastline
coastwise
coaxingly
coccolite
coccolith
coccygeal
cochineal
cochleate
cock-a-hoop
cock-fight
cockle-hat
cockneyfy
cockroach
cock's-comb
cockswain
cocoonery
coemption
coenobite
coenosarc
coequally
coercible
coeternal
coffee-bug
coffeepot
cofferdam
cofounder
cogitable
cognation
cognition
cognitive
cognizant
coheiress

coherence   columella   conciliar   conscious   co-operant
colchicum   combatant   concisely   conscript   cooperate
colcothar   combative   concision   consensus   copartner
cold-blast   comically   concocter   conserver   copestone
cold-cream   commander   concordat   consignee   copiously
coleopter   commendam   concourse   consigner   coppering
collation   commender   concreate   consonant   copperish
collative   commensal   concubine   conspirer   coprolite
colleague   commenter   condemner   constable   coprology
collector   commingle   condenser   constancy   copse-wood
collegial   comminute   condiment   constrain   copyright
collegian   committal   condition   constrict   coralline
colligate   committee   conducive   construct   corallite
collimate   committer   conductor   consulate   coralloid
collinear   commodity   conferrer   consulter   coral-reef
collision   commodore   confessed   consuming   coral-tree
collocate   commonage   confessor   contagion   coral-wood
collodion   commotion   confidant   contagium   cordately
colloidal   communion   confident   container   cordelier
collusion   communism   confiding   contemner   cordially
collusive   communist   configure   contender   cordiform
collyrium   community   confirmed   contented   coriander
colocynth   compactly   confirmee   conticent   corkscrew
colonelcy   companion   confirmer   continent   cormorant
colonizer   compeller   confluent   continual   corncrake
colonnade   competent   conformer   continued   cornelian
colophony   complaint   confucian   continuer   cornetist
colorific   complexly   confusion   contorted   cornflour
colosseum   complexus   congenial   contralto   cornopean
colostrum   compliant   congeries   contriver   corn-poppy
colouring   component   congested   contumacy   corollary
colourist   composite   congruent   contumely   corolline
colourize   composure   congruity   contusion   coroneted
colourman   comradery   congruous   conundrum   corozo-nut
coltishly   concavely   conically   converter   corporate
colt's-foot concavity   conjugate   convexity   corporeal
colubrine   concealer   connature   convivial   corposant
columbary   conceited   connector   convocate   corpulent
columbine   concentre   connexion   convolute   corpuscle
columbium   concerned   connubial   cook-chill   correctly
columbite   concerted   conqueror   cooperage   corrector

correlate
corrodent
corrosion
corrosive
corrugate
corrupted
corrupter
corruptly
corticate
corticose
coruscant
coruscate
corymbose
cosmogony
cosmology
cosmonaut
cosmorama
costively
costumier
cotangent
cothurnus
cotillion
co-trustee
cottonade
cotton-gin
cotyledon
coumarine
countable
countless
countship
courgette
courteous
courtesan
courthand
courtling
court-roll
courtship
courtyard
coverture
covert-way
covetable

cowardice
cowfeeder
coxcombry
crab-apple
crabbedly
crabstick
crackling
craftless
craftsman
cramp-iron
cranberry
crankness
crapulent
crapulous
crassness
cravatted
cravingly
craziness
creamcake
cream-laid
cream-wove
creatable
creatress
credendum
credulity
credulous
creephole
cremation
crematory
crenation
crenature
crenelate
crepitant
crepitate
crescendo
crestless
cretinism
cricketer
crimeless
criminate
criminous

crinoline
crispness
criterion
criticism
criticize
crocodile
crookedly
crop-eared
crosiered
crossbill
crossbred
crossfire
crosshead
crossness
crossover
crossroad
crosswise
crossword
crotchety
crowberry
crownless
crown-work
crow-quill
crow's-bill
crow's-feet
crow's-foot
crow's-nest
crucifier
cruciform
crudeness
crush-room
crustacea
cryometer
cryptogam
cryptonym
cubically
cubicular
cuckoldly
cuckoldom
cuckoldry
cucullate

cudgeller
cululawan
cullender
culminate
culpatory
cultivate
cumbrance
cuneiform
cunningly
cup-bearer
curbstone
curdiness
curiosity
curiously
curliness
currently
cursorial
cursorily
curstness
curtailer
curvature
cushioned
cuspidate
custodial
custodian
custodier
customary
cutaneous
cut-throat
cuttingly
cybercaf,
cyberpunk
cycloidal
cyclopean
cylindric
cymbalist
cymophane
cynegetic
cynically
cystiform
cystotomy

cytherean
cytoblast
dachshund
dairy-farm
dairy-maid
dalliance
damascene
damaskeen
damnation
damnatory
dampishly
dandelion
dandiprat
dangerous
dapple-bay
dare-devil
darwinian
darwinism
dashboard
dash-wheel
dastardly
dasymeter
date-sugar
dauntless
day-labour
day-school
dayspring
deaconess
dead-drunk
dead-house
deadlight
dead-march
deafening
death-bell
deathblow
death-fire
deathless
deathlike
death-rate
death's-man
debarment

debatable	decrement	deliriant	depravity	determine
debauched	decretist	delirious	deprecate	deterrent
debauchee	decretive	deliverer	depredate	detersion
debaucher	decretory	deludable	depressor	detersive
debenture	decumbent	demagogic	depurator	dethroner
debutante	decurrent	demagogue	derivable	detonator
decachord	decussate	demandant	derivably	detracter
decadence	dedicatee	demeaning	dermatoid	detractor
decagonal	dedicator	demeanour	derringer	detriment
decalcify	deducible	demi-devil	descanter	detrition
decalitre	deduction	demi-lance	descender	detrusion
decalogue	deductive	demi-monde	describer	devastate
decametre	deerhound	demisable	desecrate	developer
decapodal	deer-mouse	demission	desertion	deviation
decastyle	defalcate	demiurgic	deserving	devil-fish
deceitful	defaulter	democracy	dessicant	devilment
deception	defection	demulcent	dessicate	devil's-bit
deceptive	defective	demurrage	designate	devilship
decidable	defendant	dendritic	designing	deviously
decidedly	defensive	denotable	desirable	devisable
deciduate	defensory	denouncer	desirably	devitrify
deciduous	deference	denseness	desmology	devonport
decilitre	deferment	dentately	desolater	devotedly
decillion	deficient	dentiform	desolator	dewlapped
decimally	definable	dentistry	despairer	dexterity
decimator	definably	dentition	desperado	dexterous
decimetre	deflected	denyingly	desperate	dextrorse
deck-cargo	deflector	deodorant	despoiler	diablerie
declaimer	deflorate	deodorize	desponder	diabolism
declinate	defluxion	deoxidate	despotism	diabrosis
declinous	defoliate	deoxidize	destinate	diachylon
declining	defrauder	departure	destinist	diachylum
declivity	degrading	depasture	destitute	diaconate
declivous	dehiscent	dependant	destroyer	diacritic
decoction	deinornis	dependent	desuetude	diatrinic
decollate	deiparous	depicture	desultory	diaeresis
decomplex	dejection	depletion	detection	diagnosis
decompose	delicious	depletive	detective	dialectal
decorated	delighted	depletory	detention	dialectic
decorator	delineate	deposable	detergent	dialogism
decoy-duck	deliquium	depositor	determent	dialogist

dialogize	digitalin	discoidal	dispersal	divulsive
dial-plate	digitalis	discolour	disperser	dizziness
diametric	digitated	discomfit	displayer	doctorate
diametral	dignified	discommon	displease	doctoress
diamonded	dignitary	discourse	dispondee	doctrinal
diandrous	dilatable	discovery	disposure	docudrama
dianoetic	diligence	discredit	dispraise	dodecagon
diaphragm	dimension	discusser	disproval	dogmatics
diarrhoea	dimidiate	disembark	disputant	dogmatism
diastolic	dimissory	disembody	disregard	dogmatist
diathesis	dimyarian	disenable	disrelish	dogmatize
diathetic	dinginess	disengage	disrepair	dolefully
diatomite	dinoceras	disenroll	disrepute	dollybird
dicastery	dinothere	disentail	dissector	dominance
dichogamy	dioecious	disentomb	disseizor	dominator
dichotomy	dionysiac	disesteem	dissemble	dominical
dichroism	dionysian	disfavour	dissenter	dominican
dicky-bird	dioptrics	disfigure	dissident	doorplate
declinous	diphthong	disforest	dissipate	dormitive
dicoelous	diphycerc	disgorger	dissolute	dormitory
dictation	diplomacy	disgracer	dissolver	doubtable
dictature	dipterous	disguiser	dissonant	doubtless
dictatory	direction	dishcloth	distantly	doughtily
dictatrix	directive	dish-clout	distiller	dowerless
didactics	directory	dishonest	distemper	downiness
didactile	directrix	dishonour	distorted	downright
didelphia	direfully	disinfect	distraint	downscale
didelphic	dirigible	disinhume	disturber	downthrow
die-sinker	dirtiness	dislocate	dithyramb	down-train
dietarian	disaffect	dismantle	diurnally	downwards
dietetics	disaffirm	dismember	divergent	draftsman
dietetist	disappear	dismissal	diversely	dragonish
different	disavouch	disnature	diversify	dragon-fly
difficult	disavowal	disoblige	diversion	drainable
diffident	disavower	disparage	diversity	drain-tile
diffluent	disbelief	disparate	diverting	drain-trap
diffusion	disburden	disparity	dividable	dramatist
diffusive	disburser	dispauper	divisible	dramatize
digenesis	discerner	dispeller	divisibly	draperied
digestion	discharge	dispenser	divorcive	dravidian
digestive	dischurch	dispeople	divulsion	drayhorse

dreadless
dreamland
dreamless
dress-coat
driftless
drift-weed
driftwood
drinkable
driveller
dromedary
drop-press
drop-scone
drop-scene
dropsical
druidical
drum-major
drumstick
drysalter
dualistic
dubiously
ductilely
ductility
dulcamara
dumbfound
duodecimo
duodenary
duplicate
duplicity
dura-mater
duskiness
dust-brand
duteously
dutifully
dyer's-weed
dynamical
dynamiter
dyscrasia
dysentery
dyspepsia
dyspeptic
dziggetai

eagerness
eagle-eyed
eaglewood
ealdorman
ear-cockle
earliness
earnestly
earthborn
earth-flax
earthling
earthward
earth-wolf
earthwork
earthworm
easy-chair
eavesdrop
ebullient
eccentric
echinated
eclampsia
economics
economist
economize
ecstasied
ectoblast
ectoplasm
edelweiss
edibility
edificial
editorial
education
educative
eel-basket
effective
effectual
efficient
effluence
effluvial
effluvium
effluxion
effodient

effulgent
eglantine
egotheism
egotistic
egregious
egression
eider-duck
eider-down
eidograph
eightfold
eightieth
eirenicon
ejaculate
ejectment
elaborate
elaterium
elbow-room
eldership
elder-wine
electoral
electrify
electuary
elegantly
elemental
elevation
elevatory
eliminate
ellipsoid
elmo's-fire
elocution
elohistic
elopement
eloquence
elsewhere
elucidate
elutriate
emaciated
emanation
embarrass
embattled
embay-ment

embellish
ember-days
ember-tide
ember-week
embezzler
emblement
embraceor
embracery
embrasure
embrocate
embroider
embryonal
embryonic
embryotic
emendator
emergence
emergency
eminently
emmensite
emollient
emolument
emotional
emphasize
emphysema
empirical
emptiness
empyreuma
emulation
emulative
emulatory
emulously
emunctory
enactment
enamelist
encaustic
enchanted
enchanter
enchorial
enclosure
encomiast
encompass

encounter
encourage
encrimson
encrinite
endearing
endeavour
endecagon
endeictic
endemical
endlessly
endocrine
endolymph
endomorph
endoplasm
endoplast
endoscope
endosperm
endosteum
endostome
endowment
endurable
endurably
endurance
energetic
energical
enfeebler
engineman
engiscope
englishry
engrailed
engrainer
engraving
engrosser
engyscope
enhearten
enhydrous
enigmatic
enjoyable
enjoyment
enlighten
enlivener

enneander	episodial	estimably	excentric	exhibiter
enrapture	epistolic	estuarian	excepting	exhibitor
enrolment	epitaphic	estuarine	exception	existence
entelechy	epitomist	esurience	excessive	exogamous
enteralgy	epitomize	esuriency	exchanger	exogenous
enteritis	epizootic	etcaetera	exchequer	exonerate
entertain	eponymous	eternally	excipient	exorciser
enthymeme	epsom-salt	ethically	excisable	exosmosis
entomical	equalizer	ethiopian	exciseman	exosmotic
entophyte	equalness	ethmoidal	excitable	expansile
entreater	equipment	ethnicism	exclaimer	expansion
entremets	equipoise	ethnology	exclusion	expansive
entrochal	equisetum	etiquette	exclusive	expectant
entropium	equitable	etymology	excoriate	expedient
enucleate	equitably	eucharist	excrement	expensive
enumerate	equivalve	euchology	excretion	expertise
enunciate	equivocal	eulogical	excretive	expiation
enviously	equivoque	euphemism	excretory	expiatory
envoyship	eradicate	euphemize	exculpate	expirable
epaulette	erasement	euphonium	excurrent	expiscate
ephemeral	erectness	euphorbia	excursion	explainer
ephemeris	eremitism	euphrasia	excursive	expletive
ephemeron	eriometer	evaginate	excusable	expletory
epiclinal	eristical	evangelic	excusably	explicate
epicurean	erostrate	evaporate	execrable	exploiter
epicurism	erroneous	evasively	execrably	explosion
epidermal	erstwhile	eventuate	executant	explosive
epidermic	eruditely	evergreen	execution	expositor
epidermis	erudition	everybody	executive	expounder
epidictic	eruginous	evidently	executory	expressly
epigaeous	erythrite	evocation	executrix	expulsion
epigenous	escapable	evolution	exegetist	expulsive
epigraphy	escheator	evolutive	exegetics	expurgate
epigynous	esclandre	exactness	exemplary	exquisite
epileptic	esoterism	examinant	exemplify	exsertile
epilogize	espionage	examining	exemption	exsiccate
epiphragm	esplanade	exanthema	exequatur	exsiccant
epiphysis	essential	exarchate	exerciser	extempore
epiphytic	estafette	excavator	exfoliate	extensile
epiphytal	estaminet	exceeding	exhalable	extension
episcopal	estimable	excellent	exhausted	extensity

extensive
extenuate
externals
extirpate
extortion
extractor
extradite
extremely
extremist
extremity
extricate
extrinsic
extrorsal
extrusion
exuberant
exudation
eye-bright
fabaceous
fabricate
face-plate
facetious
facsimile
factitive
factorage
factorial
fagot-vote
faintness
fairyland
faith-cure
faithless
falcation
falconine
faldstool
fallopian
falsehood
falseness
falsifier
faltering
fanatical
fanciless
fancy-ball

fancy-fair
fancy-free
fancywork
fantastic
farandole
farmhouse
farmstead
far-sought
fasciated
fascicled
fascicule
fascinate
fashioner
fastening
fatefully
fattiness
faultless
faveolate
favourite
fearfully
feathered
febricula
febrifuge
feculence
fecundate
fecundity
feelingly
feignedly
fellow-man
felonious
femme-sole
fenestral
fenianism
fenugreek
feoffment
feracious
ferocious
ferrotype
ferry-boat
fertilely
fertility

fertilize
fervently
fervidity
festinate
festively
festivity
feticidal
fetidness
fetichism
fetishism
fetlocked
feudalism
feudalist
feudality
feudalize
feudatory
feu-de-joie
fibriform
fibrinous
fictional
fiddle-bow
fiduciary
field-book
fieldfare
field-work
fieriness
fife-major
fifteenth
figurable
figurante
filaceous
filiation
filigreed
filleting
fillister
filminess
filoplume
fimbriate
financial
financier
finedrawn

fin-footed
fingering
finically
finicking
fire-alarm
firebrand
firebrick
fire-eater
fireguard
fire-irons
fireplace
fireproof
firmament
first-born
first-hand
firstling
first-rate
fisherman
fishiness
fish-joint
fish-louse
fish-plate
fish-slice
fish-spear
fishwoman
fistulose
fistulous
fittingly
fixedness
flabellum
flaccidly
flagellum
flageolet
flagrancy
flakiness
flap-eared
flatterer
flatulent
flaunting
flavorous
flavoured

flayflint
fleckless
fleetness
flesh-hook
fleshings
fleshless
flesh-meat
flexitime
flightily
flintlock
flippancy
floodgate
flood-mark
flood-tide
floreated
floridity
floscular
floss-silk
flotation
flowering
flowerpot
fluctuant
fluctuate
fluor-spar
fluxional
flybitten
fly-fisher
flying-fox
foeticide
fogginess
fog-signal
foliation
following
foolhardy
foolishly
footboard
footcloth
foot-pound
footprint
footstalk
footstool

foppishly
forasmuch
forbearer
forbidden
forceless
forcemeat
foreclose
forefront
foregoing
foreigner
forejudge
forenamed
foresight
forestall
forestine
foretaste
foretoken
foretooth
forewoman
forfeiter
forgather
forgetful
forgiving
forgotten
forlornly
formalism
formalist
formality
formation
formative
formicary
formulary
formulate
formulize
fornicate
forthwith
fortifier
fortitude
fortnight
fortunate
fossilize

fosterson
foundling
foundress
foundries
fourpence
fourscore
foveolate
foxhunter
fractions
fragrance
fragrancy
franchise
francolin
frangible
franglais
frankness
fraternal
fraudless
free-range
freemason
freestone
freeze-dry
freezible
freighter
frenchman
frequency
freshness
fretfully
fricassee
fricative
frightful
frigidity
frivolity
frivolous
frontless
frostbite
frostwork
frowardly
frugality
fruiterer
fruitless

fruticose
fruticous
fugacious
fulgurite
fulgurous
fulminate
fulsomely
fundament
fungiform
fungology
funicular
funnelled
furbisher
furcation
furfurous
furiously
furnished
furnisher
furniture
furtherer
furtively
fusillade
fussiness
fustigate
fustiness
gabardine
gabionage
gainsayer
galantine
galenical
galingale
gallantly
gallantry
galleries
gallicism
gallinule
gallivant
gallooned
gallopade
gallowses
galvanism

galvanist
galvanize
gambadoes
ganglions
gannister
gardening
gargarism
garmented
garnisher
garniture
garreteer
garrotter
garrulity
garrulous
gasconade
gasholder
gasometer
gasometry
gaspingly
gastropod
gastralgy
gastritis
gathering
gaucherie
gaudeamus
gaudiness
gaugeable
gavelkind
gazetteer
gelsemium
gemmation
genealogy
generable
generally
generator
generical
genetical
geniality
genitival
genteelly
gentility

gentleman
gentlemen
genuflect
genuinely
geodesist
geography
geologist
geologian
geomancer
geomantic
geometric
geoponics
gerfalcon
germander
germanium
germicide
germinant
germinate
gerundial
gerundive
giantship
gibberish
gibbosity
gibbously
giddiness
ginglymus
gipsology
girandole
gladiator
glandered
glandular
glasswort
glaucosis
glomosity
globulose
glomerate
glowingly
glueyness
glutinate
glutinous
glycerine

glyptodon
gnathonic
gnomonics
gnomonist
godfather
godlessly
godliness
godmother
goffering
goldfinch
goldsmith
gonophore
goosander
goosefoot
gorgonean
gorgonize
gospeller
gossamery
gossipped
gothicism
goutiness
governess
graceless
gracility
gradation
gradatory
gradually
graduator
gramineal
grammatic
grandiose
grandness
grandsire
granitoid
grantable
granulate
granulite
granulous
granulose
grassable
gratifier

gratitude
gratulate
grauwacke
graveless
graveness
gravitate
grayhound
graywacke
greatcoat
greatness
greenback
greenhorn
greenness
gregorian
grenadier
grenadine
greyhound
grievance
grimalkin
griminess
gripingly
grisaille
groceries
groomsman
gropingly
grossbeak
grossness
grotesque
groundsel
groveller
gruffness
guarantee
guarantor
guardable
guardedly
guardsman
guerrilla
guideless
guildhall
guileless
guillemot

guiltless
gumminess
gunpowder
gushingly
gustatory
gymnasial
gymnasium
gymnastic
gynoecium
gynophore
gyrfalcon
gyroscope
habergeon
habitable
habituate
hackberry
hackneyed
haematoid
haggardly
hagiology
hailstone
hairiness
halfpenny
halfpence
hallowmas
halophyte
haloscope
hamadryad
hamburger
hammerman
hamstring
handiness
handiwork
handspike
haranguer
harbourer
hardihood
hardiness
harlequin
harmfully
harmonica

harmonics
harmonist
harmonium
harmonize
harmotome
harnesser
harpooner
harshness
harvester
hastiness
hatchback
hatchment
hatefully
haughtily
haversack
haymaking
hazardous
headiness
healthful
healthily
heartache
heartburn
heartfelt
heartless
heartsome
heathenry
heaviness
hebraical
hebridian
heedfully
hegemonic
heinously
heliostat
heliotype
hellebore
hellenism
hellenist
hellenize
hellishly
hematosis
hemicycle

hemiplegy
hemistich
hendiadys
hepatical
heptaglot
heptarchy
herbalist
herbarium
herbivore
herculean
hereabout
hereafter
heretical
heritable
heritably
hermitage
hermitary
heronshaw
hesitancy
hesitator
hesperian
hetairism
heterodox
heteronym
heteropox
heuristic
hexachord
hexagonal
hexameter
hexastyle
hexateuch
hibernate
hibernian
hideously
hiemation
hierarchy
hierogram
hierology
high-flier
hilarious
hilliness

hindrance	hottentot	hyperbole	imitation	imposture
hindooism	houndfish	hypertext	imitative	impotence
hippiatry	household	hypethral	immanence	impotency
hippocras	houseless	hypnotism	immanency	impounder
hirundine	housemaid	hypnotize	immediacy	imprecate
hispidity	houseroom	hypocaust	immediate	improbity
histogeny	housewife	hypocrisy	immensely	impromptu
histology	howsoever	hypocrite	immensity	improving
historian	hoydenish	hypogaeon	immersion	improvise
hoariness	huckaback	hyponasty	immigrant	imprudent
hobgoblin	huffiness	hypostyle	immigrate	impudence
hobnailed	humanness	hysterics	imminence	impulsion
hodiernal	humectate	icelander	immodesty	impulsive
hodometer	humiliate	icelandic	immolator	imputable
hoidenish	humourist	ichneumon	immorally	inability
hollyhock	hunchback	ichnolite	immovable	inamorato
holocaust	hundredth	ichnology	immovably	inamorata
holograph	hungarian	ichthyoid	immutable	inanimate
homestead	hurricane	iconology	immutably	inanition
homewards	hurriedly	idealizer	impartial	inaudible
homicidal	hurtfully	identical	impassion	inaugural
homiletic	husbandly	identikit	impassive	inbreathe
homograph	husbandry	ideograph	impatient	incapable
homologue	huskiness	idiograph	impeacher	incarnate
homophone	hybridism	idiomatic	impedance	incaution
homuncule	hybridity	idiopathy	impellent	incentive
honorabic	hybridize	idiotical	impendent	inception
honorable	hydrangea	ignitable	imperfect	inceptive
hopefully	hydraulic	ignoramus	imperious	incessant
horehound	hydrofoil	ignorance	impetrate	incidence
horologer	hydrology	iguanodon	impetuous	incipient
horometry	hydropult	illegally	impingent	inclement
horoscope	hydrosoma	illegible	impiously	inclosure
horoscopy	hydrozoan	illegibly	impleader	inclusive
horseback	hydrozoon	illiberal	implement	incognito
horsewhip	hyetology	illicitly	implicate	incognita
hortation	hygienism	illogical	impliedly	incommode
hortative	hylozoism	imaginary	impolitic	incorrect
hortatory	hymnology	imbricate	important	incorrupt
hostilely	hypallage	imbroglio	importune	incremate
hostility	hyperbola	imbuement	imposable	increment

incubator
incubuses
inculcate
inculpate
incumbent
incurably
incurvate
indecorum
indelible
indelibly
indemnify
indemnity
indenture
indexical
indicator
indiction
indigence
indignant
indignity
indispose
indolence
inducible
inductile
induction
inductive
induement
indulgent
indweller
inebriant
inebriate
inebriety
inebrious
ineffable
ineffably
inelastic
inelegant
inequable
inertness
infantile
infantine
infatuate

infection
infective
inferable
inference
infertile
infirmary
infirmity
inflation
inflexion
influence
influenza
influxion
informant
infuriate
infusible
infusoria
ingenious
ingenuity
ingenuous
ingluvies
inhabiter
inherence
inherency
inheritor
inhumanly
injection
injurious
injustice
innermost
innervate
innkeeper
innocence
innocency
innocuous
innovator
innuendos
inoculate
inodorous
inorganic
inquiline
inquiring

inquiries
insatiate
insensate
insertion
insidious
insincere
insinuate
insolence
insoluble
insolvent
inspector
instantly
instigate
institute
insularly
insulator
insulting
insurable
insurance
insurgent
integrant
integrate
integrity
intellect
intendant
intensely
intensify
intension
intensity
intensive
intention
interment
intercede
intercept
interdict
interface
interfere
interfuse
interject
interlace
interlard

interline
interlock
interlope
interlude
interment
internode
interpose
interpret
interrupt
intersect
intervene
interview
intestacy
intestate
intestine
intortion
intricacy
intricate
intriguer
intrinsic
introduce
introvert
intrusion
intrusive
intuition
intuitive
intumesce
inurement
inutility
invective
invention
inventive
inventory
inversely
inversion
invidious
inviolate
invisible
invisibly
involuted
inwreathe

inwrought
irascible
irascibly
irksomely
ironsmith
irradiant
irradiate
irregular
irriguous
irritable
irritably
irruption
irruptive
isinglass
isoclinal
isoclinic
isolation
isomerism
isometric
isosceles
israelite
issueless
itchiness
iterative
iteration
itinerant
itinerary
itinerate
jaborandi
jacobinic
jacobitic
jansenist
jansenism
jealously
jeeringly
jenneting
jeremiade
jerfalcon
jessamine
jesuitism
jettiness

jewellery
job-centre
jocundity
jocularly
jolliness
journeyer
joviality
joylessly
judgeship
judiciary
judicious
juiceless
juiciness
juniority
juridical
justifier
juxtapose
kainozoic
kentledge
keratitis
kernelled
kick-start
kidnapper
kilometre
killingly
kinematic
kingcraft
kinswoman
kissagram
kitchener
kittenish
kittiwake
kiwi-fruit
knackered
knavishly
knightage
knowingly
knowledge
krummhorn
labialize
laborious

labouring
labyrinth
lacerable
lacerated
lacertine
lachrymal
laciniate
laconical
lactation
lactifuge
lacunaria
lacustral
laevigate
lager-lout
laminated
largeness
larghetto
larviform
laryngeal
laryngean
lassitude
lastingly
laterally
laudatory
laughable
laughably
laundress
laurelled
lawgiving
lawlessly
lazaretto
leafiness
leakiness
learnedly
leasehold
leastwise
lecherous
legendary
legionary
legislate
leisurely

lengthily
leniently
lentiform
leprously
leprosity
lethargic
lettering
levantine
levelling
levelness
leviathan
levigable
levitical
lexically
liability
libellous
liberally
liberator
librarian
libration
libratory
lichenous
lickerish
lienteric
lifestyle
ligatured
lightness
lightning
light-show
lightsome
ligniform
ligulated
limaceous
limestone
limitable
limitedly
limitless
limpidity
limpingly
lineament
lineolate

lingering
lingulate
lippitude
liquation
liquefier
liquidate
liquidity
liquorice
listerism
literally
litheness
lithesome
lithoidal
lithology
lithotomy
lithotypy
litigable
litigator
liturgies
liturgist
liverwort
liveryman
lividness
lixiviate
lixivious
loathsome
lobscouse
locksmith
locomotor
lodestone
loftiness
logarithm
logically
logomachy
logomania
longevity
longevous
longicorn
longingly
longitude
loopholed

looseness
loquacity
lorgnette
loricated
lotophagi
looseness
lowermost
lowlander
lowliness
lubricate
lubricity
lucidness
lucifugal
luckiness
lucrative
lubricate
lubricity
lucidness
lucubrate
ludicrous
lumpishly
lunulated
lustfully
lustiness
luxuriant
luxuriate
luxurious
lymphatic
macaronis
macaronic
machinate
machinery
machinist
macintosh
macrocosm
macrurous
madrepore
magdalene
magically
magnalium
magnesian

magnesium   margarine   mechanist   mesmerist   migration
magnetism   margarita   mechanize   mesmerize   migratory
magnetize   marketing   medallion   messenger   milestone
magnifier   marmalade   medallist   messianic   militancy
magnitude   marmoreal   mediaeval   messieurs   milkiness
maharajah   marquetry   mediately   metalline   millipore
maharanee   marsupial   mediative   metallist   millinery
mahomedan   marsupium   mediatize   metallize   millionth
mahometan   martially   medicable   metalloid   millstone
mainframe   martinmas   medically   meteorite   mimetical
majorship   martyrdom   medicinal   metheglin   mindfully
majuscule   martyrize   medullary   methodism   miniature
malachite   masculine   megafarad   methodist   mini-skirt
maladroit   massagist   melanosis   methodize   minorship
malarious   massiness   melaphyre   methought   mirifical
malicious   massively   meliboean   methystic   mirthless
malignant   masterful   meliorate   metonymic   misbehave
malignity   masticate   melodious   metrology   misbelief
malleable   matchable   melodrama   metronome   mischance
malleolus   matchless   melodrame   mezzanine   miscreant
mammalian   matchlock   meltingly   mezzotint   misdemean
mammalogy   maternity   memoirist   miasmatic   misdirect
mammonism   matriarch   memorable   micaceous   misemploy
mammonist   matricide   memoranda   microbial   miserable
mammonite   matrimony   memorizer   microbian   miserably
mandatary   matronage   menagerie   microchip   misgiving
mandatory   matronize   mendacity   microcosm   misgovern
mandoline   matutinal   mendicant   microcyte   misinform
manducate   maunderer   mendicity   micrology   mismanage
manganese   mausolean   meniscoid   microlyte   misreport
manganite   mausoleum   menstrual   micropyle   misseltoe
manichean   mawkishly   menstruum   microtome   misshapen
manifesto   maxillary   mentation   microwave   mistiness
manipular   mayonaise   mercenary   microzoon   mistletoe
manliness   mayoralty   merciless   microzyme   mitriform
mannerism   mealiness   mercurial   micturate   mnemonics
mannerist   meaningly   mercurous   middleman   mobocracy
manoeuvre   meanwhile   merganser   midi-skirt   mockingly
manometer   meatiness   merriment   midsummer   modelling
marcasite   mechanics   mesentery   midwifery   moderator
marchpane   mechanism   mesmerism   midwinter   modernism

modernist
modernize
modillion
modulator
moistness
molecular
mollifier
momentary
momentous
monachism
monadical
monadelph
monarchal
monarchic
monastery
monatomic
moneyless
mongolian
monitress
monkeyism
monochord
monodrama
monograph
monologue
monomania
monoplane
monoptote
monosperm
monsignor
monstrous
monticule
moodiness
moonlight
moonshine
moonshiny
moonstone
moralizer
moratoria
morbidity
mordacity
mormonism

mormonist
mormonite
mortality
mortgagee
mortgager
mortgagor
mosaicist
mossiness
motorboat
mouldable
moustache
mucronate
muddiness
muffettee
multifoil
mullioned
multiform
multiplex
multitude
mumpishly
mundanely
municipal
murderess
murderous
muricated
murmuring
muscadine
muscology
muscovado
muscovite
musically
musketeer
musketoon
mussulman
mustiness
mutilator
muttering
myography
myonicity
myriorama
myrobalan

mysteries
mysticism
mythology
naileress
nakedness
nappiness
narcissus
narcotism
narcotize
narration
narrative
naseberry
nastiness
natrolite
nattiness
naturally
naughtily
nautiloid
navigable
navigably
navigator
necessary
necessity
neckcloth
necrology
nectareal
nectarean
nectarine
nectarous
needfully
neediness
nefarious
negligent
negociate
negotiate
neighbour
neolithic
neologian
neologism
neologist
neologize

neoterism
neoterize
nepenthes
nephalism
nephalist
nepheloid
nephritic
nephritis
neptunian
nervation
nerveless
nervously
nescience
nestorian
neuralgia
neuralgic
neurility
neurology
neuropter
neurotomy
neutrally
nevermore
newsagent
newspaper
newtonian
nictation
nictitate
niggardly
nightclub
nightfall
nightless
nightmare
nightward
nigritude
ninetieth
nobleness
nocturnal
noiseless
noisiness
noisomely
nominally

nominator
nonentity
nonpareil
normalize
northerly
northward
norwegian
nostalgia
notochord
notoriety
notorious
nourisher
novelette
novelties
novennial
novitiate
nowhither
noxiously
nucleolus
nullifier
numerable
numerally
numerator
numerical
nummulary
nummulite
nunneries
nutriment
nutrition
nutritive
nystagmus
oasthouse
obbligato
obconical
obcordate
obedience
obeisance
obeseness
obfuscate
objectify
objection

objective
objurgate
obliquely
obliquity
oblivious
obnoxious
osbcenely
obscenity
obscurant
obscurely
obscurity
obsecrate
obsequies
observant
observing
obsession
obstetric
obstinacy
obstinate
obstruent
obtrusion
obtrusive
obturator
obviously
obvoluted
occipital
occlusion
occultism
occupancy
ocellated
octagonal
octastyle
octennial
octopuses
oculiform
odalisque
oddfellow
odontalgy
odorously
odourless
oenanthic

offensive
offertory
officiate
officinal
officious
offspring
olecranon
oleograph
olfactory
oligarchy
ombudsman
ominously
omissible
onerously
onslaught
operation
operative
opercular
operculum
operosely
operosity
ophiology
opinioned
opodeldoc
opportune
opposable
oppressor
oppugnant
optically
optimates
optimeter
optometer
opulently
orangeade
orangeman
orangeism
orbicular
orchestra
orderless
ordinance
organical

organized
organizer
organzine
orgiastic
orientate
oriflamme
originate
orography
orphanage
orthodoxy
orthoepic
orthogamy
orthopter
oscillate
oscitancy
ossifrage
ostensive
osteology
osteotomy
ostiolate
ostracean
ostracion
ostracism
ostracize
ostrogoth
otherness
otherwise
otologist
otorrhoea
oubliette
ourselves
outermost
outfitter
outgrowth
outnumber
outrigger
outspoken
outspread
outwardly
oven-ready
overboard

overbuild
overcloud
overcrowd
overdress
overdrive
overgorge
overissue
overmatch
overnight
overpower
overreach
overshoot
oversight
oversleep
overstate
overstock
overthrow
overtrade
overvalue
overweigh
overwhelm
oviferous
ovigerous
oviparous
ovulation
ownership
oxidation
oxygenate
oxygenize
oxygenous
ozocerite
ozokerite
pachyderm
packaging
packsheet
pademelon
paedagogy
pageantry
paillasse
painfully
palaestra

palankeen
palatable
palatably
paleology
palestral
palestric
palfreyed
palladium
palmarian
palmately
palmister
palmistry
palpation
palpebral
palpiform
palpitate
palsgrave
palustral
panderess
panderism
pandurate
panegyric
panelling
panoplied
pantalets
pantaloon
pantheism
pantheist
pantomime
paperback
papillary
papillate
papillose
parabasis
parabolic
parachute
paraclete
paragraph
paralegal
paralysis
paralytic

paramatta
paramedic
parameter
paramount
paranymph
parapeted
parapodia
parataxis
parbuckle
parchment
paregoric
parenesis
parenetic
parentage
parenting
pargeting
parhelion
parochial
parodical
parotitis
parquetry
parrakeet
parricide
parseeism
parsimony
parsonage
partially
partition
partitive
partridge
passenger
passerine
passional
passively
passivity
pasticcio
pastorale
pastorate
pasturage
patchouli
patchouly

patchwork
paternity
pathology
patiently
patriarch
patrician
patrimony
patriotic
patristic
patronage
patroness
patronize
pauperism
pauperize
paymaster
peaceable
peaceably
peasantry
peccantly
peccaries
pectinate
peculator
pecuniary
pedagogic
pedagogue
pedicular
pedometer
peevishly
periastic
pelasgian
pellitory
pencilled
pendently
pendulate
pendulous
penetrant
penetrate
peninsula
penitence
penniless
pennoncel

pensioner
pensively
pentaglot
pentagram
pentander
pentarchy
pentecost
penthouse
penultima
penurious
perceiver
perchance
percolate
perdition
perennial
perfecter
perfectly
perfervid
perforate
performer
perfumery
perimeter
peripetia
periphery
periscope
perisperm
perispore
peristome
peristyle
permanent
permeable
permeably
permittee
permitter
perpetual
persecute
persimmon
personage
personate
personify
personnel

persuader
pertinent
perturber
pertusion
pervasive
perverter
pessimism
pessimist
pessimize
pestilent
petardier
petechiae
petechial
petiolary
petiolate
petrology
petroleum
petticoat
pettiness
pettishly
pettitoes
petulance
petulancy
phaenogam
phalanger
phalanges
phalanxes
phalarope
pharisaic
pharology
phenician
phenomena
philately
philippic
philogyny
philology
philomath
philomela
phlebitis
phocacean
phonation

phonetics
phonogram
phonology
phonotype
phonotypy
phosphate
phosphide
photology
phototype
phototypy
phrenetic
phrenitis
phycology
phyllopod
physician
physicism
physicist
phytogeny
phytotomy
picaninny
pickaback
pickthank
pictorial
peacemeal
pietistic
pigmental
pikestaff
pilloried
pimpernel
pinchbeck
pinnately
pipistrel
pipsqueak
piquantly
piratical
pirouette
pisciform
pisolitic
pistachio
pitchfork
pitchpipe

piteously
pithecoid
pithiness
pitifully
pituitary
pituitous
pityingly
pizzicato
placeless
placement
placental
placidity
plainness
plaintiff
plaintive
planetary
planetoid
plantless
plaquette
plasmatic
plasterer
platinize
platinoid
platinous
platitude
platonism
platonist
plausible
plausibly
playgroup
playfully
playhouse
plaything
pleasance
plenarily
plenitude
plenteous
plentiful
pleuritic
pleuritis
plication

plicature
ploughboy
ploughman
plumbeous
plumeless
plumpness
plunderer
pluralism
pluralist
plurality
pluralize
plutocrat
plutonian
plutonist
pneumatic
pneumonia
pneumonic
pocketful
poenology
poetaster
poeticule
poignancy
pointedly
pointless
pointsman
poisonous
polarizer
polemical
policeman
political
politicly
pollarchy
pollenize
pollinate
pollution
polonaise
polyandry
polyarchy
polygonal
polygraph
polyphony

polypidom
polyscope
polystyle
polyzonal
pomaceous
pompholyx
pomposity
pompously
ponderous
pontonier
poorhouse
popliteal
popularly
porbeagle
porcelain
porcupine
porterage
portfolio
porticoes
porticoed
portioner
portrayer
possessor
postilion
postulant
postulate
posturist
potassium
potentate
potential
potentite
poulterer
poussette
powerless
practical
practised
practiser
pragmatic
prayerful
preachify
preaching

prebendal
precedent
precentor
preceptor
precipice
precisely
precision
precocity
precursor
predatory
predicant
predicate
predictor
prefatory
preferrer
prefigure
prefixion
pregnable
pregnancy
prejudice
prelatist
prelature
prelector
prelusive
premature
premonish
preoccupy
preordain
prepotent
preputial
presbyter
prescient
prescribe
prescript
presentee
presently
preserver
president
presuming
pretended
pretender

preterite
pretermit
prettyish
prevalent
preventer
prevision
priceless
priestess
primarily
primatial
prime-time
primitive
princedom
principal
principia
principle
priorship
prismatic
privateer
privately
privation
privative
privatize
privilege
proactive
probation
probative
probatory
proboscis
procedure
proclitic
procoelus
proconsul
procreant
procreate
procuracy
prodigies
profanely
profanity
professed
professor

profferer	proudness	pulvinate	quakerish	rantipole
profilist	provencal	pumiceous	quakerism	rapacious
profusely	provender	punctilio	qualified	rapidness
profusion	provident	punctuate	qualities	raptorial
prognosis	provision	pungently	quarryman	rapturous
programme	provisory	purchaser	quarterly	rareeshow
projector	provoking	purgation	quartette	rascaldom
prolepsis	proximate	purgative	quartzite	rascalism
proleptic	proximity	purgatory	quartzose	rascality
proletary	prudently	puritanic	queenhood	raspberry
prolixity	prudishly	purloiner	queerness	rationale
prolusion	prurience	purposely	querulous	ravishing
promenade	pruriency	purposive	quickener	reachable
prominent	psalmodic	purpureal	quicklime	reachless
promising	pseudonym	pursiness	quickness	readdress
promotion	psoriasis	pursuance	quicksand	readiness
promotive	psychical	purulence	quiescent	readjourn
pronation	psychosis	purulency	quietness	realistic
proneness	ptarmigan	pushingly	quintette	realities
pronounce	pterygoid	pustulate	quintuple	reanimate
prooemium	ptolemaic	pustulous	quitclaim	reappoint
propagate	pubescent	putridity	quittance	rearrange
propeller	publicist	puzzolana	quixotism	reasoning
prophetic	publicity	pyramidal	quizzical	reattempt
prorogate	publisher	pyramidic	quodlibet	rebaptise
prosaical	puerilely	pyrethrum	quotation	rebaptism
proscribe	puerility	pyritical	quotidian	rebellion
prosector	puerperal	pyrogenic	rabidness	rebuilder
prosecute	puffiness	pyrolater	rackarock	rebukeful
proselyte	pugnacity	pyrometer	racketeer	recapture
prosiness	puissance	pyroxylic	radiantly	receiptor
prosodial	pulmonary	pyrrhonic	radiately	receiving
prosodian	pulpiness	pythoness	radiation	recension
prosodist	pulpiteer	pythonism	radically	reception
prostrate	pulsatile	pythonist	railingly	receptive
protector	pulsation	quadratic	raininess	recession
protester	pulsative	quadrifid	rajahship	recessive
prothorax	pulsatory	quadrille	rampantly	rechauffe
prototype	pulseless	quadruped	rancheria	recherche
protozoal	pulverize	quadruple	rancidity	recipient
protozoon	pulverous	quakeress	rancorous	reckoning

reclinate
reclusely
reclusive
recognise
recollect
recommend
reconcile
recondite
reconduct
reconquer
recoverer
recreancy
recrement
recruiter
rectangle
rectifier
rectitude
rectorial
rectorate
recumbent
recurring
recurvate
recusance
recusancy
recycling
redaction
redbreast
reddition
redeliver
redolence
redolency
redoubted
reducible
reduction
redundant
refection
refectory
referable
reference
referment
refinedly

refitment
reflector
reflexion
reflexive
reforming
refortify
refractor
refresher
refulgent
refurbish
refurnish
refusable
refutable
regardant
regardful
regarding
regenesis
regicidal
regiminal
registrar
regretful
regularly
regulator
rehearsal
rehearser
reimburse
reimplant
reimprint
reinforce
reinspect
reinspire
reinstall
reinsurer
reiterate
rejection
rejoicing
rejoinder
relevance
relevancy
relieving
religious

reliquary
remainder
remigrate
remindful
remission
remissive
remissory
remittent
removable
renascent
rendition
renewable
renitence
renitency
renouncer
renovator
reparable
reparably
repayable
repayment
repeating
repellent
repentant
repercuss
repertory
reperusal
replenish
repletion
repletory
replicant
reporting
reposeful
repossess
reprehend
represent
represser
reprimand
reprobate
reproduce
reptatory
reptilian

republish
repudiate
repugnant
repulsion
repulsive
reputable
reputedly
requisite
rescuable
resection
resentful
reservoir
residence
residency
residuary
resilient
resistant
resistent
resolvent
resonancy
resonator
respecter
restfully
restiform
restively
restraint
resultant
resumable
resurgent
retaining
retaliate
retention
retentive
reticence
reticulum
retinitis
retiredly
retractor
retrieval
retriever
retrocede

retrousse
reverence
reversely
reversion
reversive
revetment
revivable
revocable
revolting
revulsion
revulsive
rhachitis
rhapsodic
rheometer
rheumatic
rhinolith
rhizodont
rhymeless
rhythmics
ribbonism
ribbonman
riddlings
rightness
rigidness
rigmarole
ringleted
riotously
ritualism
ritualist
rivalship
roadstead
rocambole
rockiness
roguishly
roisterer
rokambole
romancist
romanizer
rompishly
roominess
rosaceous

rostellum
rostrated
rotatable
rotundity
roughness
roundelay
roundhead
roundness
round-trip
rubescent
ruddiness
ruffianly
ruination
ruinously
ruminator
runcinate
runecraft
rusticate
rusticity
rustiness
ruthenium
sabadilla
sabretash
saccharic
saccharin
sacciform
sackcloth
sacrament
sacrifice
sacrilege
sacristan
sadducean
safeguard
safe-house
safflower
sagacious
sagittate
sailborne
saintfoin
sainthood
saintship

salacious
salangane
saleratus
salicylic
saliently
salimeter
salmonoid
saltation
saltatory
saltpetre
salubrity
salvation
samaritan
sanctuary
sandalled
sandarach
sandiness
sandpiper
sandstone
sanjakate
sapidness
sapiently
sapodilla
sappiness
sarcastic
sarcocarp
sargassum
sarmentum
sartorial
sartorius
sassafras
sassenach
satanical
satellite
satiation
saturable
saturnian
saturnine
sauciness
saunterer
savourily

saxifrage
saxophone
scagliola
scaliness
scalloped
scansores
scantling
scantness
scapement
scapiform
scapolite
scapulary
scarecrow
scarifier
scarpines
scatheful
scattered
scatterer
scavenger
scentless
sceptical
schematic
schemeful
schistose
schistous
schmaltzy
scholarly
scholiast
scholiums
schooling
schoolman
schorlous
sciatical
sciential
scientist
scintilla
sciomachy
sciomancy
scioptric
scirrhoid
scirrhous

scissible
sclerosis
sclerotic
scorbutic
scorching
scorpioid
scotchman
scoundrel
scraggily
scrambler
scratcher
screaming
scribbler
scrimmage
scriptory
scripture
scrivener
scrutoire
sculpture
scumbling
scummings
scutcheon
scutellum
scutiform
scytheman
seafaring
searching
seasoning
sebaceous
secernent
secession
seclusion
seclusive
secondary
secretary
secretion
secretive
secretory
sectarian
sectional
secularly

secundine
securable
sedentary
seditious
seducible
seduction
seductive
seediness
seemingly
segmental
segregate
seigniory
selachian
selection
selective
selenious
selfishly
selvedged
semantics
semaphore
semblance
semibreve
semicolon
semiology
semiotics
semitonic
senescent
seneschal
seniority
sensation
senseless
sensitive
sensitize
sensorial
sensorium
sensually
sentencer
sentiment
separable
separably
separator

september
septenary
sepulchre
sepulture
sequester
seraskier
serenader
sergeancy
sergeanty
seriality
sericeous
seriously
sermonize
serration
serrature
serricorn
serviette
servilely
servility
servitude
sessional
setaceous
sevenfold
seventeen
seventhly
severable
severance
severally
sexennial
sex-object
sexuality
sexualize
sforzando
shadiness
shakiness
shallowly
shamanism
shambling
shameless
shapeable
shapeless

sharpness
shaveling
shearling
sheathing
shebeener
sheepfold
sheephook
sheldrake
shiftless
shiftwork
shillelah
shingling
shipboard
shipshape
shipwreck
shoeblack
shoemaker
shoreless
shorthand
shortness
short-term
shovelful
shoveller
showiness
shrinkage
shrubbery
shuffling
sibilance
sibilancy
sibylline
siccation
siccative
sickening
sickleman
sideboard
sidelines
sighingly
sightless
sigmoidal
signalize
signatory

signature
signifier
signitary
signorina
siliceous
siliquose
silkiness
silliness
silvering
silverize
similarly
simpering
simpleton
simulator
sincerely
sincerity
sinewless
singleton
sinistral
sinlessly
sinologue
sinuation
sinuosity
sinuously
siphonage
siphuncle
situation
siveralty
sixteenmo
sixteenth
sizarship
sketchily
skilfully
skinflint
slackness
slakeness
slanderer
slantwise
slatiness
slaughter
slavishly

slavonian
sleekness
sleepless
slenderly
sliminess
slippered
slouching
slumberer
slumbrous
smallness
smart-card
smartness
smatterer
smilingly
smokeless
smokiness
smuggling
sniveller
snowboard
soap-opera
soapstone
soberness
sobriquet
socialism
socialist
sociality
socialize
societies
sociology
softening
sojourner
soldering
soldierly
solemness
solemnity
solemnize
solfatara
solfeggio
solicitor
solidness
soliloquy

solitaire
something
sometimes
somewhere
somnolent
sonneteer
sonnetize
sonometer
sootiness
sophister
sophistic
sophistry
sophomore
soporific
sopranist
sorceress
sorriness
sorrowful
sortilege
sottishly
soubrette
soundable
sound-bite
soundings
soundless
soundness
southerly
southmost
southward
sovereign
spaghetti
spareness
sparingly
sparkling
sparterie
spasmodic
spatially
spatulate
speakable
spearmint
specially

specialty
spectacle
spectator
speculate
speculums
speechify
speed-read
speedwell
spermatic
sphacelus
spherical
sphincter
spiciness
spiculate
spikenard
spillikin
spindrift
spininess
spinnaker
spinneret
spinosity
spirillum
spiritual
spleenful
spleenish
splendent
splendour
splenetic
splenitis
splintery
spokesman
spoliator
spongiole
sporangia
sporidium
sporocyst
sportsman
spoutless
sprightly
springing
springlet

sprinkler
spuminess
sputterer
squalidly
squarrose
squeamish
stableboy
stableman
stability
stagnancy
staidness
stainless
staircase
stalactic
staleness
stalkless
stalworth
staminate
stammerer
stanchion
starboard
starchily
staringly
starlight
startling
statement
statesman
stational
stationer
statistic
statuette
statusful
statutory
staymaker
steadfast
steelyard
steepness
steersman
stellular
stellated
stepchild

sterility
sterilize
sternmost
sternness
stevedore
stewartry
stiffener
stiffness
stigmatic
stillness
stimulant
stimulate
stintless
stipitate
stipulate
stitching
stock-cube
stockdove
stoically
stolidity
stomachal
stomacher
stomachic
stonewall
stoniness
stoutness
straggler
strangely
strangles
strangury
strapping
stratagem
strategic
streamlet
strenuous
stretcher
striation
stricture
stringent
stripling
strobilus

strontium
structure
struggler
strychnia
studiedly
stupefier
stupidity
stutterer
stylishly
stylistic
stylobate
suability
suasively
subaerial
subalpine
subaltern
subarctic
subcostal
subdeacon
subdivide
subduable
subereous
subfamily
subgenera
subjacent
subjugate
sublessee
sublimate
sublimely
sublimity
sublunary
submarine
submersed
subregion
subscribe
subscript
subsidies
subsidize
substance
subsultus
subtenant

subtilely
subtilize
subtorrid
subverter
succeeder
successor
succourer
succulent
succursal
suctorial
sudorific
suffering
suffixion
suffocate
suffragan
suffusion
suggester
sulcation
sulkiness
sulphuret
sulphuric
sultanate
sultaness
summaries
summarily
summarist
summarize
summation
summerset
summonses
sumptuary
sumptuous
sunflower
sunniness
sunrising
sunstroke
superable
superfine
super-glue
superheat
superpose

supersede	sycophant	tantalize	temperate	theandric
supervene	syllabify	tarantara	tempering	thematist
supervise	syllogism	tarantism	temporary	theme-park
suppliant	syllogize	tarantula	temporize	theocracy
supporter	symbiosis	taraxacum	temptable	theocrasy
suppurate	symbiotic	tarbouche	temptress	theogonic
supremacy	symbolism	tardiness	temulence	theologic
supremely	symbolist	tarentula	tenacious	theomachy
surcharge	symbolize	targeteer	tendinous	theomancy
surcingle	symbology	targetier	tenebrous	theophany
surfboard	symphonic	tarnisher	tenseness	theoremic
surgeoncy	symphysis	tarpaulin	tensility	theoretic
surliness	symposiac	tartarean	tentacled	theorizer
surmising	symposium	tartarize	tentative	theosophy
surmullet	synagogue	tartarous	tepidness	therapist
surpliced	synchrony	tasimeter	terebinth	thereaway
surprisal	synclinal	tasmanian	termagant	therefore
surprised	syncopate	tasselled	terminate	therefrom
surrender	syncopize	tasteless	termitary	thereinto
surrogate	syndicate	tattooing	territory	thereupon
surveying	syneresis	tauriform	terrorism	therewith
suspender	synizesis	tautology	terrorist	thermally
suspensor	synodical	tawniness	terrorize	thesaurus
suspicion	synonymic	taxidermy	terseness	theurgist
sustainer	syntactic	taxonomic	tessellar	thickness
swaggerer	synthesis	teachable	testacean	thinkable
swallower	synthetic	techiness	testament	thirstily
swansdown	syphilize	technical	testatrix	thirtieth
swarthily	systemize	tectonics	testifier	thrashing
sweepings	tabasheer	tediously	testimony	threshing
sweetener	tabularly	tegulated	testiness	threefold
sweetmeat	tacamahac	telegraph	tetralogy	threnetic
sweetness	tactician	telemeter	tetrarchy	threshold
swiftness	tae-kwon-do	telemetry	textorial	thriftily
swimmeret	tailoress	teteology	textually	thrilling
swindling	tailoring	telepathy	thallogen	throbless
swineherd	taintless	telephone	thanatoid	throttler
swingeing	talegalla	telephony	thanehood	throwster
swinishly	talkative	telescope	thaneship	thumbless
swordsman	talmudist	telescopy	thankless	thunderer
sybaritic	tangerine	tellurian	thatching	thylacine

tiercelet
tightness
timbering
time-share
timidness
tipsiness
tiredness
titillate
titration
tittlebat
titularly
tolerable
tolerably
tolerance
tolerator
tollbooth
tombstone
tomentose
tomentous
tonguelet
tonsillar
tonsorial
toothache
toothless
toothpick
toothsome
topiarian
topically
tormenter
tormentil
tormentor
tornadoes
torpedoes
torpidity
torquated
torridity
torsional
tortility
totalness
touchable
touch-tone

touchwood
toughness
tourmalin
towelling
town-house
townsfolk
townwards
trabecula
traceable
traceably
tracheary
trachytic
trackball
trackless
tractable
tractably
tradesman
tradition
traditive
tragedian
trainable
traitress
transcend
transform
transfuse
transient
translate
transmute
transpire
transport
transpose
trapezium
trapezoid
trappings
traumatic
travelled
traveller
traverser
travertin
treachery
treadmill

treasurer
treatment
trematode
trematoid
trembling
tremulous
trenchant
triatomic
tribalism
tribesman
tribunate
tributory
tricksome
trickster
triclinic
tricolour
tricuspid
tricyclic
triennial
trifacial
trifloral
triforium
trigamist
trigonous
trigynian
trigynous
trihedral
trihedron
trilinear
trilithon
trilithic
trilobate
trilobite
trilogies
trimerous
trimester
trinerved
trinketer
trinketry
trinomial
triserial

triteness
tritheism
triturate
triumphal
triumpher
trivially
trochlear
tropology
troublous
trousered
trousseau
troutling
truceless
truculent
truepenny
trumpeter
truncated
truncheon
trustless
truthless
tubercled
tubicolar
tubulated
tufaceous
tug-of-love
tumidness
tunefully
tunicated
turbidity
turbinate
turbulent
turfiness
turgidity
turnround
turnstile
turnstone
turpitude
turquoise
tussilago
tutorship
twentieth

twinkling
typically
tyrannize
tyrannous
uliginous
ultimatum
umbellate
umbilical
umbilicus
umbonated
unabashed
unadorned
unadvised
unalloyed
unamiable
unanimity
unanimous
unassured
unavenged
unbending
unbiassed
unblessed
unbounded
unbridled
unburthen
unceasing
uncertain
uncivilly
uncleanly
unclouded
unconcern
uncorrupt
uncourtly
uncouthly
uncrossed
uncrowned
undaunted
undeceive
undefined
underbred
undergrid

underhand	unguarded	unquietly	unwarlike	vaporable
underhung	unguiform	unreality	unwatched	vaporific
underline	unhandily	unrefined	unwatered	vapourish
underling	unhappily	unrelated	unwearied	variation
undermine	unharness	unresting	unweighed	varicella
undermost	unhealthy	unruffled	unwelcome	variegate
underpass	unheedful	unsavoury	unwilling	varieties
underplot	unheeding	unscathed	unwinking	variolous
underprop	unhopeful	unselfish	unwitting	varioloid
underrate	unifacial	unsettled	unwomanly	variously
undersell	uniformly	unshackle	unworldly	varnisher
undershot	unigenous	unshapely	unwounded	vasculose
undersign	uninjured	unsheathe	unwreathe	vasomotor
undertake	uninvited	unsightly	unwritten	vassalage
underwear	uniparous	unskilful	unwrought	veeringly
underwood	uniserial	unskilled	upholster	vegetable
undesired	unisexual	unsoundly	uppermost	vehemence
undiluted	unisonant	unsparing	uprightly	vehemency
undivided	unisonous	unspotted	urceolate	vehicular
undoubted	unitarian	unstained	urticaria	vellicate
undreamed	univalent	unstamped	uselessly	velveteen
undressed	univalved	unstinted	usherette	velveting
undulated	universal	unstudied	ushership	veneering
undutiful	unjointed	unsubdued	utilities	venerable
unearthly	unknowing	unsullied	utricular	venerably
uneatable	unlearned	untainted	utterable	venerator
unendowed	unlimited	untamable	utterance	vengeance
unengaged	unluckily	untenable	uttermost	veniality
unenglish	unmatched	unthanked	vacancies	ventilate
unequable	unmeaning	unthought	vaccinate	ventricle
unequally	unmerited	unthrifty	vacillate	venturous
unexpired	unmindful	untimeous	vaginated	veracious
unexposed	unmixedly	untouched	vagueness	veratrine
unfeeling	unmortise	untracked	vainglory	verbalism
unfeigned	unmusical	untrained	valentine	verbalist
unfitness	unnatural	untrodden	valiantly	verbalize
unfitting	unnoticed	untunable	valuation	verbosely
unfledged	unopposed	untutored	valueless	verbosity
unfounded	unpitying	unusually	vampirism	verdantly
ungallant	unplumbed	unvarying	vandalism	verdigris
ungenteel	unpopular	unvisited	vapidness	veridical

veritable	villiform	vulcanian	weathered	windingly
veritably	villosity	vulvanite	weatherly	winningly
vermicide	vinaceous	vulcanize	wednesday	wingfully
vermiform	vindicate	vulgarism	weepingly	wistfully
vermifuge	violation	vulgarity	weighable	withering
verminate	violently	vulgarize	weevilled	withstand
verminous	violinist	vulnerary	weightily	witlessly
vernation	virescent	vulpicide	weirdness	witnesser
verrucose	virgilian	vulpinite	westering	witticism
verrucous	virginity	vulturine	westwards	wittiness
versatile	virtually	vulturish	whalebone	wittingly
versifier	virtuosos	vulturous	wheedling	woebegone
vertebrae	virulence	waggishly	wherefore	wofulness
vertebral	viscerate	wagonette	whereinto	wolfishly
vesicular	viscidity	wailingly	whereness	wolverene
vestibule	viscounty	waistband	whereunto	womanhood
vestigial	visionary	waistcoat	whereupon	womankind
vetchling	visuality	wakefully	wherewith	womanlike
vexatious	vitelline	waldenses	wherryman	wonderful
vexillary	vitiation	walkabout	whetstone	woodcraft
viability	vitrified	wallabies	whichever	woodiness
vibracula	vitriform	wandering	whimperer	wordiness
vibratile	vitriolic	wapenshaw	whimsical	workforce
vibration	vitruvian	wapentake	whiningly	workhouse
vibratory	vivacious	warehouse	whinstone	workmanly
vibrissae	vividness	warningly	whirligig	workwoman
vicariate	vizierate	warranter	whirlpool	worldling
vicarious	vizierial	warrantor	whirlwind	worriment
vicarship	vocalness	washiness	whiskered	worshiper
vicennial	voiceless	waspishly	whisperer	worthless
viciously	volcanism	wassailer	whiteness	woundable
victimize	volcanist	wasteness	whitewash	wristband
victoress	volcanoes	watchword	wholefood	wrongness
victorine	volumeter	waterfall	wholeness	wrynecked
victories	voluntary	waterless	wholesale	xenophile
videlicet	volunteer	watershed	wholesome	xeroderma
video-game	voodooism	wayfaring	whosoever	xylograph
videotext	voracious	waywardly	widowhood	xylophone
viewpoint	vorticose	wealthily	wieldable	yachtsman
vigesimal	vouchsafe	weariness	willingly	yankeeism
vigilance	vulcanism	wearisome	windiness	yellowish

yesterday	youngster	zemindary	zoography	zumbooruk
yestereve	ytterbium	zeuglodon	zoologist	zygomatic
youngling	zealously	zeugmatic	zoophytic	zymometer
youngness	Zeitgeist	zirconium	zootomist	

10-Letter Words

abbreviate
abdication
abdominous
aberdevine
aberration
abhorrence
abiogenist
abjectness
abjuration
abjuratory
able-bodied
abnegation
abnormally
abominable
abominably
aboriginal
aborigines
abortively
above-board
abridgment
abrogation
abrogative
abruptness
abscission
absentment
absinthian
absolutely
absolution
absolutism
absolutory
absorbable
absorbedly
absorption
absorptive
abstemious
abstention
abstergent

abstersion
abstinence
abstracted
abstractly
abstrusely
absurdness
abundantly
abyssinian
academical
accelerate
accentuate
acceptable
acceptably
acceptance
acceptancy
accessible
accessibly
accidental
accipitral
accomplice
accomplish
accordance
accoucheur
accountant
accrescent
accubation
accumbency
accumulate
accurately
accusation
accusative
accusatory
accustomed
acephalous
acetabulum
acetarious
acetimeter

acetopathy
achievance
achromatic
acidimeter
acinaceous
acorn-shell
acotyledon
acquainted
acquirable
acroamatic
acrogenous
acronychal
acroterium
actinolite
actinozoon
actionable
activeness
adamantine
adam's-apple
adaptation
adder-stone
adder's-wort
additional
adequately
adherently
adhesively
adhibition
adiactinic
adjacently
adjectival
adjudgment
adjudicate
adjunction
adjunctive
adjuration
adjuratory
adjustable

adjustment
admeasurer
administer
admiration
admiringly
admissible
admittable
admittance
admittatur
admittedly
admonisher
admonition
admonitive
admonitory
adolescent
adroitness
adulterant
adulterate
adulteress
adulterine
adulterous
advance-man
adventurer
advertence
advertiser
aeriferous
aerologist
aeronautic
aerostatic
aeruginous
aesthetics
affability
affectedly
affiliable
affirmable
afflicting
affliction

afflictive	alliaceous	amphibrach	anisomeric
affronting	alligation	amphimacer	annexation
aforenamed	alliterate	amputation	annihilate
africander	allocation	amygdalate	annotation
afterbirth	allocution	amygdaline	annunciate
after-grass	allopathic	amygdaloid	anointment
afterimage	allurement	amylaceous	answerable
afterpains	alluringly	anabaptism	answerably
afterpiece	allusively	anabaptist	answerless
afterstate	almond-cake	anacamptic	antagonism
aftertaste	almond-tree	anaclastic	antagonist
afterwards	alms-giving	anadromous	antecedent
agallochum	alongshore	anagogical	ante-chapel
aggrandize	alpenstock	analogical	antepenult
aggression	alphabetic	analysable	anteriorly
aggressive	altar-bread	anamniotic	anthracene
agony-uncle	altar-cloth	anaplastic	anthropoid
agrypnotic	altarpiece	anarthrous	antichrist
aide-de-camp	altazimuth	anastomose	anticipate
air-bladder	alteration	anatomical	anticlimax
air-cushion	alterative	ancestress	anticlinal
alarmingly	altogether	anchoretic	antiemetic
albescence	altruistic	anchor-hold	antilithic
albuminoid	alum-schist	androecium	antinonial
albuminous	amalgamate	androgynal	antinomian
alcoholism	amanuensis	androphagi	antiphonal
alcoholize	amateurish	anecdotist	antiquated
aldermancy	amazedness	anelectric	antiseptic
aldermanic	ambassador	anemograph	antithesis
aldermanry	ambidexter	anemometer	antithetic
alexanders	ambulacrum	anemometry	aphaeresis
algebraist	ambulation	anemoscope	aphoristic
alienation	ambulatory	aneurismal	apiculture
alimentary	ambushment	angiosperm	aplacental
alineation	ameliorate	anglo-irish	apocalypse
allegation	amendatory	anglomania	apocarpous
allegiance	amerceable	anglo-saxon	apocryphal
allegorist	amercement	angora-wool	apodeictic
allegorize	amiability	angularity	apologetic
allegretto	ammunition	animadvert	apologizer
alleviator	amphibious	animalcule	apophthegm

apoplectic	arrestment	atmosphere	baby-farmer
apostatize	arrogantly	atrabiliar	baby-sitter
apostolate	arrogation	atramental	babylonian
apostrophe	artfulness	attachable	backgammon
apothecary	articulate	attachment	background
apothecium	artificial	attackable	backhander
apotheosis	ascendable	attainable	backslider
apparently	ascendancy	attainment	backwardly
apparition	asceticism	attendance	bafflingly
appealable	ascribable	attraction	balderdash
appearance	ascription	attractive	balneology
appeasable	asphyxiate	auctioneer	balustrade
appetitive	aspiration	audibility	banishment
applausive	aspiringly	audiometer	bankruptcy
applicable	assailable	auditorium	baptistery
applicancy	assemblage	augustness	barcarolle
appositely	assentient	auriculate	barebacked
apposition	assessable	auriferous	bareheaded
appositive	assessment	aurigation	bargeboard
appreciate	asseverate	auspicious	barkentine
apprentice	assibilate	australian	barleycorn
approacher	assignable	authorship	barometric
approvable	assignment	autochthon	barrenness
aquamari ne	assimilate	autocratic	base-minded
aquiferous	assistance	autogenous	basket-case
arachnidan	associable	autography	basket-hilt
arbitrator	assortment	automobile	basset-horn
arbor-vitae	assumption	autonomous	bassoonist
archbishop	assumptive	autoptical	bass-relief
archdeacon	asteroidal	avant-garde	bastardize
archerfish	astomatous	avant-guard	bastionary
archetypal	astonished	avanturine	bat-fowling
architrave	astounding	avaricious	bathing-box
arefaction	astringent	aventurine	bathometer
arenaceous	astrolatry	averseness	bathymetry
areolation	astrologer	aviculture	baton-round
areopagite	astrometer	avouchment	batrachian
argumental	astronomer	awakenment	battledore
aristocrat	astronomic	babblement	battlement
arithmetic	astuteness	babiroussa	battleship
armipotent	athanasian	baby-boomer	beadleship

beard-grass
bear-garden
beautifier
beauty-spot
bechedemer
becomingly
bedchamber
beer-engine
beforehand
behindhand
believable
belladonna
bellflower
bell-hanger
bell-ringer
bell-turret
bellwether
benedicite
benedictus
benefactor
beneficent
beneficial
benevolent
benumbment
bequeather
besottedly
besprinkle
bestiality
bestialize
bestiarian
bestseller
betterment
bettermost
betterness
bevel-wheel
bewitchery
bewitching
biblically
bibliology
bibliopegy
bichromate

bicorporal
biennially
bijouterie
bilge-water
bilinguist
bill-broker
billet-doux
bimaculate
bimetallic
biogenesis
biographer
biological
bioplasmic
bird-cherry
bird-spider
birostrate
birthnight
birthplace
birthright
bishop-weed
bismuthite
bissextile
bisulphate
bisulphite
bitterness
bituminize
bituminous
blackamoor
blackberry
blackboard
black-chalk
blackfriar
blackguard
black-sheep
blacksmith
blackthorn
blamefully
blancmange
blandisher
blanketing
blank-verse

blasphemer
blastoderm
blazonment
blissfully
blitheness
blithesome
blockhouse
bloodhorse
bloodhound
bloodiness
blood-money
bloodstone
bloody-flux
bloomingly
bluebottle
bluejacket
bluishness
blushingly
blustering
blusterous
board-wages
boastfully
boastingly
body-armour
body-colour
bogtrotter
boisterous
bombardier
bomb-vessel
bondholder
bondswoman
bone-setter
bone-spavin
book-hunter
book-keeper
book-muslin
bookseller
bootlessly
borderland
bottle-bank
bottle-fish

bottlenose
bottle-tree
bottomless
bouts-rimes
bowdlerize
bowie-knife
boyishness
brachiopod
brachylogy
brachyural
bracketing
bracteated
braggingly
brahmanism
brain-death
brain-drain
brain-fever
branchiate
branchless
brant-goose
brawlingly
brawniness
brazenness
brazil-wood
braziletto
breadfruit
breadstuff
breakwater
breastbone
breast-deep
breast-knot
breast-wall
breastwork
breathable
breathless
brent-goose
bricklayer
bridegroom
bridesmaid
bridge-deck
bridle-hand

bridle-path
bridle-road
bridle-rein
brigandage
brigandism
brigantine
brightness
brightsome
brilliance
broadcloth
broadsheet
broadsword
broken-down
brokenness
broken-wind
brome-grass
bronchitis
broomstick
broomstaff
browbeater
brown-study
brusquerie
bubonocele
buccinator
buck-basket
buckjumper
buddhistic
buffoonery
buffoonish
bullionist
bunglingly
burdensome
bureaucrat
burrow-duck
bush-harrow
bushranger
bush-shrike
butlership
butter-bird
butter-boat
buttermilk

butter-tree
butterwort
buttery-bar
button-push
buttonhole
buttonhook
buttonwood
cacography
cadaverous
caddice-fly
caespitose
calamitous
calcareous
calcinable
calcsinter
calculable
calculated
calculator
caledonian
caliginous
caligraphy
calumniate
calumnious
calyciform
calyptrate
camelopard
cameronian
campaigner
campestral
camphorate
camphor-oil
canary-wood
cancellate
cancellous
candescent
candidness
candle-coal
candlefish
candlewick
candy-sugar
canephorus

cankerworm
cannel-coal
cannonball
cannon-shot
canonicals
canonicity
cantatrice
canterbury
cantilever
cantonment
canvasback
caoutchouc
capability
capacitate
capillaire
capitalize
capitation
capitulate
capnomancy
capricious
captiously
carabineer
caravaneer
carbazotic
carbonated
carbuncled
cardialgia
carelessly
caricature
carnallite
carpellary
carthusian
cartwright
cascarilla
case-bottle
case-harden
casemented
cassia-bark
cassia-buds
cassiopeia
cassolette

castigator
castration
catafalque
catalectic
cataleptic
catamenial
cataphract
catarrhine
catchpenny
catechetic
catechumen
categorial
catenarian
catenation
catholicon
catoptrics
cat-scanner
cattle-show
caulescent
causticity
cautionary
cautiously
cavalierly
celebrated
celebrater
cellulated
cenobitism
censorious
censorship
censurable
censurably
centaurian
centennial
centesimal
centigrade
centimetre
centipedal
centralism
centrality
centralize
centricity

centrifuge
cephalitis
cephalopod
cerebellar
cerebellum
cerebritis
ceremonial
ceregraphy
certiorari
ceruminous
cessionary
cestiodean
cestracion
chain-cable
chalcedony
chalkiness
challenged
challenger
chalybeate
chamaeleon
chamber-pot
chambertin
champignon
chancellor
chandelier
changeable
changeably
changeless
changeling
channelled
chapel-cart
chapfallen
chaplaincy
chargeable
charioteer
charitable
charitably
charmingly
chartreuse
chartulary
chasteness

chatelaine
chatterbox
chaucerian
chauvinism
chauvinist
cheek-pouch
cheek-tooth
cheerfully
cheeriness
cheeringly
cheesecake
cheesiness
cheiropter
chemically
chemisette
chequebook
chersonese
cherubimic
chessboard
chickenpox
chiffonier
childbirth
childishly
chiliastic
chilliness
chillingly
chimerical
chimney-can
chimney-pot
chimpanzee
china-aster
chinchilla
chip-bonnet
chirognomy
chirograph
chiromancy
chirurgeon
chiselling
chivalrous
chloralism
chloridize

chloridate
chlorodyne
chloroform
choiceless
cholagogue
choliambus
chop-fallen
chopsticks
choriambus
christhood
christless
chromatics
chronicler
chronogram
chronology
chrysolite
chubbiness
chumenical
churchgoer
churchless
church-rate
churchyard
churlishly
ciceronian
cinchonism
cinenchyma
cinquefoil
cinque-pace
circensian
circuitous
circulable
circularly
circulator
circumcise
circumflex
circumfuse
circummure
circumvent
cismontane
cistercian
citizenize

clack-valve
clamminess
clangorous
clannishly
clarenceux
clasp-knife
classicism
classicist
clavichord
clavicular
claw-hammer
clay-ground
cleansable
clearstory
clerestory
clergiable
cleverness
clientship
clingstone
clinically
clinkstone
clinometer
clodhopper
cloisterer
cloudberry
cloudbuilt
cloudburst
cloudiness
clownishly
club-footed
clumsiness
coach-stand
coadjutrix
coagulable
coagulator
coalescent
coal-heaver
coal-master
coarseness
coastguard
coastwards

coat-armour
cockatrice
cockchafer
cockneydom
cockneyish
cockneyism
coequality
coercively
coetaneous
coeternity
coexecutor
coexistent
coffee-mill
coffee-room
cogitation
cogitative
cognizable
cognizably
cognizance
cognominal
coherently
cohesively
coincident
cold-chisel
coleorhiza
collarless
collatable
collateral
collection
collective
collegiate
collimator
collingual
colliquate
collocutor
colloquial
colloquist
colloquize
coloration
colourable
colourably

colourless
colporteur
combatable
combinable
combinedly
combustion
comedietta
comeliness
comestible
comforting
comicality
commandant
commandeer
commentary
commercial
commissary
commission
commissure
commitment
commixture
commodious
commonable
commonalty
commonness
commonweal
commutable
comparable
comparably
comparison
compassion
compatible
compatibly
compatriot
compendium
compensate
competence
competitor
complacent
complainer
complement
completely

completion
completive
completory
complexion
complexity
compliance
complicacy
complicate
complicity
compliment
composedly
compositor
compounder
comprehend
compressed
compressor
compromise
compulsion
compulsive
compulsory
computable
concentric
conception
conceptual
concerning
concertina
concession
concessive
conchoidal
conchology
conciliate
concinnity
conclavist
concluding
conclusion
conclusive
concoction
concordant
concretely
concretion
concubinal

concurrent
concussion
concussive
condescend
condolence
conduction
conductive
confection
conference
confervoid
confession
confidante
confidence
confinable
confiscate
confluence
conformist
conformity
confounded
confounder
confusedly
confutable
congeneric
congenital
congestion
congestive
conglobate
congregate
congruence
coniferous
conjecture
conjointly
conjugally
conjunctly
connascent
connatural
connection
connective
connivance
connivence
conquering

conscience
consecrate
consensual
consequent
consistent
consistory
consociate
consolable
consonance
conspectus
conspiracy
constantly
constipate
constitute
constraint
constringe
consubsist
consuetude
consulship
consulting
consultive
consumable
consumedly
consummate
contactual
contagious
containant
contention
contestant
contextual
contexture
contiguity
contiguous
continence
contingent
continuity
continuous
contortion
contraband
contracted
contractor

contradict
contrarily
contravene
contribute
contritely
contrition
controller
controvert
convalesce
convection
convective
convenable
convenance
convenient
convention
conventual
convergent
conversant
conversely
conversion
convexness
conveyable
conveyance
conviction
convincing
convulsion
convulsive
cool-headed
cooperator
coordinate
coparcener
copernican
copper-head
coprolitic
copulation
copulative
copulatory
copyholder
coquettish
co-radicate
cordiality

cordillera
cordwainer
corelative
coriaceous
corinthian
corn-beetle
corncockle
cornerwise
corn-factor
cornflower
cornucopia
coronation
coroniform
corporally
corporeity
corpse-gate
corpulence
correction
corrective
correctory
correspond
corrigenda
corrigible
corrodible
corrugated
corrugator
corruption
corruptive
corseleted
coryphaeus
cosmically
cosmogonal
cosmoramic
costliness
cothurnate
cottierism
cottonseed
cotton-tree
cottonwood
cotton-wool
cotyliform

couch-grass
councillor
councilman
council-tax
counsellor
counteract
countryman
courageous
court-baron
court-dress
courthouse
court-sword
cousinhood
cousinship
covenantee
covenanter
covenantor
covered-way
covetingly
covetously
cow-bunting
cowcatcher
cow-chervil
cow-parsley
cow-parsnip
cowrie-pine
crackbrain
craftiness
cragginess
crane's-bill
craniology
crapulence
crassament
crassitude
crawlingly
creaminess
creational
credential
creditable
creditably
crenellate

crescented
crescentic
cretaceous
cribriform
criminally
cringeling
crio-sphinx
crispation
crisscross
critically
criticizer
crossbones
crossbreed
crossroads
cross-staff
cross-stone
crosstrees
crotcheted
crow-flower
crown-grass
crown-wheel
cruet-stand
crumb-brush
crumb-cloth
crustacean
crustation
crustiness
cryophorus
cryptogamy
cryptogram
cryptology
ctenophora
cuckoo-spit
cucurbital
cuirassier
cultivable
cultivator
culturable
culvertail
cumberless
cumbersome

cumbrously
cummerbund
cumulation
cumulative
curability
curateship
curmudgeon
curriculum
cursedness
customable
cuttlebone
cuttlefish
cyathiform
cyclometer
cylindroid
czarevitch
daggle-tail
daintiness
damageable
damask-plum
damask-rose
dapple-grey
dark-browed
daughterly
dauphiness
daydreamer
dazzlingly
deaconhood
deaconship
dead-letter
deadliness
dead-nettle
dead-weight
dear-bought
deaspirate
death-agony
death's-door
death's-head
death-token
deathwatch
debasement

debauchery
debentured
debilitate
debonairly
debouchure
decagynian
decagynous
decahedral
decalogist
decampment
decandrian
decandrous
decangular
decapitate
decapodous
deceivable
decemviral
decigramme
decimalize
decimation
decipherer
decisively
declaimant
declarable
declarator
declaredly
declension
declinable
declinator
decolorant
decolorate
decolorize
decompound
decoration
decorative
decorously
decreeable
decrescent
decumbence
decumbency
decurrency

dedication
dedicatory
defacement
defalcator
defamation
defeasance
defeasible
defecation
defendable
defensible
deficience
deficiency
defilement
definitely
definition
definitive
deflagrate
deflection
deflowerer
deformedly
defrayment
degeneracy
degenerate
dehiscence
dehumanize
dejectedly
dejudicate
del credere
delectable
delectably
delegation
deliberate
delicately
delightful
delineator
delinquent
deliquesce
delusively
demonetize
demagogism
demandable

demiquaver
demobilize
democratic
demogorgon
demography
demoiselle
demolisher
demolition
demonology
demoralize
demureness
demurrable
dendriform
dendrolite
dendrology
denization
denominate
denotation
denotative
denouement
densimeter
dentifrice
denudation
denunciate
deobstruct
deodorizer
deontology
department
dependable
dependance
dependence
dependency
depilation
depilatory
deplorable
deplorably
deployment
depolarize
depopulate
deportment
depositary

deposition
depravedly
deprecator
depreciate
depredator
depression
depressive
depuration
depuratory
deputation
deracinate
deridingly
derisively
derivation
derivative
derogation
derogatory
descendant
descendent
descending
descension
desecrater
deservedly
deshabille
desiccator
desiderate
designator
designedly
desolately
desolation
despairing
despatcher
despicable
despicably
despisable
despiteful
despondent
desquamate
desudation
detachment
detainment

detectable
detergence
detergency
determined
detestable
detestably
detonating
detonation
detraction
detractive
detractory
detruncate
deutoplasm
devastator
devilishly
devil's-dust
devitalize
devolution
devotement
devotional
devourable
diabetical
diabolical
diacaustic
diacoustic
diaglyphic
diagnostic
diagonally
dialectics
dialogical
diapedesis
diaphanous
diaphonics
diaskeuast
diathermal
diathermic
diatribist
dictatress
dictionary
didactical
didelphian

didunculus
didynamous
dielectric
die-sinking
dietetical
difference
difficulty
diffidence
difformity
diffusible
digestible
digitately
digitation
digitiform
digitorium
digression
digressive
dilacerate
dilapidate
dilatation
dilatorily
dilettante
diligently
dilly-dally
dilucidate
diminisher
diminuendo
diminution
diminutive
dimorphism
dimorphous
dining-room
dinner-hour
dinnerless
dinnertime
dioptrical
dipetalous
diphtheria
diphyllous
diphyodont
diplomatic

diprotodon
dipsomania
directness
directress
disability
disanimate
disapparel
disappoint
disapprove
disarrange
disastrous
disbelieve
disburthen
discerning
discharger
discipline
disclaimer
disclosure
discomfort
discommend
discompose
disconcert
disconnect
discontent
discophora
discordant
discounter
discourage
discourser
discoverer
discreetly
discrepant
discretion
discretive
discursive
discussion
discussive
discutient
disdainful
disembogue
disembosom

disembowel
disembroil
disenchant
disengaged
disennoble
disenslave
disentitle
disfeature
disfigurer
disfurnish
disgustful
disgusting
dishabille
dishearten
dishonesty
dishwasher
disincline
disinherit
disjointed
disloyally
disloyalty
dismalness
dismission
dismissory
disomatous
disordered
disorderly
disownment
disparager
dispassion
dispensary
dispensing
dispeopler
dispermous
dispersive
dispersion
dispirited
displeased
displeaser
disposable
dispossess

disputable
disqualify
disrespect
disruption
dissatisfy
dissecting
dissection
dissembler
dissension
dissenting
disservice
dissidence
dissilient
dissimilar
dissipated
dissociate
dissoluble
dissolvent
dissonance
dissuasion
dissuasive
dissymetry
distensive
distention
distichous
distillate
distinctly
distortion
distortive
distracted
distrainer
distrainor
distraught
distressed
distribute
ditheistic
divagation
divaricate
divergence
divergency
divination

divineness
diving-bell
divisional
docimastic
doctorship
documental
doggedness
dogmatizer
dog-parsley
dolorously
domination
doorkeeper
double-bass
double-dyed
double-lock
doubleness
double-star
doubtfully
downlooked
downmarket
downstairs
dragon-tree
dramatical
dramaturgy
draught-bar
drawbridge
drawlingly
dreadfully
dreadlocks
dreaminess
dreariness
dressmaker
droopingly
drop-hammer
drosometer
drossiness
drowsiness
drudgingly
drupaceous
drysaltery
dubitation

duck-billed
dullwitted
dumbwaiter
duniwassal
duodecimal
dupability
durability
duumvirate
dwarfishly
dynamitard
dysenteric
earthbound
earthiness
earth-plate
earthquake
earthshine
ear-trumpet
easterling
eastertide
eboulement
ebracteate
ebullience
ebulliency
ebullition
ecchymosis
ecclesiast
eccoprotic
echinoderm
economical
ecthlipsis
eczematous
edaciously
edentulous
edibleness
edifyingly
editorship
edulcorate
effaceable
effacement
effectible
effectless

effectuate
effeminacy
effeminate
effervesce
efficiency
effloresce
effleurage
effortless
effrontery
effulgence
egyptology
eighteenmo
eighteenth
eisteddfod
elaborator
elasticity
elderberry
elecampane
electorate
electrical
electronic
elementary
elenchical
eleusinian
eliminable
eliquation
elliptical
elongation
eloquently
elucidator
emaciation
emancipate
emarginate
emasculate
embankment
embassador
ember-goose
emblazoner
emblematic
embodiment
embolismal

embolismic
embonpoint
embossment
embouchure
embroidery
embryogeny
embryology
embryonary
embryotomy
emendation
emendatory
emergently
emetically
emigration
emmetropia
emphatical
empiricism
employable
employment
enamellist
enantiosis
encampment
encephalic
encephalon
enchanting
enclitical
encourager
encrinital
encrinitic
encroacher
encyclical
encystment
endearment
endemicity
endermatic
endogamous
endogenous
endopleura
endorhizal
endorsable
endosmosis

endosmotic
endostitis
enduringly
enervation
enforcible
engagement
engagingly
englishman
enharmonic
enigmatist
enjoinment
enlacement
enlistment
enormously
enrichment
enrockment
ensanguine
ensignship
entailment
enteralgia
enterocele
enterolite
enterolith
enterotomy
enterprise
enthronize
enthusiasm
enthusiast
enticeable
enticement
enticingly
entireness
entombment
entomology
entophytic
entrochite
entry-money
enumerator
enunciable
enunciator
epaulement

epauletted
epenthesis
epenthetic
epexegesis
ephemerist
epicycloid
epideictic
epidemical
epigastric
epigenesis
epigenetic
epiglottic
epiglottis
epigraphic
epileptoid
epilogical
epiloguize
epiphloeum
epirhizous
episcopacy
episcopate
episodical
epispastic
epistolist
epistolize
epitaphian
epitaphist
epithelial
epithelium
epitomator
epitomizer
eprouvette
equability
equanimity
equanimous
equatorial
equestrian
equitation
equivalent
equivocate
eradicable

eradicator
erectility
eremitical
erethistic
ericaceous
erotomania
erpetology
erubescent
eructation
eruptional
erysipelas
escalation
escapement
escarpment
escharotic
escritoire
esculapian
escutcheon
esophagous
especially
essayistic
esteemable
estimation
estivation
esuriently
eternalist
eternalize
ethereally
etheriform
ethnically
ethnologic
etiolation
etymologic
eucalyptol
eucalyptus
eudemonism
eudemonist
eudiometer
eudiometry
euhemerism
eulogistic

euphonious
euphorbium
euphuistic
eurodollar
eustachian
euthanasia
evacuation
evaluation
evanescent
evangelist
evangelize
evaporable
even-handed
eventually
everliving
everywhere
evidential
eviscerate
evolvement
exacerbate
exactitude
exaggerate
exaltation
examinable
examinator
exasperate
ex-cathedra
excavation
excellence
excellency
excerption
excitation
excitative
excitatory
excitement
excogitate
excrescent
excruciate
excusatory
excuseless
execration

execrative
execratory
executable
exegitical
exhalation
exhalement
exhausting
exhaustion
exhaustive
exhibition
exhibitive
exhibitory
exhilarant
exhilarate
exhumation
exorbitant
exoterical
expansible
expatiator
expatriate
expectance
expectancy
expediency
expedition
expellable
experience
experiment
expertness
expiratory
explicable
explicitly
exploitage
explorable
exportable
exposition
expositive
expository
expression
expressive
expurgator
exsiccator

extendible
extensible
extenuator
exteriorly
externally
extincteur
extinction
extinguish
extirpable
extirpator
extraction
extractive
extramural
extraneous
extricable
exuberance
exuberancy
exulcerate
exultation
exuviation
eyelet-hole
eye-servant
eye-service
eyewitness
fabricator
fabulously
fabulosity
facileness
facilitate
factionary
factionist
factiously
factitious
factorship
fagot-voter
fahrenheit
fair-minded
fair-spoken
faithfully
fallacious
fallow-chat

fallow-deer
familiarly
famishment
fanaticism
fanaticize
fancifully
fantoccini
fan-tracery
farcically
far-fetched
farmership
far-sighted
fasciation
fascicular
fasciculus
fastidious
fastigiate
fat-brained
fatalistic
fatherhood
fatherland
fatherless
fathership
fathomable
fathomless
faultiness
favourable
favourably
fearlessly
feathering
febrifugal
federalism
federalist
federalize
federation
federative
feebleness
felicitate
felicitous
fellmonger
fellow-heir

fellowship
felspathic
feme-covert
femininely
femininity
fenestrate
fer-de-lance
fertilizer
fervidness
fetterless
fetterlock
feuilleton
feverishly
fibrillous
fictionist
fictitious
fiddlewood
field-glass
fieldmouse
field-sport
field-study
field-train
field-trial
fierceness
figuration
figurative
figurehead
file-cutter
filibuster
filthiness
filtration
fimbriated
fine-spoken
finger-bowl
finger-post
finicality
finiteness
fire-bucket
fire-engine
fire-escape
fire-screen

first-fruit
first-water
fishfinger
fishing-rod
fishmonger
fisticuffs
fitfulness
flabbiness
flabellate
flaccidity
flagellant
flagellate
flagginess
flagitious
flagrantly
flamboyant
flattering
flatulence
flatulency
flavescent
flavourous
fleabitten
flectional
fledgeling
fleshiness
flintiness
flippantly
flirtation
floatation
flocculent
floppy-disk
florentine
floridness
flosculous
flunkeyisy
fluviatile
fluxionary
foliaceous
footbridge
footlights
foraminule

foraminous
forbearant
forbearing
forbidding
forcefully
forcipated
forclosure
forecastle
forechosen
forefather
foreground
forehanded
foreordain
forerunner
foreshadow
foreteller
forfeiture
forgivable
formidable
formidably
fornicator
forthgoing
fortuitous
fosterling
foundation
fourchette
foursquare
fourteenth
fractional
fragmental
fragrantly
framboesia
franciscan
fraternise
fratricide
fraudfully
fraudulent
freakishly
freebooter
freehanded
freeholder

freemartin
freightage
frenetical
frenziedly
frequenter
fricandeau
frictional
friendless
friendship
frigorific
friskiness
fritillary
frolicsome
frostiness
frothiness
frowningly
fruiteress
fruitfully
frustrable
frutescent
fucivorous
fugitively
fulfilment
fumigation
functional
funereally
fungaceous
furbelowed
gabionnade
galimatias
gallowglas
galvanizer
gamekeeper
ganglionic
gangrenous
garishness
garnishing
gasteropod
gastralgia
gastronome
gastronomy

gelatinate
gelatinize
gelatinoid
gelatinous
gemination
gemmaceous
generality
generalize
generation
generative
generatrix
generosity
generously
genethliac
genialness
geniculate
gentlefolk
gentleness
geocentric
geognostic
geographer
geological
geophagism
geoponical
geoselenic
geotropism
gingerbeer
glacialist
glaciation
glancingly
glandiform
glandulous
glassiness
glimmering
glitterati
globularly
gloriously
glossarial
glossarist
glossiness
glossology

glottology
glucosuria
glumaceous
gluttonize
gnosticism
gobsmacked
goniometer
goodliness
gorgeously
gorgoneion
gorgonzola
gormandize
gracefully
graciously
gramophone
granadilla
grandchild
grandniece
granduncle
grangerism
graphology
graphotype
graptolite
grassiness
gratefully
gratifying
gratuitous
graveolent
gravigrade
gravimeter
greasiness
gregarious
gressorial
grievously
grittiness
grogginess
groundless
groundsill
groundwork
grovelling
grudgingly

guillotine	henceforth	hopelessly	iconoclast
guiltiness	henotheism	horizontal	iconolatry
gutturally	hentachord	horography	ideography
gymnasiums	heptagonal	horologist	ideologist
gymnastics	heptarchic	horoscopic	idiopathic
gymnosperm	heptateuch	hospitable	idolatrous
gynandrous	herbescent	hospitably	idoloclast
gyrational	hereabouts	housewives	ignipotent
habiliment	hereditary	hovercraft	ignorantly
habilitate	heresiarch	hullabaloo	illatively
habitually	hermetical	humbleness	illegality
hackmatack	herpetical	humoralism	illiteracy
haematosis	hesitation	humoralist	illiterate
haematozoa	heterodoxy	humoristic	illuminant
haematuria	heterotopy	humorously	illuminate
hagiocracy	hexagynian	humoursome	illuminati
halberdier	hexahedral	humpbacked	illustrate
halleluiah	hexahedron	husbandman	imaginable
handicraft	hexametric	hydraulics	imaginably
handmaiden	hexandrian	hydromancy	immaculate
hang-glider	hiddenness	hydromania	immanation
harassment	hierarchal	hydropathy	immaterial
harbourage	hierophant	hydrophane	immaturely
harmlessly	highwayman	hydrophyte	immaturity
harmonious	hinderance	hygrometer	immemorial
harquebuse	hindustani	hylotheism	immersible
haustellum	hippogryph	hymenopter	immobility
headstrong	hippophile	hymenotomy	immoderate
heartiness	hippophagy	hypaethral	immodestly
heavenward	hithermost	hyperbolic	immolation
hebdomadal	hitherward	hyperdulia	immorality
hectically	hoarseness	hypermeter	immortelle
heedlessly	hollowness	hypnotizer	impalpably
helicoidal	holophotal	hypodermal	impanation
heliograph	homeliness	hypodermic	impassable
heliotrope	homeopathy	hypogynous	impassible
helminthic	homiletics	hypotenuse	impatience
hemipteran	homosexual	hypsometer	impeccable
hemihedral	homotonous	hypsometry	impediment
hemihedron	honorarium	hysterical	impenitent
hemorrhage	honourable	iconoclasm	imperative

imperially	incidental	infallibly	innateness
impersonal	incinerate	infamously	innocently
implacable	inclinable	infatuated	innominate
implacably	includible	infectious	innovation
implicitly	incomplete	infeftment	innuendoes
importable	inconstant	infelicity	inoculable
importance	incredible	inferiorly	inoculator
imposingly	incredibly	inferrible	inofficial
imposition	increscent	infidelity	inosculate
impossible	incubation	infiltrate	inquietude
impossibly	incubative	infinitely	inquisitor
imposthume	incumbency	infinitive	insalutary
impotently	indagation	infinitude	insaneness
impoundage	indecently	inflection	insatiable
impoverish	indecision	inflective	insecurely
impregnate	indecisive	inflexible	insecurity
impresario	indecorous	infliction	insensible
impression	indefinite	inflictive	insensibly
imprimatur	indelicate	informally	insinuator
improbable	indication	infraction	insipidity
improbably	indicative	infrequent	insobriety
improperly	indictable	infusorial	insolation
imprudence	indictment	infusorian	insolently
impudently	indigenous	inglorious	insolvable
impugnable	indirectly	ingredient	insolvency
imputation	indiscreet	ingulfment	insouciant
imputative	indistinct	inhabitant	inspection
inaccuracy	inditement	inhalation	inspirable
inaccurate	individual	inherently	inspissate
inactively	indocility	inheritrix	instalment
inactivity	inducement	inhibition	instigator
inadequate	indulgence	inhibitory	instilment
inaptitude	induration	inhumanity	institutor
inaugurate	industrial	inhumation	instructor
incapacity	inelegance	inimically	instrument
incasement	ineligible	inimitable	insularity
incautious	ineloquent	iniquitous	insulation
incendiary	inequality	initiation	intangible
incestuous	inevitable	initiative	intangibly
inchoately	inexpiable	initiatory	integument
inchoative	infallible	injudicial	intendancy

interbreed
intercross
interested
interferon
interloper
interlunar
intermarry
intermezzo
intermural
internally
interspace
interweave
intestable
intestinal
intimately
intimation
intimidate
intonation
intoxicate
intramural
intrepidly
introducer
introspect
inundation
invaginate
invalidate
invaluable
invariable
invariably
inventible
investment
inveterate
invigorate
inviolable
invitation
invitatory
invitingly
invocation
invocatory
involucral
involucrum

involution
inwardness
iridescent
iridosmium
ironmonger
irradiance
irradiancy
irrational
irrelevant
irreligion
irremeable
irresolute
irreverent
irrigation
irritating
irritation
isagogical
ishmaelite
isochronal
isodynamic
isomerical
israelitic
jackanapes
jaggedness
janizaries
jardiniere
jargonelle
jeopardize
jeopardous
jesuitical
jinrikisha
jocularity
jolterhead
journeyman
jovialness
joyfulness
joyousness
jubilation
judaically
judicially
juggernaut

juncaceous
juvenility
juxtaposit
kerchiefed
kerseymere
kindliness
kilogramme
kinematics
kingfisher
kingliness
knighthood
knobkerrie
knottiness
kriegspiel
krugerrand
laboratory
laceration
lachrymose
lackadaisy
laconicism
lactometer
lactoscope
lacustrine
lambdacism
lambdoidal
lamentable
lamentably
lamination
lanceolate
landholder
landlocked
landlubber
landspring
languorous
laniferous
lanigerous
lansquenet
lardaceous
laryngitis
lascivious
laughingly

laureation
lawfulness
leaderette
leadership
legateship
legislator
legitimacy
legitimate
legitimize
leguminous
lemongrass
lenticular
lethargize
leucopathy
levigation
levitation
levogyrate
lexicology
liberalism
liberality
liberalize
liberation
liberatory
libidinist
librettist
licentiate
licentious
lieutenant
lifelessly
ligamental
lighthouse
likelihood
likeliness
limberness
limitation
linguiform
linguistic
liquescent
literalism
literalist
literality

literalize	maceration	marionette	megalithic
literature	machinator	marketable	megalosaur
lithograph	mach-number	marlaceous	megapodius
lithologic	mackintosh	marmorated	melanaemia
lithophyte	maculation	marquisate	melancholy
lithotrity	magistracy	marrowless	membership
litigation	magistrate	marshaller	membranous
littleness	magnetizer	marshiness	memorandum
liturgical	magnifical	martingale	menacingly
livelihood	maidenhair	marvellous	mendacious
liveliness	maidenhead	mascarpone	mendicancy
locomotion	maidenhood	masquerade	menstruate
locomotive	maintainer	massasauga	menstruums
loculament	malacology	masterless	mensurable
loggerhead	malapropos	mastership	mephitical
logistical	malcontent	masticable	mercantile
logography	malefactor	masticator	merchantry
lollardism	malevolent	mastodynia	mercifully
loneliness	malignance	matchmaker	mesenteric
lonesomely	malingerer	materially	mesmerizer
longheaded	malodorous	maternally	mesothorax
loquacious	malpighian	mathematic	metabolism
lordliness	malvaceous	matriarchy	metacarpus
lorication	mammillate	matronhood	metacarpal
loveliness	manageable	maturation	metacentre
loweringly	management	maturative	metaphoric
loxodromic	manchineel	matureness	metaphrase
lubricator	mandibular	maxilliped	metaphrast
lucifugous	manfulness	mayonnaise	metaphysic
lucklessly	mangosteen	meagreness	metastasis
luculently	maniacally	measurable	metatarsus
lugubrious	manifestly	measurably	metatarsal
luminosity	manifoldly	mechanical	metathesis
luminously	manipulate	medallurgy	metathorax
lumpsucker	manoeuvrer	meddlesome	methodical
lusciously	manuscript	medicament	methylated
lustration	maraschino	medication	meticulous
lustreless	marcescent	mediocrity	metrically
luxuriance	marginally	meditation	metrograph
lutestring	margravine	meditative	metronymic
macadamize	mariolatry	meerschaum	metropolis

mettlesome
michaelmas
microfarad
micrometer
micrometry
microphone
microphyte
microscope
microscopy
microseism
midi-system
midshipman
mightiness
mignonette
militarism
militarist
militiaman
millennial
millennium
millesimal
mineralize
mineralogy
minimalism
minimalist
mini-series
ministrant
minorities
minstrelsy
minuteness
miraculous
mirthfully
misadvised
misarrange
misbelieve
miscellany
misconduct
misfortune
mismeasure
misogamist
misogynist
misprision

missionary
mistakable
mistakenly
mnemonical
moderation
moderately
moderatism
modernizer
modernness
modifiable
modishness
modulation
mohammedan
molybdenum
monarchism
monarchist
monasticon
monetarism
monetarist
moniliform
monitorial
monochrome
monochromy
monoculous
monoecious
monogamist
monogamous
monolithic
monologist
monomaniac
monopolize
monotheism
monotheist
monotonous
monsignore
monumental
mopishness
moratorium
morbidness
mordacious
morganatic

moroseness
morphology
mortifying
mosaically
motherhood
motherless
motionless
mouldiness
mountebank
mournfully
movability
mucedinous
mucousness
mulattress
mulishness
multimedia
multiplier
multivalve
mumblingly
mutability
mutilation
mutinously
mycologist
mystagogue
mysterious
mythically
mythologic
namelessly
nanosecond
naphthalic
natatorial
nativeness
natterjack
naturalism
naturalist
naturalize
nautically
navigation
nebulosity
necrolatry
necromancy

necropolis
needle-time
negatively
neglectful
negligence
negligible
negotiable
negotiator
neological
neoterical
nephrotomy
nethermost
networking
neuropathy
neurotonic
neutrality
neutralize
newsagency
newscaster
newsmonger
newsreader
nidamental
nidificate
nightshade
nigrescent
nihilistic
nimbleness
nincompoop
nineteenth
noblewoman
nominalism
nominately
nomination
nominative
non-aligned
nonchalant
non-patrial
northerner
northwards
nosologist
notability

notarially
noteworthy
noticeable
noticeably
nourishing
noviceship
nubiferous
nuciferous
numeration
numerously
numismatic
nurseryman
nutritious
nyctalopia
nympholept
obdurately
obediently
objectless
objuration
oblateness
obligation
obligatory
obligement
obligingly
obliterate
obsequious
observable
observably
observance
obsidional
obsoletely
obstetrics
obstructor
obtainable
obtainment
obturation
obtuseness
occultness
occupation
ochlocracy
ochraceous

octahedral
octahedron
octandrian
octangular
octogenary
octohedron
odiousness
odontalgic
odontology
oesophagus
officially
officiator
oftentimes
oleaginous
oleraceous
oligarchic
oligoclase
olivaceous
omniferous
omnigenous
omnipotent
omniscient
omnivorous
oneirology
ontologist
opalescent
operameter
ophthalmia
ophthalmic
oppositely
opposition
oppression
oppressive
opprobrium
oppugnancy
opsiometer
optatively
optimistic
optionally
oracularly
oratorical

orchestral
orchideous
ordainable
ordainment
ordination
oreography
organogeny
organology
originally
originated
originator
ornamental
ornamenter
orological
orphanhood
orthoceras
orthoclase
orthodoxly
orthoepist
orthopraxy
oscillancy
osculation
osculatory
ossiferous
ossivorous
ostensible
osteoblast
osteocolla
osteologic
otherwhere
outlandish
outrageous
outstretch
ovariotomy
overbridge
overburden
overcanopy
overcharge
overgrowth
overmasted
overstrain

overturner
overwisely
ovipositor
oxidizable
ozone-layer
ozonoscope
pachymeter
pacifiable
paedophile
pagination
paideutics
painkiller
painstaker
palaeozoic
palatalize
palatinate
palimpsest
palindrome
palinodist
palliation
palliative
pallidness
palmaceous
palpitated
paltriness
paludinous
pancratium
pancreatic
panegyrist
panegyrize
pangenesis
paniculate
panslavism
papistical
parallelly
paralogism
paraphrase
paraplegia
parapodium
paraselene
parasitism

pardonable
pardonably
parenchyma
parentless
parisienne
parliament
parnassian
paronomasy
paronymous
paroxysmal
paroxysmic
paroxytone
partiality
participle
particular
parturient
pasigraphy
pasquinade
passionary
passionate
pasteboard
patentable
patriarchy
patriciate
patriotism
patristics
patronizer
patronymic
pawnbroker
peacefully
peccadillo
peculation
peculiarly
pedantical
pedestrian
peduncular
peerlessly
peirameter
pejorative
pellicular
penannular

pendentive
penetrable
penetralia
penetrator
penguinery
pennyroyal
pennyworth
pensionary
pentachord
pentagonal
pentameter
pentastyle
pentateuch
peppermint
percentage
perceptive
perchloric
percipient
percolator
percurrent
percussion
percussive
percutient
perdurable
perdurably
perfidious
perforator
performing
perihelion
perilously
periodical
periosteal
periosteum
peripheral
periphrase
peripteral
perishable
peritoneal
peritoneum
periwinkle
perlaceous

permanence
permeation
permission
permissive
pernicious
pernickety
perpetrate
perpetuate
perpetuity
perplexing
perplexity
perquisite
perruquier
persiflage
persistent
persistive
personable
personally
personalty
personator
perstringe
persuasion
persuasive
pertinence
perversion
perversity
perversive
pestilence
petitgrain
petitioner
petrissage
pettichaps
pettychaps
petulantly
phagedaena
phalangeal
phanerogam
phantasmal
pharisaism
pharyngeal
pheasantry

phenomenal
phenomenon
philosophy
phlebotomy
phlegmasia
phlegmatic
phlogistic
phlogiston
phlyctaena
phoenician
phonetical
phonometer
phosphoric
phosphorus
photograph
photometer
photometry
photophone
phrenology
phylloxera
physically
phytophagy
pianoforte
pickaninny
pickpocket
pierceable
piercingly
piezometer
pilgrimage
piliferous
pinnatifid
pistillary
pistillate
pitchiness
pitilessly
pityriasis
plagiarism
plagiarist
plagiarize
planimeter
planimetry

planometer	polytheist	preconcert	procreator
plastering	pomiferous	precursory	proctorial
placticity	pomologist	predaceous	procumbent
platelayer	ponderable	predacious	procurable
platyrhine	pontifical	predecease	procurator
plauditory	popularity	predestine	producible
playground	popularize	predicable	productile
playwright	population	prediction	production
pleadingly	populously	predictive	productive
pleasantly	porousness	prefecture	profession
plebiscite	porphyrite	preferable	profitable
pleonastic	porraceous	preferably	profitably
pleximeter	portcullis	preference	profligacy
plexometer	portentous	preferment	profligate
ploddingly	portliness	prehensile	progenitor
ploughable	portuguese	prelatical	prognathic
plumassier	positively	premonitor	projectile
pluperfect	positivism	prepayment	projection
pneumatics	positivist	presbyopia	prolocutor
poachiness	possession	presbytery	prominence
poculiform	possessive	prescience	promissory
poephagous	possessory	presentive	promontory
poetically	postmaster	presidency	promptness
poignantly	postscript	presignify	promulgate
politeness	pourparler	pressingly	pronominal
politician	powerfully	presumable	propaganda
pollutedly	practising	presumably	propagator
polyanthus	praemunire	presuppose	properness
polycarpic	praetorium	pretension	propertied
polychrome	prayerless	prevailing	propitious
polychromy	preadamite	prevalence	proportion
polygamist	prebendary	priesthood	propulsion
polygamous	precarious	priestlike	propulsive
polygenous	precaution	primevally	proscenium
polygraphy	precedence	primordial	proscriber
polyhedral	precedency	principled	prosecutor
polyhedron	precession	prioritize	prospectus
polymerism	preciously	proceeding	prosperity
polynomial	preclusion	proclivity	prosperous
polyporous	preclusive	proclivous	prostitute
polytheism	precocious	procoelian	protection

protective
protectrix
protestant
prothallus
protophyte
protoplasm
protoplast
protractor
protrusive
protrusion
provenance
proverbial
providence
provincial
prudential
psalmodist
psalmodize
psittacine
pubescence
publicness
pugilistic
pugnacious
puissantly
pulsometer
pulverizer
punctually
pupilarity
pupiparous
pupivorous
purblindly
puritanism
purulently
putrescent
puzzlement
pyramidion
pyrometric
pyrotechny
pyrrhonism
pyrrhonist
pythogenic
quadrantal

quadrature
quadricorn
quadrivial
quadrumana
quandaries
quarantine
quarriable
quartering
quaterfoil
quaternary
quaternion
queasiness
quenchable
quenchless
quercitron
questioner
quiescence
rabbinical
rabblement
radicalism
radiometer
ragamuffin
rainforest
ramblingly
rancidness
rangership
ransomable
ransomless
ratability
rattlewort
ravenously
ravishment
reactively
readership
reafforest
realizable
reapproach
reassemble
rebellious
rebukingly
recallable

receivable
recentness
receptacle
recipiency
reciprocal
recitation
recklessly
recommence
recompense
reconciler
reconquest
reconsider
recoupment
recreantly
recreation
recreative
recrudesce
rectorship
recumbency
recuperate
recurrence
redeemable
redelivery
rediscover
redressive
redundancy
redundance
referrible
refinement
reflecting
reflection
reflective
reflexible
reformable
refraction
refracting
refractive
refragable
refreshing
refringent
refulgence

refulgency
refutation
refutatory
regalement
regardless
regelation
regenerate
regeneracy
regentship
regimental
registered
regression
regressive
regulation
regulative
rejuvenate
relational
relatively
relaxation
relaxative
releasable
relegation
relentless
relievable
relinquish
relishable
reluctance
reluctancy
remarkable
remarkably
remarriage
remedially
remediless
rememberer
remissible
remissness
remittance
remonetize
remorseful
remoteness
remunerate

renascence
renascency
rencounter
renderable
rendezvous
renownedly
repairable
reparation
reparative
repatriate
repealable
repeatable
repeatedly
repellence
repellency
repentance
repertoire
repetition
repetitive
repiningly
replevisor
reportable
reposition
repository
repression
repressive
reproacher
reprobater
reproducer
reprovable
reprovably
republican
repudiator
repugnance
repurchase
reputation
requitable
rescission
researcher
resentment
reservedly

reshipment
residented
resilience
resiliency
resistance
resonantly
respectful
respecting
respirable
respondent
responsive
responsory
restaurant
restharrow
restlessly
restorable
restrainer
resultless
resumption
resumptive
retainable
retardment
reticulate
retractile
retraction
retractive
retrochoir
retrograde
retrospect
returnable
revealable
revelation
revengeful
reverencer
reversible
revertible
reviewable
revivalism
revocation
revolution
rewardable

rhabdoidal
rhapsodist
rhapsodize
rhapsodist
rhetorical
rheumatism
rhinoceros
rhinoscope
rhomboidal
ridiculous
rightfully
rigorously
rinderpest
ringleader
risibility
robustness
romanesque
rootedness
roquelaure
rosaniline
rotational
rottenness
roundabout
rubiginous
rubbishing
rubricator
rudimental
ruefulness
ruffianish
ruffianism
ruggedness
rumination
runologist
ruthlessly
saccharify
saccharine
sacerdotal
sacredness
sacrificer
safari-park
safari-suit

salamander
salineness
salivation
sallowness
salmagundi
salmagundy
salubrious
salutarily
salutation
salutatory
sanatorium
sanctified
sanctifier
sanctimony
sandalwood
sanderling
sanguinary
sanguinely
sanitarian
sanitation
sapphirine
sarcolemma
sarcophagi
sarcophile
saturation
satisfying
saturnalia
satyriasis
savageness
savourless
saxicavous
saxicolous
scabbiness
scandalize
scandalous
scantiness
scaramouch
scarceness
scarlatina
scatheless
scepticism

scepticize
schematize
schemingly
schismatic
scholastic
sciagraphy
scientific
sciography
sciolistic
scirrosity
scirrhosis
scoffingly
scornfully
scorzonera
scotograph
scotticism
scowlingly
scrambling
screenings
scrimpness
scriptural
scrofulous
scrupulous
scrutineer
scrutinize
scrutinous
scullionly
sculptural
sculptured
scurrility
scurrilous
scurviness
searchable
searchless
searedness
seasonable
seasonably
seasonless
sebiferous
secretness
secularist

secularize
secureness
sedateness
seducement
sedulously
seemliness
seguidilla
selectness
semeiology
semeiotics
semicircle
sempstress
senatorial
sensualist
sensualize
separately
separation
separatism
separatist
septennial
septicidal
septillion
sequacious
sereneness
seventieth
sexagenary
sextillion
shadowless
shagginess
shamefaced
shampooing
shandygaff
shellshock
shibboleth
shieldless
shipwright
shockingly
shoemaking
shopaholic
shopkeeper
shortening

shrewdness
shrewishly
shrievalty
shrillness
shrink-wrap
shuddering
sialagogue
sialogogue
sibilatory
sickliness
siderostat
silentness
silhouette
similarity
similitude
simoniacal
simplicity
simulacrum
simulation
simulatory
sinecurist
sinfulness
singularly
sinisterly
sinistrous
sinologist
sisterhood
sisterless
skateboard
skittishly
skulkingly
slanderous
slantingly
sleetiness
sleeveless
slightness
slipperily
sloppiness
slothfully
sluggishly
slumberous

sluttishly
smattering
smuttiness
snappishly
sneakingly
sneeringly
snivelling
snobbishly
sociologic
socratical
solacement
soldiering
solecistic
solemnizer
solicitant
solicitous
solicitude
solidarity
solitarily
solstitial
solubility
somatology
sombreness
somersault
somnolence
sonorously
soothingly
soothsayer
sordidness
sororicide
soundproof
southerner
spaciously
spadiceous
sparseness
specialism
specialist
speciality
specialize
speciously
spectacled

spectrally
speculator
speechless
spermaceti
sphenogram
sphenoidal
sphericity
spheroidal
sphrigosis
spin-doctor
spinescent
spiritedly
spiritless
spirituous
spirometer
spissitude
splanchnic
spleenwort
splendidly
splenology
spoliation
spondaical
sponginess
sponsorial
spotlessly
spring-roll
sprinkling
spruceness
spumescent
spuriously
squadroned
squalidity
squareness
squeezable
squirehood
squireship
stableness
stagnantly
stagnation
stalactite
stalagmite

staminated
stamineous
stammering
stanchless
stanchness
standpoint
starriness
starvation
starveling
statically
stationary
stationery
statistics
statuesque
statutable
statutably
staurolite
steadiness
steakhouse
stealthily
steaminess
stelliform
stenciller
stenograph
stentorian
stepfather
stepmother
stercorate
stereogram
stereotype
sterilizer
stertorous
stewardess
stickiness
stiffening
stigmatist
stigmatize
stipulator
stolidness
stomatitis
stoopingly

storehouse
strabismus
strabotomy
straighten
stramonium
strategist
strathspey
stratiform
street-cred
streetwise
strengthen
strictness
stridulous
stringency
stronghold
structural
structured
strychnine
stubbornly
studiously
stuffiness
stultifier
stupendous
stupidness
sturdiness
subaquatic
subaqueous
subclavian
subduction
subjection
subjective
subjoinder
subjugator
subkingdom
sublimable
sublingual
submersion
submission
submissive
subprefect
subscriber

subsection
subsequent
subsidence
subsidiary
subsistent
subspecies
substitute
substratum
subtangent
subterfuge
subtleness
subtleties
subtracter
subtrahend
subvention
subversion
subversive
succedanea
succeeding
successful
succession
successive
succinctly
succulence
succulency
succussion
successive
sudatorium
suddenness
sufferable
sufferance
sufferably
sufficient
suffragist
sugariness
suggestion
suggestive
suicidally
sullenness
sulphurate
sultanship

sultriness
sunsetting
supercargo
supergrass
superhuman
superlunar
superstore
supertonic
supervisal
supervisor
superwoman
supination
supperless
supplanter
supplement
suppleness
suppletory
suppliance
supplicate
supply-side
supposable
suppressor
suprarenal
suretyship
surfaceman
surgically
surpassing
surplusage
surprising
susceptive
suscipient
suspension
suspensive
suspensory
suspicious
sustenance
suzerainty
swaggering
sweatiness
sweepingly
sweepstake

sweetbread
sweetening
sweetheart
swimmingly
sybaritism
sycophancy
syllabical
symbolical
symmetrize
syncarpous
synchronal
syncretism
synecdoche
syngenetic
synonymist
syphilitic
systematic
systemless
tabernacle
tabularize
tabulation
tachometer
taciturnly
tactically
talismanic
talmudical
tambourine
tangential
tantamount
tardigrade
tarmacadam
tarpauling
tartareous
tastefully
tauntingly
tautologic
tawdriness
taxability
tax-bracket
taxidermic
tax-shelter

tetchiness
technology
teetotaler
telegraphy
teleostean
telepathic
telescopic
television
televisual
tellership
telpherage
temperable
temperance
temporizer
temptation
temptingly
tenability
tenantable
tenantless
tenderness
tendrilled
tenebrific
tenemental
tentacular
teratology
tessellate
testicular
tetrachord
tetragonal
tetrameter
tetrastich
tetrastyle
textualist
thankfully
theatrical
themselves
theodicean
theodolite
theogonist
theologian
theologize

theophanic
theoretics
theosophic
theosopher
thereabout
thereafter
thereunder
theriotomy
thermostat
thermotics
thickening
thievishly
thimbleful
thinkingly
third-world
thirteenth
thoroughly
thoughtful
thousandth
threadbare
threatener
threepence
threepenny
threescore
thriftless
thrivingly
thrombosis
throneless
throughout
thundering
ticklishly
timeliness
timorously
tinctorial
tiresomely
titularity
toilsomely
tolerantly
toleration
tomfoolery
tongueless

topography
tormenting
torpidness
torrential
torrentine
torridness
tortuously
torturable
touchiness
touchingly
touchstone
tourmaline
tournament
tourniquet
tower-block
toxicology
trabecular
tracheitis
tractarian
tradecraft
tradesfolk
trafficker
tragacanth
tragically
traitorous
trajectory
trammelled
trammeller
tramontane
tranquilly
transactor
transcribe
transferee
transgress
transience
transiency
transition
transitive
transitory
translator
translucid

translunar
transpires
transplant
transposal
transposer
transputer
transverse
trashiness
traumatism
travailing
travelling
treadwheel
treasuries
tremendous
trendiness
trepanning
trespasser
triangular
tricennial
trichotomy
trickiness
triclinium
tricostate
tridentate
tridentine
trifarious
triflingly
trifoliate
trifurcate
trigeminal
trilateral
trilingual
triliteral
trilocular
trimembral
trimestral
trimmingly
trimorphic
trinervate
trinoctial
tripartite

triphthong
tripinnate
triplicate
trippingly
triradiate
trisection
trisulcate
triternate
triturable
triumphant
triviality
trochanter
troglodyte
tropaeolum
tropically
troubadour
trousering
truculence
truculency
trunnioned
trustfully
trustiness
trustingly
truthfully
tubercular
tuberosity
tubuliform
tuitionary
tumblerful
tumultancy
tumultuous
tungstenic
turbulence
turbulency
turbidness
turgescent
turgidness
turpentine
twittering
twittingly
tympanitic

tympanitis
typography
tyrannical
ubiquitous
ulceration
ultimately
ultroneous
umbellifer
umbrageous
unaffected
unaspiring
unassisted
unattached
unattended
unattested
unavailing
unbalanced
unbearable
unblushing
unchanging
unchastity
unclerical
uncoloured
uncommonly
unconfined
uncritical
unctuosity
undecaying
undefended
undeniably
underbrace
underbrush
underclass
underdrain
undershrub
understate
undertaker
undervalue
underworld
underwrite
undeterred

undismayed
undisposed
undisputed
undulating
undulation
undulatory
uneasiness
unedifying
uneducated
unemployed
unenviable
unerringly
unevenness
unexamined
unexecuted
unexpected
unexplored
unfairness
unfaithful
unfamiliar
unfastened
unfathered
unfatherly
unfeminine
unfettered
unfinished
unflagging
unforeseen
unforgiven
ungenerous
ungoverned
ungraceful
ungracious
ungrateful
ungrounded
ungrudging
unhallowed
unhampered
unhandsome
unhistoric
unholiness

unhonoured
unicostate
uniflorous
uniformity
unilateral
unilocular
unimagined
unimpaired
unimposing
unimproved
uninclosed
uninspired
uninviting
unisonance
university
univocally
unkindness
unlamented
unleavened
unlettered
unlicensed
unmannerly
unmeasured
unmerciful
unmolested
unmotherly
unnameable
unnumbered
unofficial
unpleasant
unpleasing
unpoetical
unpolished
unpolluted
unprepared
unprovided
unprovoked
unpunctual
unpunished
unreadable
unrecorded

unredeemed
unreformed
unregarded
unreliable
unrelieved
unrepealed
unrepented
unrequited
unreserved
unresisted
unresolved
unrestored
unrevenged
unrewarded
unrivalled
unromantic
unruliness
unsaleable
unschooled
unseasoned
unseconded
unsisterly
unsmirched
unsociable
unsociably
unsteadily
unstrained
unsuitable
unsuitably
unswerving
untameable
untempered
untenanted
unthankful
unthinking
untidiness
untillable
untowardly
untroubled
untruthful
unwariness

unwavering
unwearable
unweighing
unwieldily
unwontedly
unworthily
unyielding
upbraiding
upbringing
upholstery
uppishness
uproarious
urinoscopy
urtication
usefulness
usurpation
utriculate
uxoriously
valorously
vanquished
vanquisher
varicosity
variegated
variolitic
vaticanism
vaticinate
vaudeville
vauntingly
vegetality
vegetarian
vegetation
vegetative
vehemently
vehiculary
velocipede
velocities
velutinous
veneration
vengefully
venialness
venomously

ventilator
ventricous
ventricose
verifiable
vermicelli
vermicular
vernacular
vertebrata
vertebrate
vertically
vesication
vesicatory
vesiculate
vesiculose
vesiculous
vespertine
vestibular
veterinary
vibraculum
viceregent
victorious
victualler
vigilantly
vigorously
villainous
villeinage
vinaigrous
vindicator
vindictive

violaceous
virtueless
virtuously
virulently
visitation
vitrescent
vitriolate
vitriolize
vituperate
vivandiere
viviparity
vivisector
vocabulary
vocational
vociferate
vociferous
volatility
volatilize
volitional
voltameter
volubility
volumetric
voluminous
voluptuary
voluptuous
vomitories
vortiginal
voyageable
vulnerable

wapinschaw
wardenship
wastefully
watchfully
watercress
wateriness
waterproof
watertight
waveringly
weathering
weatherman
wellington
westwardly
wharfinger
whatsoever
wheelie-bin
whensoever
whereabout
whispering
whispering
whitsunday
whizzingly
wickedness
wilderedly
wilderment
wilderness
wilfulness
windsurfer
witchcraft

withdrawal
withholder
woefulness
womanishly
wonderment
wondrously
woodpecker
workaholic
worryingly
worshipful
worshipper
worthiness
worthwhile
wrathfully
wretchedly
writership
wrongfully
xylography
yearningly
yeastiness
yestereven
yestermorn
ylang-ylang
yourselves
youthfully
zincograph
zoomorphic
zoophagous
zootomical

11-Letter Words

aaron's-beard
abandonment
abbreviator
abecedarian
abhorrently
abiogenesis
ablactation
abnormality
abolishable
abomination
above-ground
abracadabra
abranchiate
absentation
absenteeism
absolvatory
abstinently
abstraction
abstractive
abusiveness
academician
acatalectic
accelerator
acceptation
accessional
accessorial
accessorily
accipitrine
acclamation
acclamatory
acclimatize
accommodate
accompanier
accompanist
accordantly
accordingly
accoucheuse

accountable
accountably
accumulator
achievement
acidifiable
acinaciform
acknowledge
acoustician
acquiescent
acquirement
acquisition
acquisitive
acquittance
acrimonious
actinometer
acumination
acupressure
acupuncture
adam's-needle
addle-headed
adiaphorous
adiathermic
adjectively
adjournment
adjudicator
adminicular
admiralship
adolescence
adolescency
adstriction
adumbration
adumbrative
advancement
adventuress
adventurous
adverbially
adversative

adverseness
advertising
advertorial
advisedness
aerological
aeronautics
aerostatics
aerostation
aesculapian
aestivation
affectation
affectingly
affectioned
affiliation
affirmation
affirmative
affranchise
after-growth
agatiferous
agglomerate
agglutinant
agglutinate
aggrandizer
aggravating
aggravation
aggregately
aggregation
agnosticism
agnus-castus
agonizingly
agrarianism
agriculture
aguardiente
aimlessness
albuminuria
alchemistic
alexandrian

alexandrine
alkalescent
alkalimeter
alkalimetry
alleviation
alleviative
all-fools' day
allophylian
all-souls' day
altercation
alternately
alternation
alternative
alto-rilievo
amalgamator
amaranthine
amativeness
ambiguously
ambitiously
ambrosially
amelanchier
ameliorator
amenorrhoea
amentaceous
americanism
americanize
amethystine
amiableness
amoenomania
amontillado
amorousness
amphetamine
amphibology
amphisbaena
amplexicaul
anacanthous
anachronism
anacoluthon
anacreontic
anaesthesia
anaesthetic

anallantoic
analogously
anaplerotic
anastomosis
anastomotic
anchoritess
anchovy-pear
ancientness
androsphinx
anecdotical
anfractuous
angelically
angelolatry
angelophany
anglicanism
anglo-indian
anglophobia
animalcular
animatingly
annihilable
annihilator
anniversary
annunciator
anomalistic
anonymously
antecedence
antechamber
antemundane
antenuptial
antepaschal
antependium
anteriority
anthracitic
antibilious
anticardium
anticyclone
antifebrile
antifederal
antiphrasis
antipyretic
antiquarian

antiqueness
antirrhinum
antispastic
antistrophe
antitypical
antonomasia
anxiousness
aphrodisiac
apocalyptic
apologetics
aponeurosis
apopetalous
aposiopesis
aposteriori
apostleship
apostrophic
appallingly
appellation
appellative
apple-blight
application
applicative
applicatory
appointment
apportioner
appreciable
appreciably
apprehender
approbation
appropriate
approvingly
approximate
appurtenant
arbitrament
arbitrarily
arbitration
arbitrament
arborescent
archaeology
archangelic
archduchess

archegonium

archimedean

archipelago

arduousness

aristocracy

arminianism

armour-plate

arquebusier

arraignment

arrangement

arrow-headed

arterialize

arteriotomy

artillerist

artlessness

ascensional

ascertainer

ascititious

asportation

assafoetida

assassinate

assestation

assentingly

assertively

assessorial

assiduously

assignation

association

associative

assuagement

assuredness

assyriology

astigmatism

astonishing

astringency

athermanous

athleticism

atmidometer

atmospheric

atomization

atrabilious

atrociously

attemptable

attentively

attenuation

attestation

attitudinal

attractable

attribution

attributive

audaciously

audibleness

auditorship

auricularly

auscultator

austereness

autographic

avoirdupois

awkwardness

bacchanalia

bacciferous

baccivorous

bacillicide

balefulness

bandy-legged

barbarously

barefacedly

barley-sugar

barley-water

barn-swallow

barquentine

barrel-organ

barycentric

bashfulness

bastard-wing

beam-compass

bear-baiting

bearing-rein

bear's-grease

beastliness

beauteously

beautifully

bedizenment

beguilement

believingly

bell-bottoms

bell-founder

belligerent

bellows-fish

benedictine

benediction

benedictive

benefaction

beneficence

beneficiary

benevolence

bengal-light

benignantly

bereavement

beseemingly

bestselling

beta-blocker

bewitchment

bibliolater

bibliolatry

bibliomancy

bibliomania

bibliophile

bibliotheca

bicarbonate

bicentenary

bifurcation

biliousness

bill-sticker

bilophodont

bimetallism

bimetallist

biodynamics

biofeedback

biogenesist

bipartition

biquadratic

bitter-sweet

bituminated
black-beetle
black-letter
black-monday
bladder-fern
bladderwort
blamelessly
blameworthy
blasphemous
bleachfield
blepharitis
blessedness
block-system
blood-bought
blood-guilty
bloodlessly
bloodsucker
blood-vessel
blue-coat-boy
blunderbuss
board-school
body-servant
bohemianism
bolting-mill
bolt-upright
bombardment
bonapartist
bonnet-rouge
bookbinding
bookishness
book-keeping
book-learned
book-selling
boorishness
borborygmus
botanically
botheration
bottlebrush
bottle-chart
bottle-glass
bottle-green

bottle-nosed
boulder-clay
boundlessly
bounteously
bountifully
bourgeoisie
boxing-glove
boxing-match
brabblement
brachiopoda
braggadocio
branchiopod
brazen-faced
breadthways
breadwinner
breast-plate
breast-wheel
breech-block
bricklaying
brilliantly
brine-shrimp
bristliness
brittleness
bronchocele
bronchotomy
bronze-steel
brotherhood
brotherless
brush-turkey
brusqueness
brutishness
bucket-wheel
buffalo-robe
bull-baiting
bullet-mould
bulletproof
bullfighter
bull-terrier
bunch-backed
bureaucracy
burgess-ship

burglarious
burgomaster
burnt-sienna
busybodyism
butcher-bird
butter-knife
butter-mould
butter-print
butyraceous
byssiferous
cabbage-moth
cabbage-palm
cabbage-tree
cabbage-rose
cabbage-worm
cabbalistic
cacogastric
cacophonous
calceolaria
calciferous
calcination
calcography
calculating
calculation
calculative
calefacient
calefaction
calefactory
calibration
calligraphy
calling-card
callousness
calorimeter
calorimetry
calumniator
calvinistic
camaraderie
camel's-thorn
campanology
campanulate
camphor-tree

canary-grass
canceration
candelabrum
candescence
candidature
candleberry
candlelight
candlepower
candlestick
cannibalism
canonically
cantharides
capaciously
capillament
capillarity
capilliform
capitulator
captainship
captivating
caravansary
carbonpoint
carbuncular
carburetted
carcinology
cardinalate
cardiograph
card-sharper
carefulness
caressingly
carminative
carnationed
carnivorous
carolingian
carriageway
carrion-crow
cartography
carunculate
carvel-built
cassiterite
castellated
castigation

castigatory
castile-soap
casting-vote
catacaustic
catachresis
cataclysmal
cataclysmic
cataphonics
catastrophe
catechetics
categorical
cater-cousin
caterpillar
cathedratic
catholicism
catholicity
catholicize
cauliflower
causatively
causativity
causelessly
caustically
cave-dweller
cavernulous
cavo-rilievo
ceaselessly
celebration
celestially
celliferous
cementation
centenarian
centreboard
centrepiece
centrically
centrifugal
centripetal
centrobaric
cephalalgic
cephalapsis
cephalotomy
cerebralism

cerebration
cerebriform
ceremonious
ceroplastic
certainness
certificate
cesarewitch
chafing-dish
chain-bridge
chain-stitch
chairperson
chalcedonic
chalcedonyx
chalkstones
chamberlain
chambermaid
championess
changefully
chanterelle
chanticleer
chaos-theory
chaotically
chaperonage
charismatic
charlatanic
charlatanry
chartaceous
chastisable
check-string
cheerleader
cheerlessly
cheese-press
chef-d'oeuvre
chequer-work
cherry-stone
chess-player
cheval-glass
chiaroscuro
chieftaincy
chieftainry
chilognatha

chirography
chiromancer
chiromantic
chiropodist
chirurgical
chisel-tooth
chitterling
chlorometer
chlorophyll
choir-screen
chondrology
chorography
chrismatory
christendom
christening
christology
chromatrope
chronograph
chronologer
chronologic
chronometer
chronometry
chronoscope
chrysoberyl
chrysocolla
chrysophyll
chrysoprase
church-court
church-going
churchwoman
cicatricule
cineraceous
cineritious
cinnabarine
cinque-ports
circularity
circulating
circulation
circulative
circulatory
circumpolar

circumspect
circumvolve
citizenship
clairvoyant
clamorously
clandestine
class-fellow
classically
clean-handed
clean-limbed
cleanliness
clear-headed
clearing-nut
clear-starch
cleft-palate
cleptomania
clericalism
climacteric
climatology
clinometric
clog-almanac
close-fisted
close-handed
close-hauled
clothes-moth
cloud-capped
clover-grass
coach-office
coagulation
coagulative
coalescence
coal-trimmer
coal-whipper
cobble-stone
cochin-china
cock-and-bull
codicillary
cod-liver-oil
coefficient
coessential
coeternally

coexistence
coextensive
coffee-berry
coffee-house
cognoscible
coincidence
cold-blooded
cold-hearted
collaborate
collapsible
collectanea
collectedly
collectible
collimation
collocation
collusively
colonialism
colorimeter
columbarium
columnarity
combination
combustible
comet-finder
comfortable
comfortably
comfortless
commandment
commemorate
commendable
commendably
commendator
commentator
commination
comminatory
comminution
commiserate
commissural
commonplace
communalism
communalist
communicant

communicate
communistic
commutation
commutative
compactness
comparative
compartment
compassable
compass-card
compellable
commendious
compensator
competently
competition
competitive
compilation
complacence
complacency
complainant
complaisant
compliantly
complicated
comportment
compositely
composition
compossible
compression
compressive
compressure
compromiser
comptroller
compunction
compurgator
computation
computerize
comradeship
concatenate
concealable
concealment
conceitedly
conceivable

conceivably
concentrate
conceptacle
concernment
conciliable
conciliator
conciseness
concomitant
concordance
concubinage
concubinary
concurrence
condemnable
condensable
conditional
conditioned
condolatory
condolement
condominium
condonation
conductible
conductress
confabulate
confederacy
confederate
conferrable
confessedly
confidently
confidingly
confinement
confirmable
confiscable
confiscator
conflagrate
conflicting
confliction
conformable
conformably
confutation
congealable
congelation

congruously
conirostral
conjectural
conjugality
conjugation
conjunction
conjunctive
conjuncture
conjuration
connectedly
connoisseur
connotation
connotative
connubially
conquerable
consciously
consecrator
consecution
consecutive
consentient
consequence
conservable
conservancy
conservator
considerate
considering
consignment
consilience
consistence
consolation
consolatory
consolidant
consolidate
consonantal
consortship
conspicuous
conspirator
constellate
consternate
constituent
constituter

constrained
constrainer
constrictor
constructer
constructor
consumption
consumptive
containable
contaminate
contemplate
contentedly
contentious
contestable
continental
continently
contingence
contingency
continuable
continually
continuance
continuator
continuedly
contrabasso
contractile
contraction
contrajerva
contrariant
contrariety
contrarious
contra-tenor
contravener
contrayerva
contretemps
contributor
contrivable
contrivance
controlment
controversy
convenience
conveniency
conventicle

convergence
conversable
conversably
convertible
convertibly
conveyancer
convincible
convivially
convocation
convolution
convolvulus
convulsible
cool-tankard
cooperation
cooperative
coparcenary
copiousness
copperplate
coppersmith
coquilla-nut
coralliform
corbeltable
cornerstone
corniculate
cornigerous
corporality
corporately
corporation
corporeally
corpulently
corpuscular
correctable
correctness
correlation
correlative
corroborant
corroborate
corrosively
corrugation
corruptible
corruptibly

corruptless
corruptness
coruscation
co-signatory
cosmogonist
cosmography
cosmologist
costiveness
coterminous
cotton-grass
cotton-plant
cotton-press
cotyledonal
couch-potato
countenance
counterfeit
counterfoil
counterfort
countermand
countermark
countermine
countermove
counterpane
counterpart
counterplot
counterseal
countersign
countersink
countervail
counterwork
countrified
countryside
courteously
courtliness
coxcombical
crabbedness
cracovienne
craniometer
craniometry
cranioscopy
crateriform

cream-cheese
creatorship
credibility
credulously
crematorium
creophagous
crepitation
crepuscular
crestfallen
criminalist
criminality
crimination
criminative
criticaster
crocidolite
crocodilian
crook-backed
crookedness
cross-action
cross-legged
crotcheteer
crown-prince
cruciferous
crucifixion
crucigerous
crustaceous
cryptogamic
cryptograph
crystalline
crystallize
crystalloid
cubicalness
cuir-bouilli
culmiferous
culmination
culpability
cultivation
cupellation
cupriferous
curatorship
curly-headed

currant-wine
curry-powder
cursoriness
curtailment
curvilinear
curvilineal
customarily
custom-house
cycadaceous
cyclopaedia
cyclopaedic
cynophilist
cyperaceous
cytogenesis
dactylology
dampishness
dancing-girl
dangerously
dauntlessly
day-labourer
death-rattle
death-stroke
debarkation
debauchment
decarbonize
deceitfully
decemvirate
deceptively
declamation
declamatory
declaration
declarative
declaratory
declination
declinatory
declinature
decollation
decomposite
decorticate
decrepitate
decrepitude

decrescendo
decumbently
decurrently
decussately
decussation
deductively
deep-mouthed
deerstalker
defalcation
defectively
defenceless
defensively
deferential
defiantness
defibrinize
defibrinate
deficiently
deflagrator
defloration
defoliation
deforcement
deformation
deglutition
deglutitory
degradation
degradingly
dehortation
dehortative
dehortatory
dehydration
deictically
deification
deistically
delectation
deleterious
deliciously
delightedly
delightless
delightsome
delineation
delinquency

deliriously
delitescent
deliverable
deliverance
demagnetize
demarcation
demesmerize
demi-bastion
demi-cadence
democratize
demographic
demoniacism
demonolatry
demonologic
demonstrate
denizenship
denominable
denominator
denticulate
dentigerous
denunciator
deobstruent
deoxidation
depauperate
depauperize
dependently
dephlegmate
depopulator
deportation
depravation
deprecation
deprecatory
deprecative
depredation
depredatory
deprivation
deprivement
derangement
dereliction
dermatology
descendable

descendible
describable
description
descriptive
desecration
deservingly
desiccation
desideratum
designation
designative
desperately
desperation
despisingly
despondence
despondency
destination
destitution
destroyable
destruction
destructive
desultorily
deteriorate
determinant
determinate
determinism
determinist
detestation
detrimental
deuterogamy
deuteronomy
devastation
developable
development
deviousness
devolvement
devotedness
dexterously
diacritical
diagnostics
dialectical
dialogistic

diamagnetic
diametrical
diaphaneity
diaphoresis
diaphoretic
diarthrosis
diathermous
dicephalous
dichogamous
dichotomous
dichromatic
dichroscope
dicotyledon
dictatorial
didactylous
differentia
differently
difficultly
diffidently
diffraction
diffractive
diffuseness
diffusively
digitigrade
dilapidated
dilapidator
diluvialist
dimensional
dimensioned
dinner-table
dinosaurian
dinotherium
diphthongal
diphycercal
diplomatics
diplomatist
diplomatize
diprismatic
dipsomaniac
directorate
directorial

direfulness
disaccustom
disaffected
disafforest
disapproval
disarmament
disbandment
disbeliever
discernible
discernibly
discernment
discontinue
discordance
discordancy
discotheque
discourager
discourtesy
discrepance
discrepancy
discussable
disembitter
disencumber
disentangle
disenthrall
disenthrone
disentrance
disgraceful
disguisedly
dishonestly
disinthrall
disjunction
disjunctive
dislocation
dismastment
disobedient
disobliging
disorganize
dispensable
dispersedly
dispiriting
displeasing

displeasure
disposition
disputation
disputative
disquieting
disquietude
dissectible
dissentient
dissepiment
dissertator
dissilience
dissimulate
dissipation
dissolutely
dissolution
dissolvable
dissyllabic
dissyllable
distasteful
distempered
distensible
distillable
distinction
distinctive
distinguish
distracting
distraction
distressful
distressing
distributor
distrustful
disturbance
dithyrambic
dithyrambus
diversified
divertingly
diving-dress
divining-rod
divorceable
divorcement
dock-warrant

doctrinaire
doctrinally
documentary
dolabriform
dolefulness
domesticate
domesticity
domiciliary
domciliated
domineering
double-edged
double-entry
double-faced
double-first
double-quick
doublespeak
doubtlessly
doughtiness
downtrodden
doxological
dramaturgic
draughtsman
dreadnought
dreamlessly
drunkenness
dubiousness
ductileness
duplication
duplicative
duplicature
dutifulness
dynamically
dyslogistic
earnestness
earthenware
earthliness
eccentrical
eclecticism
edification
editorially
educational

effectively
efficacious
efficiently
effoliation
effulgently
eglandulose
eglandulous
egregiously
eidoloclast
ejaculation
elaborately
elaborative
elaboration
elastically
electioneer
electorship
electrician
electrocute
electrogild
electrolyse
electrolyte
electrotype
elementally
elephantine
elephantoid
eligibility
elizabethan
ellipsoidal
ellipticity
elucidation
elucidative
elusoriness
elutriation
emancipator
embarkation
embarrassed
emblematist
emblematize
embowelment
embracement
embrocation

embroilment
embryologic
emmenagogue
emmenagogic
empirically
emulatively
emulsionize
enarthrosis
encephaloid
encephalous
enchainment
enchantment
enchantress
encomiastic
encouraging
encumbrance
encystation
endocardiac
endemically
endlessness
endocardium
endorhizous
endorsement
endosmosmic
endospermic
energetical
enfeoffment
enforceable
enforcement
enfranchise
engineering
engorgement
engrailment
engrossment
enhancement
enigmatical
enlargement
enlightened
enlivenment
enneagynous
enneahedral

enneahedron
ennoblement
enouncement
enslavement
entablature
enteropathy
entertainer
enthralment
entomologic
entozoology
entreatable
entwinement
enucleation
enumeration
enunciation
enunciative
enunciatory
envelopment
environment
epidictacal
epigastrium
epigraphics
epilogistic
epipetalous
epiphyllous
epiphytical
episcopally
epistolical
epithalamic
epithelioma
epithetical
equableness
equiangular
equidistant
equilateral
equilibrate
equilibrist
equilibrium
equinoctial
equipollent
equivalence

equivalency
equivocally
equivocator
eradication
eradicative
erastianism
eremacausis
erratically
erroneously
erubescence
erythematic
eschatology
escheatable
esotericism
essentially
established
establisher
ethereality
etherealize
ethnography
ethnologist
etymologist
etymologize
eucharistic
eudaemonism
eudaemonist
euphemistic
europeanize
evanescence
evangelical
evaporation
evaporative
eventuality
eventuation
everlasting
evolutional
exaggerator
examination
exceedingly
excellently
exceptional

excessively
exclamation
exclamatory
exclusively
exclusivism
excoriation
excorticate
excrescence
exculpation
exculpatory
excursively
executioner
executorial
exemplarily
exemplifier
exfoliation
exhaustible
exhaustless
exhortation
exhortative
exhortatory
existential
exoneration
exonerative
exorbitance
exorbitancy
exoskeleton
exoskeletal
exotericism
expansively
expatiation
expatiatory
expectation
expectative
expectorant
expectorate
expediently
expeditious
expenditure
expensively
experienced

expiscation
explanation
explanatory
explication
explicative
explicatory
exploitable
exploration
exploratory
explosively
exponential
exportation
exposedness
expostulate
expressible
expropriate
expurgation
expurgatory
exquisitely
extemporary
extemporize
extensively
extenuation
extenuatory
exteriority
exterminate
externalism
externality
externalize
extirpation
extirpatory
extortioner
extractible
extradition
extravagant
extravasate
extrication
extrinsical
exuberantly
fabrication
facetiously

facsimilist
facultative
faddishness
faithlessly
fallibility
falteringly
familiarity
familiarize
fanatically
fanfaronade
fantastical
farthermore
farthermost
farthingale
fascinating
fascination
fashionable
fastigiated
faultlessly
faussebraye
favouritism
fearfulness
feasibility
featherless
featureless
febriculose
febriferous
fecundation
feloniously
felspathose
fermentable
ferociously
ferriferous
ferruginous
ferulaceous
fidgetiness
filamentary
filamentose
filamentous
filamentoid
fillibuster

fimetarious
financially
fingerprint
finicalness
firmamental
fissiparous
flabbergast
flaccidness
flatulently
flavourless
flexibility
flightiness
flocculence
florescence
florilegium
flourishing
floweriness
fluctuating
fluctuation
fluorescent
fomentation
foolishness
foppishness
foraminated
foraminifer
forbearance
forcipation
foreclosure
foreignness
forepayment
foreshorten
forestaller
forethought
forfeitable
forgiveness
formication
formularize
formulation
fornication
forthcoming
fortifiable

fortnightly
fortunately
forwardness
fractionize
fractionate
fractiously
fragileness
fragmentary
frangipanni
frankfurter
frantically
fraternally
fratricidal
fraudlessly
fraudulence
freebooting
freemasonry
freethinker
freeze-frame
fretfulness
frightfully
frivolously
frowardness
faugiferous
frugivorous
fruitlessly
frustration
fulguration
fulminating
fulmination
fulsomeness
funambulist
functionate
functionary
fundamental
fungivorous
furiousness
furtherance
furthermore
furthermost
gainfulness

gallimaufry
gallowglass
gamogenesis
garnishment
garrulously
gastronomer
gemmiparous
gendarmerie
genealogist
generalship
generically
genetically
geniculated
genteelness
gentlemanly
gentlewoman
gentlewomen
genuflexion
genuineness
geometrical
germination
germinative
gerrymander
gesticulate
ghastliness
ghostliness
gigantesque
gillyflower
gingerbread
girlishness
glaucescent
globigerina
globularity
glomeration
glumiferous
glyptotheca
goatishness
goddaughter
godlessness
gonfalonier
gormandizer

gourmandize
gracelessly
gradational
grammatical
grandfather
grandiosity
grandmother
grandnephew
graniferous
granitiform
granivorous
granulation
graphically
gratulation
gratulatory
gravimetric
gravitation
gravitative
greengrocer
gristliness
grotesquely
grotesquery
guaniferous
guardedness
guesstimate
guilelessly
guiltlessly
gullibility
gummiferous
guttiferous
gutturalize
gynecocracy
gynaecology
gynaeolatry
haberdasher
habituation
haemoglobin
haemophilia
haemoptysis
haemorrhage
hagiography

hagiologist
handbreadth
handicapper
handwriting
harbourless
harmfulness
harpsichord
hatefulness
haughtiness
haustellate
hazardously
healthfully
healthiness
hearthstone
heartlessly
heavenwards
hebdomadary
heedfulness
heinousness
heliochromy
heliography
hellenistic
hellishness
helminthoid
helpfulness
hematoxylin
hemeralopia
hemihedrism
hemipterous
hemispheric
hemitropous
hemorrhagic
hemorrhoids
heptagynous
heptagynian
heptahedron
heptahedral
heptamerous
heptandrous
heptangular
herbivorous

hereditable
hereinafter
heresiology
heretically
hermeneutic
herpetology
hesperornis
heteroclite
heterophemy
hexagonally
hibernation
hibernicism
hideousness
hierarchism
hippocampus
historiette
histrionism
hobbledehoy
holographic
holothurian
homiletical
homoeopathy
homogeneity
homogeneous
homogenesis
homogenetic
homoiousian
homomorphic
homoplastic
honeysuckle
honourables
hopefulness
horological
horoscopist
hospitality
hospitaller
householder
housekeeper
housewifely
housewifery
huckleberry

hucksterage
humectation
humiliating
humiliation
humorsomely
hunchbacked
hurtfulness
hyacinthine
hyalography
hydrocarbon
hydrocyanic
hydrogenous
hydrography
hydrometric
hydropathic
hydrophobia
hydrophobic
hydrostatic
hydrothorax
hyetography
hygrometric
hygroscopic
hymnography
hyperbolism
hyperbolize
hyperborean
hypercritic
hypermarket
hypersthene
hypertrophy
hypnologist
hypogastric
hypoglossal
hypostasize
hypostatize
hypothecate
hypothenuse
hypothermia
hypothesize
hysterotomy
ichthyolite

ichthyology
ichthyornis
iconography
icosahedral
identically
ideographic
idiomatical
idiomorphic
idiotically
ignobleness
ignominious
ignoramuses
illiberally
illimitable
illogically
illuminator
illusionist
illustrator
illustrious
imagination
imaginative
imbrication
imitability
imitatively
immediately
immenseness
immigration
immortality
immortalize
impanelment
impartation
impartially
impassioned
impassively
impatiently
impeachable
impeachment
impecunious
impenitence
imperfectly
imperforate

imperialism
imperialist
imperialize
imperiously
impermeable
impermeably
impersonate
impertinent
impetuosity
impetuously
impiousness
implacental
implemental
implication
implicative
imploration
imploratory
importantly
importation
importunate
importunity
imprecation
imprecatory
impregnable
impregnably
impressible
impressibly
impressment
impropriate
impropriety
improvement
imprudently
impulsively
inadvertent
inalienable
inalienably
inalterable
inalterably
inattention
inattentive
inaugurator

incantation
incantatory
incarcerate
incarnadine
incarnation
inceptively
incertitude
incessantly
inclemently
inclination
inclusively
incogitable
incoherence
incoherency
incompetent
incongruent
incongruous
inconsonant
inconstancy
incontinent
incorporate
incorporeal
incorrectly
increasable
incredulity
incredulous
incrimation
incriminate
inculcation
inculpation
inculpatory
incumbrance
incuriously
incurvation
incurvature
indeciduate
indefinable
indentation
independent
indexterity
indifferent

indigestion
indignantly
indignation
individuate
indivisible
indivisibly
indomitable
indomitably
indorsement
indubitable
indubitably
inductional
inductively
indulgently
induplicate
industrious
inebriation
ineffective
ineffectual
inefficient
inelegantly
inequitable
inescapable
inessential
inestimable
inestimably
inexcusable
inexcusably
inexpedient
inexpensive
inexplosive
infanticide
infatuation
infecundity
inferential
inferiority
infertilely
infertility
infestation
infeudation
infinitival

inflammable
inflammably
influential
informality
information
infracostal
infrangible
infrequency
ingathering
ingeniously
ingenuously
ingratitude
ingurgitate
inhabitable
inheritable
inheritably
inheritance
injudicious
injuriously
innavigable
innervation
innocuously
innoxiously
innumerable
innumerably
innutrition
inobservant
inobtrusive
inoculation
inoffensive
inoperative
inopportune
inorganized
inquisition
inquisitive
insalubrity
insatiately
inscription
inscriptive
inscrutable
inscrutably

insecticide
insectivore
insensitive
inseparable
inseparably
insessorial
insidiously
insincerely
insincerity
insinuating
insinuation
insinuative
insouciance
inspiration
inspiratory
instability
instigation
instinctive
institution
instruction
institutive
instructive
insultingly
insuperably
integration
intelligent
intemperant
intemperate
intenseness
intensively
intentional
intentioned
interaction
intercalary
intercalate
intercessor
interchange
intercostal
intercourse
interesting
interfluent

interfusion
interiority
interjacent
interlinear
interlineal
intermeddle
intermedial
intermedium
interminate
intermingle
internality
internecine
internuncio
interocular
interpolate
interpreter
interregnum
interrogate
interrupted
intersperse
interviewer
intolerable
intolerably
intolerance
intractable
intractably
intrepidity
intricately
intrinsical
intrusively
intuitional
intuitively
intumescent
invectively
inventively
inventorial
investigate
investiture
invidiously
inviolately
involuntary

involvement
ipecacuanha
iridescence
irksomeness
ironmongery
irradiation
irreducible
irreducibly
irrefutable
irrefutably
irregularly
irrelevance
irrelevancy
irreligious
irremovable
irremovably
irreparable
irreparably
irreverence
irrevocable
irrevocably
isochronous
isochronism
isometrical
isomorphism
isomorphous
israelitish
ithyphallic
jacobitical
jactitation
joylessness
judiciously
juridically
justiceship
justifiably
juvenescent
kinematical
kleptomania
knavishness
labefaction
laboriously

labradorite
laconically
lacrymatory
lactescence
lactiferous
lamellicorn
lamelliform
lamentation
lammergeier
lanceolated
lancinating
lancination
languidness
languishing
laryngotomy
latifoliate
latifolious
latifundium
latitudinal
laurustinus
lawlessness
leaseholder
lecherously
lectureship
legerdemain
legislation
legislative
legislature
lengthiness
lentiginous
lepidosiren
lethargical
leucorrhoea
libellously
libertarian
liberticide
libertinism
lichenology
lickerishly
lickspittle
lieutenancy

ligamentous
lightkeeper
lilliputian
lingeringly
linguistics
liquefiable
liquescency
liquidambar
liquidation
lissomeness
literalness
lithography
lithotomist
lithotripsy
lithotritor
litigiously
litterateur
loathliness
loathsomely
logarithmic
logicalness
logomachist
long-sighted
loose-limbed
loudspeaker
low-spirited
loxodromics
loyalty card
lubrication
ludicrously
lumpishness
lustfulness
lutheranism
luxuriantly
luxuriously
lycanthrope
lycanthropy
machination
macrobiotic
magisterial
magistratic

magnanimity	matriarchal	metamorphic
magnetician	matriculate	metaphysics
magnifiable	matrimonial	meteorolite
magnificent	mawkishness	meteorology
magnificoes	meaningless	methodistic
maintenance	measureless	methodology
malediction	measurement	metonymical
maleficence	mechanician	micrococcus
malevolence	mechanology	micrography
malfeasance	mediastinum	microlithic
maliciously	mediateness	micrometric
malignantly	mediatorial	microscopic
malposition	medicinally	micturition
malpractice	medievalism	millenarian
mammiferous	medievalist	milligramme
mandarinate	megalomania	millionaire
mandibulate	megatherium	mindfulness
manducation	melancholia	mineralizer
manducatory	melioration	mineralogic
manganesian	melliferous	miniaturist
manipulator	mellifluent	ministerial
manufactory	mellifluous	ministering
manufacture	mellivorous	minnesinger
manumission	melodiously	misalliance
marchioness	memorabilia	misanthrope
marginalize	memorandums	misanthropy
market-maker	memorialist	misbecoming
marmoration	memorialize	misbegotten
marshalling	menorrhagic	misbeliever
marshalship	mensuration	miscarriage
martyrology	mentionable	mischievous
masculinity	mercenarily	misconceive
masquerader	merchandise	misconstrue
master-class	merchantman	misfeasance
mastication	mercilessly	misspelling
masticatory	mercurially	mistrustful
matchlessly	meritorious	mitigations
materialism	mesalliance	mixtilineal
materialist	mesophloeum	mixtilinear
materialize	messiahship	mobile-phone
mathematics	metagenesis	molestation

momentarily
momentously
monarchical
monasticism
monodelphic
monogenesis
monographer
monographic
monomorphic
monophthong
monophysite
monopolizer
monotremata
monstrosity
monstrously
moonlighter
moravianism
morphologic
mountaineer
mountainous
movableness
multangular
multanimous
multilineal
multipotent
multiserial
multisonous
mumpishness
munificence
murderously
murmuringly
muscularity
musculature
music-centre
mutableness
mycological
mythologist
mythologian
mythologize
mythopoetic
narratively

nationalism
nationalist
nationality
nationalize
naturalness
naughtiness
necessarily
necessitate
necessitous
neckerchief
necrobiosis
necrologist
necromancer
necromantic
needfulness
nefariously
negligently
negotiation
negotiatory
neighbourly
neotropical
nephritical
neutralizer
neutron-bomb
nictitation
nightingale
nimbiferous
nitrogenize
nitrogenous
noctilucous
noctivagant
nocturnally
noiselessly
noisomeness
nomenclator
nominatival
nonchalance
nondescript
nonsensical
northeaster
northwester

northwardly
nosological
notableness
nothingness
notoriously
nourishable
nourishment
noxiousness
numerically
numlSmatics
numismatist
nuncupative
nuncupatory
nutrimental
nutritively
nyctitropic
nympholepsy
nymphomania
obediential
obfuscation
objectively
objectivity
objurgation
objurgatory
obliqueness
obliviously
obnoxiously
obsceneness
obscuration
obscurement
obscureness
obsecration
obsecratory
observantly
observation
observative
observatory
obsolescent
obstetrical
obstinately
obstipation

obstruction
obstructive
obtestation
obtrusively
obviousness
occultation
ochlocratic
oenophilist
oesophageal
offensively
officialism
officiously
offscouring
ominousness
omnifarious
omnipotence
omnipresent
omniscience
omnisciency
omphalotomy
oneiromancy
onirocritic
onomasticon
onomatology
ontogenesis
ontological
opalescence
operatively
operoseness
opinionable
opinionated
opportunely
opportunism
opportunist
opportunity
opprobrious
orbicularly
orbiculated
orchestrion
orchidology
orderliness

organically
organizable
orientalism
orientalist
orientalize
originality
origination
originative
ornamentist
ornitholite
ornithology
orthography
orthopaedia
orthopaedic
orthopedist
orthotropal
oscillating
oscillation
oscillatory
ostentation
osteography
osteologist
osteoplasty
ostreaceous
outdistance
outstanding
overbalance
overbearing
overflowing
overweening
overwrought
oxygenation
oxyhydrogen
ozone-shield
pacifically
pacificator
paedagogics
paedophilia
painfulness
painstaking
palaearctic

paleography
palmiferous
palpability
palpitation
palpigerous
palsgravine
pamphleteer
pampiniform
pandemonium
panduriform
panegyrical
panhellenic
pantheistic
papyraceous
papyrograph
parabolical
paracentric
parachutist
paradoxical
paragogical
paragraphic
parallactic
parallelism
parasitical
parchedness
parenthesis
parentheses
parenthetic
parenticide
paripinnate
parishioner
parochially
paronomasia
partibility
participate
participial
particulate
partitively
partnership
parturition
parvanimity

passibility
passionless
passiveness
pastureless
paternoster
pathologist
patriarchic
patrimonial
patronizing
pearlaceous
peccability
pectination
peculiarity
pecuniarily
pedagogical
pedicellate
pedobaptism
pedobaptist
pedunculate
peevishness
pelagianism
pelargonium
pellucidity
penetrating
penetration
penetrative
peninsulate
penitential
pennoncelle
pennyweight
pensiveness
pentagynian
pentagynous
pentahedral
pentahedron
pentandrous
pentangular
pentecostal
penultimate
penuriously
people-mover

perambulate
perceivable
perceivably
perceptible
perceptibly
percipience
percipiency
percolation
peregrinate
perennially
perfectible
perfectness
perforation
perforative
performable
performance
perfumatory
perfunctory
pericardial
pericardiac
pericardium
pericarpial
pericranium
perigastric
periodicity
periosteous
peripatetic
periphrasis
periphrases
peristaltic
peristroika
peritonaeal
peritonaeum
peritonitis
permanently
permissible
permissibly
permutation
perpetrator
perpetuable
perpetually

persecution
persecutrix
persevering
persistence
persistency
personalism
personality
personalize
personation
perspective
perspicuity
perspicuous
perspirable
persuadable
persuasible
pertinacity
pertinently
perturbable
perturbance
pervertible
pessimistic
pestiferous
pestilently
petitionary
petrifiable
petrodollar
petrography
petrologist
pettifogger
phagedaenic
phantomatic
pharisaical
pharyngitis
phenomenism
phenomenist
philatelist
philhellene
philologist
philologian
philomathic
philosopher

philosophic
phosphorate
phosphorize
phosphorous
photochromy
photocopier
photoglyphy
photography
photometric
photosphere
phraseology
phthiriasis
phylacteric
phyllotaxis
physiognomy
physiolatry
physiologic
phytography
phytologist
picrotoxine
pictorially
picturesque
pietistical
pinnatisect
piperaceous
pipistrelle
piratically
piscatorial
piscivorous
piteousness
pitifulness
placability
plagiostome
plaintively
planetarium
planetoidal
planisphere
plantigrade
platinotype
playfulness
pleasurable

pleasurably
plebeianism
plebeianize
pleistocene
plenariness
plenipotent
plenteously
plentifully
plethorical
pleuritical
pliableness
ploughshare
pluriparous
plutocratic
pluviometer
pneumometer
pneumonitis
pococurante
podophyllin
pointedness
poisonously
polarimeter
polariscope
polarizable
polemically
politically
poltroonery
polycarpous
polychromic
polygastric
polygenesis
polymorphic
polyonymous
polyphonism
polyphonist
polyplastic
polyrhizous
polysporous
polytechnic
pomegranate
pompelmoose

pompousness
ponderosity
ponderously
pontificate
pornography
porphyritic
portability
portmanteau
portraiture
possibility
posteriorly
postulatory
potentially
powerlessly
practicable
practicably
practically
pragmatical
prayerfully
preaudience
preceptress
precipitant
precipitate
precipitous
preciseness
precognosce
preconceive
precontract
predecessor
predicament
predication
predicative
predicatory
predominant
predominate
prehistoric
prejudgment
prejudicate
prejudicial
prelateship
prelibation

preliminary
prematurely
prematurity
premeditate
premiership
premonition
premonitory
preoccupied
preparation
preparative
preparatory
preposition
prepositive
prerogative
presagement
presentable
presentness
preservable
presumption
presumptive
pretendedly
pretentious
preterition
preteritive
prevalently
preventable
prickliness
priestcraft
primateship
primigenial
primitively
principally
prismatical
privatively
probability
probationer
problematic
proboscides
proconsular
procreation
proctorship

procuration
procurement
prodigality
profanation
profaneness
proficiency
profuseness
prognathism
prognathous
progression
progressive
prohibition
prohibitive
prohibitory
prolegomena
proleptical
proletarian
prominently
promiscuous
promisingly
promptitude
promulgator
pronouncing
propagation
propagative
prophetical
propinquity
propitiable
propitiator
proposition
proprietary
proprietrix
proprieties
prorogation
prosaically
prosecution
prosecutrix
proselytism
proselytize
prosenchyma
prosopopeia

prospection
prospective
prostitutor
prostration
protectoral
protectress
protomartyr
protractile
protraction
protractive
protrusible
protuberant
protuberate
providently
provocation
provocative
provokingly
provostship
proximately
prudishness
pruriginous
psalmodical
pseudopodia
psittaceous
psychologic
pteridology
pterodactyl
publication
publishable
puerilities
pulverulent
pulviniform
punctilious
punctuality
punctuation
purchasable
purgatively
purgatorial
purgatorian
puritanical
purposeless

putridinous
putrifiable
putrescence
putrescible
pyramidical
pyramidally
pyrotechnic
pythagorian
pythagorism
quacksalver
quadrennial
quadrillion
qualitative
quarrelsome
querulously
questionary
quibblingly
quicksilver
quiescently
quincuncial
quintillion
quiveringly
rallentando
rapaciously
rapscallion
rapturously
rarefaction
ratiocinate
rationalism
rationalist
rationality
rationalize
ravishingly
reactionary
reactionist
readability
readmission
realization
reanimation
reassertion
reassurance

recantation
recelebrate
receptivity
reciprocate
reciprocity
reclaimable
reclamation
reclination
recommender
reconnoitre
reconstruct
recoverable
recremental
recriminate
recruitment
rectangular
rectifiable
rectilineal
rectilinear
rectiserial
recumbently
reddishness
rediscovery
redoubtable
redressible
reduplicate
redundantly
referential
reflectible
reflexively
reflexology
reformation
reformative
reformatory
refractable
refrainment
refrangible
refreshment
refrigerant
refrigerate
refulgently

regardfully
regimentals
regretfully
regrettable
regurgitate
reinsertion
reintroduce
reiteration
reiterative
reliability
religionism
religionist
religiously
reluctantly
remembrance
remigration
reminiscent
remonstrant
remonstrate
remorseless
remunerable
renaissance
repentantly
replacement
replenished
repleviable
replication
reportorial
reprehender
representer
repressible
repressibly
reproachful
reprobation
reprovingly
repudiation
repugnantly
repulsively
requirement
requisition
rescindment

resemblance
resentfully
reservation
residential
resignation
respectable
respectably
respiration
respiratory
resplendent
respondence
respondency
responsible
responsibly
responsions
restitution
restiveness
restoration
restorative
restriction
restrictive
resuscitate
retaliation
retaliative
retaliatory
retardation
retardative
retentively
reticularly
reticulated
retiredness
retractable
retranslate
retribution
retributive
retributory
retrievable
retrievably
retroactive
reverberant
reverberate

reverential
reverseless
reversioner
revoltingly
rhabdomancy
rhapsodical
rhetorician
rhinocerial
rifacimento
righteously
riotousness
risibleness
ritualistic
rodomontade
rollerblade
rollerskate
romanticism
romanticist
rompishness
rosicrucian
rubefacient
rudimentary
rustication
sabbatarian
sacramental
sacrificial
sadduceeism
sagaciously
salinometer
salvability
sanskritist
saponaceous
saracenical
sarcastical
sarcomatous
sarcophagus
satirically
saturnalian
savouriness
saxifragous
scaffolding

scalpriform
scandinavia
scapularies
scaremonger
scenography
sceptically
scholarship
scholiastic
schottische
sciatically
scintillant
scintillate
scirrhosity
sclerobasic
sclerometer
sclerotitis
scolopendra
scopiferous
scoundrelly
scragginess
scrutinizer
searchingly
secondarily
secondaries
secretarial
sectionally
secularness
sedentarily
sedimentary
seditionary
seditiously
seductively
segregation
seigniorage
seigniorial
seismograph
seismometer
siesmoscope
siesmometry
selfishness
self-starter

213

semiography
sempiternal
sensational
senselessly
sensibility
sensiferous
sensitively
sensitivity
sententious
sentimental
sentinelled
septicaemia
septiferous
sequestered
sequestrate
sericulture
seriousness
serviceable
serviceably
sesquipedal
seventeenth
sexagesimal
sexennially
shadowiness
shallowness
shamelessly
shapeliness
shareholder
shelterless
shepherdess
sheriffalty
sheriffship
shiftlessly
shipbuilder
shiveringly
shopkeeping
shortcoming
showeriness
shrinkingly
shrubbiness
shufflingly

sideroscope
sightliness
significant
silversmith
simperingly
singularity
sinistrally
sinistrorse
sinlessness
sketchiness
skilfulness
slaughterer
sleeplessly
sleepwalker
slenderness
slightingly
slumberless
sociability
socinianism
sojournment
solanaceous
soldatesque
soldiership
solemnities
soliloquies
soliloquize
solmization
solubleness
solvability
somewhither
somnambulic
soothsaying
sophistical
sorrowfully
soteriology
sottishness
sound-system
sovereignty
sparklingly
spathaceous
spectacular

spectatress
spectrology
speculation
speculative
spendthrift
spherically
spherometer
spiciferous
spiniferous
spokeswoman
sponsorship
spontaneity
spontaneous
sportswoman
spreadsheet
springiness
spumiferous
squalidness
squeamishly
squirearchy
stalactical
stalactitic
staphylosis
starchiness
stateliness
statistical
steadfastly
steeplejack
stenography
stepbrother
stereoscope
stereotrope
stereotyped
stereotyper
stereotypic
stethometer
stethoscope
stethoscopy
stewardship
stichomancy
stichometry

stickleback
stigmatical
stimulating
stimulation
stimulative
stintedness
stipendiary
stipulation
stockbroker
stockholder
straightway
stramineous
strangeness
strangulate
strategetic
strategical
strenuously
stringently
stringiness
strippagram
strip-search
studentship
stuntedness
stylishness
stylography
subaxillary
subcontract
subcontrary
subdeaconry
subdivision
subdominant
subglobular
subjugation
subjunctive
sublimation
sublimatory
sublimeness
submergence
submetallic
submultiple
subordinacy

subordinate
subornation
subscapular
subsensible
subsequence
subservient
subsistence
substantial
substantive
subtileness
subtraction
subtropical
succedaneum
succourless
sufficiency
suffocating
suffocation
suffocative
suffragette
suffumigate
suggestible
suitability
sulphurator
sulphureous
summersault
sumptuously
superabound
superfetate
superficial
superficies
superfluity
superfluous
superimpose
superinduce
superintend
superioress
superiority
superjacent
superlative
superlunary
supermarket

supernatant
superscribe
supersubtle
supervision
supervisory
suppliantly
supportable
supportably
supposition
suppression
suppressive
suppuration
suppurative
supracostal
supraorbits
supraspinal
surgeonship
surrebutter
surrounding
susceptible
susceptibly
swarthiness
sweepstakes
swinishness
sycophantic
syllabarium
syllabicate
syllogistic
symmetrical
sympathetic
sympathizer
symphonious
symposiarch
symptomatic
synchronism
synchronize
synchronous
syncopation
synergistic
synodically
syntactical

synthesizer
systematize
tabefaction
tachygraphy
taciturnity
talkatively
talking-head
tangibility
tastelessly
tautologist
tautologize
taxableness
tearfulness
technomania
tediousness
teenybopper
teetotaller
teetotalism
tegumentary
telebanking
telecottage
telegrammic
telegraphic
telekinesis
telekinetic
telescopist
temerarious
temperately
temperature
tempestuous
temporality
temporarily
temporizing
tenableness
tenebrosity
tenementary
tentatively
tepefaction
terebratula
termination
terminative

terminology
terraqueous
terrestrial
terricolous
terrigenous
territorial
tessellated
testamental
testiculate
tetragynous
tetrahedral
tetrahedron
tetramerous
tetrandrous
thallophyte
thanatology
thanklessly
thanksgiver
thatcherism
thatcherite
thaumatrope
thaumaturge
thaumaturgy
theatricals
thenceforth
theodolitic
theologizer
theopneusty
theorematic
theoretical
theosophist
theotechnic
thereabouts
therewithal
thermometer
thermoscope
thitherward
thoughtless
thrasonical
threadiness
threatening

thriftiness
thrillingly
thunderbolt
titillation
titillative
tobacconist
tonsillitis
topographer
topographic
tormentilla
torpescence
torturingly
totipalmate
totteringly
tower-system
toxophilite
tracheotome
tracheotomy
tracklessly
track-record
traditional
traducement
trafficking
trafficless
tragedienne
transaction
transalpine
transcriber
transferrer
transfixion
transfluent
transfusion
transfusive
transiently
translation
translatory
translucent
transmarine
transmittal
transmitter
transparent

transported
transporter
transversal
trapeziform
trapezoidal
treacherous
treasonable
treasonably
tremblingly
tremulously
trendsetter
trepidation
triangulate
tribulation
tribunician
tribunitial
tributarily
tributaries
tricapsular
tricksiness
tricoloured
tricuspidal
triennially
trifoliated
trigeminous
trimestrial
trinitarian
tripersonal
tripetalous
triphyllous
triquetrous
trisepalous
tristichous
trisyllable
trituration
triturature
triumvirate
trivialness
trochoidals
troglodytic
trojan-horse

troublesome
truculently
truehearted
truncheoned
truncheoner
trusteeship
trustworthy
tuberculate
tuberculine
tuberculize
tuberculose
tuberculous
tumefaction
tunableness
turbulently
turgescence
typographer
typographic
tyrannicide
tyrannously
ultramarine
unabolished
unadvisable
unadvisably
unadvisedly
unalterable
unambiguous
unambitious
unapostolic
unaspirated
unbefitting
unblemished
uncanonical
unceasingly
uncertainty
unchristian
uncivilized
uncommitted
unconcealed
unconcerned
uncondemned

unconfirmed
unconnected
unconscious
uncontested
unconverted
uncorrected
uncourteous
uncouthness
undauntedly
undefinably
undercharge
underground
undergrowth
understroke
undertaking
undeserving
undesirable
undeviating
undignified
undisguised
undisturbed
undoubtedly
undutifully
unemotional
unendurable
unenlivened
unessential
unexercised
unexhausted
unfailingly
unfaltering
unfeelingly
unfeignedly
unfermented
unflinching
unforgiving
unforgotten
unfortunate
unfulfilled
unfurnished
ungallantly

ungenteelly
ungodliness
unguardedly
unguiculate
unharboured
unhealthily
unheedfully
unicellular
unification
uniformness
unimportant
uninhabited
unipersonal
unipetalous
univalvular
universally
unknowingly
unluckiness
unmanliness
unmeaningly
unmelodious
unmindfully
unmitigable
unmitigated
unnaturally
unnecessary
unobservant
unobserving
unobtrusive
unoffending
unorganised
unpalatable
unparagoned
unpatriotic
unperformed
unperverted
unpopularly
unpractical
unpractised
unpresuming
unpromising

unprotected
unpublished
unqualified
unreadiness
unreasoning
unreclaimed
unredressed
unrelenting
unremitting
unrepentant
unresisting
unrighteous
unsatisfied
unseaworthy
unsectarian
unsentenced
unshrinking
unsmirching
unsolicited
unsoundness
unspeakable
unspeakably
unspecified
unspiritual
unsupported
unsurpassed
unsuspected
untarnished
unteachable
unthinkable
unthriftily
untinctured
untractable
untravelled
unutterable
unutterably
unvarnished
unveracious
unwarranted
unwedgeable
unwholesome

unwillingly
unwitnessed
unwittingly
upholsterer
uranography
urticaceous
uselessness
utilitarian
vaccination
vacillating
vacillation
vagabondage
vagabondism
valediction
valedictory
variability
variegation
varsovienne
vascularity
vaticinator
vellication
vendibility
venesection
ventilation
ventricular
ventriloquy
venturesome
venturously
veraciously
verboseness
verisimilar
vermiculate
vermiculous
vermivorous
versatilely
versatility
versicolour
vertebrated
vertiginous
vexatiously
vicariously

viceregency
viceroyalty
viceroyship
viciousness
vicissitude
vinaigrette
vincibility
vindication
vindicative
vindicatory
vinegarette
violoncello
viscountess
visibleness
visionaries
viticulture
vitrescence
vitrifiable
vituperable
vituperator
vivaciously
vivisection
volcanicity
volubleness
voluntarily
voluntaries
voraciously
vulcanicity

waggishness
wakefulness
wanderingly
warrantable
warrantably
washerwoman
waspishness
watercolour
waywardness
wealthiness
wearisomely
weathermost
weenybopper
weightiness
wesleyanism
westernmost
whereabouts
wheresoever
wherewithal
whichsoever
whimsically
white-knight
whitsuntide
wholesomely
whoremonger
willingness
winsomeness
wishfulness

witenagemot
witheringly
withstander
witlessness
womanliness
wonderfully
wonderingly
workmanlike
workmanship
workstation
worldliness
worthlessly
xanthophyll
xylographer
xylographic
xylophagous
xylophylous
yesternight
zealousness
zinciferous
zincography
zip-fastener
zoantharian
zoomorphism
zoroastrian
zygodactyle
zymotically

12-Letter Words

abbreviation
abbreviatory
abolitionist
abortiveness
absoluteness
absorptivity
abstemiously
abstractedly
abstractness
abstruseness
academically
acanthaceous
acceleration
accelerative
acceleratory
accentuation
accidentally
accommodator
accomplisher
accouchement
accumulation
accumulative
accurateness
achlamydeous
acknowledger
acoustically
acquaintance
acquiescence
acrocephalic
acrostically
adaptability
adder's-tongue
addictedness
additionally
adhesiveness
adjudication
adjunctively

admonitorial
adorableness
adscititious
adulteration
adulterously
advantageous
adventitious
adventureful
advocateship
aerodynamics
aerosiderite
aestheticism
aetiological
affectedness
affectionate
affinity-card
afflictingly
after-thought
agalmatolite
agamogenesis
agribusiness
agricultural
alcoholmeter
alexipharmic
alienability
alimentation
alkalescence
alliteration
alliterative
allomorphism
all-saints'day
allusiveness
almightiness
alterability
amalgamation
ambassadress
ambidextrous

amelioration
ameliorative
amenableness
amicableness
ammoniaphone
amortization
amortizement
amphicoelous
amphistomous
amphitheatre
amygdaloidal
anabaptistic
anaesthetize
analogically
analytically
anamorphosis
anapodeictic
anarthropoda
anathematize
anatomically
anemophilous
angiocarpous
anguilliform
animalculine
anitrogenous
annihilation
annomination
announcement
annunciation
annunciatory
another-guess
antagonistic
antarthritic
antasthmatic
antebrachial
antecedently
antediluvian

antemeridian
antepileptic
anteprandial
anthelmintic
anthocarpous
anthological
anthropogeny
anthropology
anthropotomy
anticipation
anticipative
anticipatory
antidemocrat
antifriction
antihypnotic
antilegomena
anti-macassar
antimoniated
antipathetic
antiphrastic
antistrophic
antitheistic
antivenereal
aphorismatic
apostrophize
apparitional
appendicitis
appendicular
apperception
appoggiatura
appositional
appraisement
appreciation
appreciatory
apprehension
apprehensive
approachable
appropriable
appropriator
appurtenance
arborescence

arborization
archdeaconry
archipelagic
architecture
argillaceous
aristocratic
aristotelian
arithmetical
arithmometer
armour-bearer
armour-plated
aromatherapy
articulately
articulation
artificially
artiodactyle
artistically
ash-wednesday
asphyxiation
aspirational
assassinator
asseveration
assimilation
assimilative
astonishment
astringently
astrological
asymmetrical
asymptotical
atheromatous
attitudinize
attorneyship
attractively
attributable
augmentation
augmentative
auscultation
auspiciously
australasian
authenticate
authenticity

avant-courier
avariciously
averruncator
bacchanalian
bachelorhood
bachelorship
backwardness
bacteriology
balance-sheet
balance-wheel
balladmonger
barbette-ship
battering-ram
battlemented
beatifically
beetle-browed
benefactress
beneficently
beneficially
benevolently
bequeathable
bequeathment
beseechingly
besottedness
bewilderment
bewitchingly
biarticulate
bibliography
bibliomaniac
bibliopolist
bicentennial
billingsgate
biographical
blackcurrant
black-draught
black-economy
blackguardly
black-hearted
black-mouthed
black-pudding
blamableness

blandishment
blast-furnace
blennorrhoea
blissfulness
blister-steel
blood-letting
bloodshedder
bloodstained
bloodthirsty
blue-stocking
boarding-pike
body-language
body-snatcher
boisterously
book-learning
bootlessness
bottle-holder
bow-compasses
bowling-alley
bowling-green
brachygraphy
brackishness
branchiopoda
brass-founder
breathalyser
breathlessly
breech-loaded
brevipennate
bride-chamber
brigade-major
bristolboard
bristol-brick
bristol-paper
brother-in-law
brownie-point
buccaneering
buffle-headed
burdensomely
bureaucratic
burning-glass
butterscotch

buttery-hatch
cabinet-maker
cachinnation
cadaverously
calabash-tree
calamitously
calisthenics
calligrapher
calligraphic
callisthenic
calorescence
calumniation
calumniatory
calumniously
calycifloral
campbedstead
camp-follower
canaliculate
cancellarian
cancellation
candle-holder
canonization
cantabrigian
cantankerous
cantharidine
capercailzie
capitulation
capriciously
captiousness
carbonaceous
cardinal-bird
carelessness
caricaturist
carlovingian
carpetbagger
carpet-knight
carriageable
carte-blanche
carthaginian
cartridge-box
case-hardened

catachrestic
catacoustics
catadioptric
catallactics
catastrophic
catelectrode
causationism
cautiousness
cementitious
censoriously
centennially
centifolious
centuplicate
ceremonially
ceroplastics
chairmanship
chalcography
championship
chance-medley
chaplainship
chapterhouse
characterize
charles's-wain
charnel-house
charter-party
chartography
chastisement
chauvinistic
checker-board
cheerfulness
cheesemonger
cheese-paring
cheiropodist
chequerboard
cherry brandy
cherry-laurel
cherry-pepper
chief-justice
chieftainess
child-bearing
child-growing

childishness
chimerically
chimneypiece
chimney-shaft
chimney-stack
chimney-stalk
chimney-sweep
chirographer
chirographic
chivalrously
cholesterine
chrestomathy
christianity
christianize
christmas-box
christmas-day
christmas-eve
christ's-thorn
chromatology
chromosphere
chronography
chronologist
chronometric
chrysophanic
church-warden
churlishness
chylifactive
circuitously
circumcision
circumfluent
circumfusion
circumgyrate
circumjacent
circumnutate
circumscribe
circumstance
civilization
clairvoyance
clairvoyante
clannishness
classicalism

classifiable
clear-sighted
cleistogamic
climatically
clinker-built
clothes-horse
cloven-footed
cloven-hoofed
clownishness
coachmanship
coalitionist
coal-measures
codification
coelenterate
coenesthesis
cohabitation
cohesiveness
coincidently
coleopterous
collaborator
collaterally
collectively
collectivism
collectivist
collectorate
colliguative
colloquially
cologne-earth
colonization
coloquintida
commemorable
commemorator
commencement
commendation
commendatory
commensalism
commensurate
commentation
commentative
commercially
commiserator

commissarial
commissariat
commissioned
commissioner
commodiously
commonwealth
communicable
communicably
communicator
compellation
compensation
compensative
compensatory
complacently
complaisance
complemental
completeness
complexional
complexioned
complication
complicative
complimenter
composedness
comprehender
compressible
compulsively
compunctious
compurgation
concentrated
conchiferoijs
conchologist
conciliation
conciliatory
conclamation
conclusively
concomitance
concomitancy
concordantly
concremation
concrescence
concreteness

concupiscent
concurrently
condemnation
condemnatory
condensation
confabulator
confectioner
conferential
confessional
confidential
confirmation
confirmative
confirmatory
confiscation
confiscatory
conformation
confoundedly
confucianism
congeniality
conglobation
conglomerate
conglutinate
congratulant
congratulate
congregation
connubiality
conscionable
conscription
consecration
consentience
consequently
conservation
conservatism
conservative
conservatory
considerable
considerably
consignation
consistently
consistorial
consociation

console-table
consolidator
constabulary
constipation
constituency
constitution
constitutive
constriction
constrictive
constringent
construction
constructive
consultation
consultative
consummately
consummation
consummative
contabescent
contagiously
contaminable
contemplator
contemporary
contemptible
contemptibly
contemptuous
conterminous
contestation
contiguously
contingently
continuation
continuously
contractedly
contractible
contradicter
contrapuntal
contrariness
contrariwise
contribution
contributive
contributory
contriteness

controllable
controverter
contumacious
contumelious
convalescent
convectively
conveniently
conventicler
conventional
conversantly
conversation
convexo-plane
conveyancing
convincingly
convivialist
conviviality
convulsional
convulsively
coordinately
coordination
coordinative
coprophagous
copulatively
coquettishly
corallaceous
corespondent
corn-exchange
corn-marigold
corollaceous
corporalship
corporealism
corporealist
corporeality
corpse-candle
corradiation
correctional
correlatable
corroborator
cosmographer
cosmographic
cosmological

cosmoplastic
cosmopolitan
costermonger
cotyledonary
cotyledonous
council-board
counsellable
countenancer
counter-agent
countercharm
countercheck
counter-force
countermarch
counterpoint
counterpoise
counter-proof
counterscarp
counter-tenor
counterweigh
country-dance
courageously
court-martial
court-plaster
cousin-german
covetousness
cowardliness
coxcomically
crack-brained
craniologist
credibleness
cremationist
crenellation
criticizable
cross-examine
cross-grained
cross-purpose
cryptogamous
cryptography
cucking-stool
culpableness
cupping-glass

cupuliferous
curling-irons
curling-tongs
curling-stone
currant-jelly
curvirostral
custard-apple
cyclostomous
cylindriform
dactyliology
dactylorhiza
damnableness
danger-signal
deambulatory
death-warrant
debilitating
debilitation
decapitation
decasyllabic
decentralize
decipherable
decipherment
decisiveness
declinometer
decoloration
decomposable
deconsecrate
decreasingly
decrepitness
decrustation
dedicatorial
deducibility
deer-stalking
defamatorily
definiteness
definitional
definitively
deflagration
deforciation
deformedness
defraudation

degenerately
degeneration
dejectedness
deliberately
deliberation
deliberative
delicateness
delightfully
delimitation
deliquescent
delitescence
delitescency
delusiveness
demoniacally
demonologist
demonstrable
demonstrably
demonstrator
demoralizing
denaturalize
dendrologist
denomination
denominative
denouncement
denticulated
dentirostral
denunciation
denunciatory
denunciative
deontologist
departmental
depopulation
depravedness
depreciation
depreciative
depreciatory
depressingly
derivational
derivatively
dermatophyte
descensional

desiderative
desirability
desolateness
despairingly
despitefully
despoliation
despondently
despotically
desquamation
desquamative
desquamatory
dessertspoon
destructible
desulphurize
desulphurate
desynonymize
determinable
determinator
determinedly
dethronement
detonization
detruncation
deuteropathy
deuteroscopy
devilishness
devil-may-care
devotionally
dextro-gyrate
diabolically
diagrammatic
dialectician
dialectology
dialling-tone
dialogically
diamagnetism
diamond-drill
diaphanously
diatomaceous
diatonically
dibranchiate
dichroscopic

dictatorship
didactically
dietetically
differential
digressional
digressively
dijudication
dilaceration
dilapidation
dilatability
dilatoriness
dilettantism
diminishable
diminutively
diphtheritic
diphthongize
diplomatical
directorship
disadvantage
disaffection
disaggregate
disagreeable
disagreeably
disagreement
disallowable
disallowance
disannulment
disappointed
disassociate
disastrously
disbursement
discerningly
discipleship
disciplinary
discomfiture
discommodity
discomposure
disconsolate
discontented
discordantly
discountable

discouraging
discourteous
discoverable
discreetness
discretional
discretively
discriminate
discursively
disdainfully
diseasedness
disembarrass
disembellish
disenchanter
disendowment
disestablish
disfranchise
disgorgement
disguisement
disgustingly
disinfectant
disinfection
disingenuous
disintegrate
disinterment
dislodgement
disobedience
disorganizer
dispauperize
dispensation
dispensatory
dispiritedly
displaceable
displacement
displeasedly
disputatious
disquisition
disquisitory
disregardful
disreputable
disreputably
dissatisfied

disseminator
dissenterism
dissertation
disseverance
dissimilarly
dissimulator
dissociation
dissuasively
dissyllabism
distillation
distillatory
distinctness
distractedly
distrainable
distribution
distributive
ditheistical
divarication
divisibility
doctrinarian
dodecahedral
dodecahedron
dodecandrous
dogmatically
domestically
donkey-engine
double-acting
double-dealer
double-minded
doubtfulness
dragon's-blood
dramatically
draught-board
drawing-board
drawing-paper
dreadfulness
dressing-case
dressing-gown
dressing-room
driving-shaft
driving-wheel

droughtiness
ducking-stool
dwarfishness
earnest-money
eau-de-cologne
eavesdropper
eccentricity
ecclesiastes
ecclesiastic
ecclesiology
eclectically
economically
ecstatically
ectoparasite
educationist
eduction-pipe
edulcoration
edulcorative
effectuation
effeminately
effervescent
efflorescent
effusiveness
egoistically
egyptologist
electrically
electrolysis
electrolytic
electrometer
electrometry
electromotor
electroplate
electroscope
electrotypic
eleemosynary
elementarily
elliptically
elocutionist
emancipation
emargination
emasculation

emasculatory
embezzlement
embitterment
emblazonment
emigrational
emollescence
emotionalism
emphatically
empressement
empyreumatic
encephalitis
enchantingly
enclitically
encroachment
encumbrancer
encyclopedia
endocarditis
endoparasite
endophyllous
endosmometer
endoskeleton
enfeeblement
enharmonical
entanglement
enterprising
entertaining
enthronement
enthusiastic
entomologist
entomostraca
entrancement
entreatingly
envisagement
epencephalon
epexegetical
ephemerality
ephemeridian
epicureanism
epicycloidal
epideictical
epidemically

epidemiology	exchangeable	fastidiously
epigrammatic	excitability	fearlessness
episcopalian	exclusionist	febrifacient
episodically	excogitation	felicitation
epistemology	excruciating	felicitously
epithalamium	excursionist	feminineness
equalization	executorship	fenestration
equanimously	exercitation	fermentation
equatorially	exhaustively	fermentative
equestrienne	exhibitioner	feverishness
equimultiple	exhilaration	fictitiously
equipollence	exorbitantly	fissilingual
equipollency	exoterically	fissirostral
equivalently	expatriation	flagellation
equivocatory	experiential	flagitiously
erythematous	experimental	flatteringly
eschatologic	experimenter	flexibleness
escutcheoned	explicitness	flittermouse
esoterically	exploitation	floriculture
essentiality	expostulator	fluorescence
essential-oil	expressional	foraminifera
estrangement	exsanguinous	forbiddingly
etherization	extemporizer	forcibleness
ethnographer	exterminator	fordableness
ethnological	exterminable	forebodement
etymological	extinguisher	foreknowable
euphoniously	extortionary	fornicatress
evanescently	extramundane	fortuitously
evangelicism	extraneously	foundationer
evidentially	extravagancE	frankincense
evisceration	extravagancy	fraudulently
evolutionary	extravaganza	frequentness
evolutionist	factiousness	frolicsomely
exacerbation	factitiously	fromage-frais
exaggeration	faithfulness	frondescence
exaggerative	fallaciously	frondiferous
exaggeratory	fancifulness	frontispiece
exalbuminous	faradization	fructescence
exanthematic	farcicalness	fugitiveness
exasperation	fascicularly	functionally
exasperating	fasciculated	furfuraceous

futilitarian
galactagogue
galactometer
galligaskins
gallinaceous
galvanometry
galvanoscope
gamopetalous
gasification
gelatination
genealogical
geniculation
gentilitious
genuflection
geographical
geologically
geometrician
gerontocracy
gesticulator
gladiatorial
glandiferous
glaucomatous
glossography
glossologist
glottologist
gluttonously
glyphography
governmental
governorship
gracefulness
graciousness
graduateship
grallatorial
grammaticize
gratefulness
gratuitously
greenishness
gregariously
grievousness
groundlessly
gymnosophist

haberdashery
hagiographer
hagiographic
handkerchief
harmoniously
headquarters
heliocentric
heliotropism
henceforward
hermeneutics
hermetically
herpetologic
hesitatingly
heterogamous
heterologous
heterosexual
hibernaculum
hibernianism
hieroglyphic
hindoostanee
hippocentaur
hippophagist
hippopotamus
historically
histrionical
homoeopathic
homologation
homomorphism
horizontally
horticulture
house-husband
housekeeping
humorousness
hydrofluoric
hydrographer
hydropathist
hydrostatics
hydrothermal
hygienically
hymnographer
hyperbolical

hypertension
hypnotizable
hypochondria
hypocritical
hypostatical
hypothecator
hypothetical
hysterically
iambographer
ichthyolatry
ichthyopsida
identifiable
idioelectric
idiosyncrasy
idolatrously
illegibility
illegitimacy
illegitimate
illiberality
illumination
immaculately
immatureness
immeasurable
immeasurably
immemorially
immensurable
immersionist
immethodical
immoderately
immutability
impartiality
impenetrable
impenetrably
impenitently
imperatorial
imperatively
imperfection
imperforable
imperishable
imperishably
impersonally

impersonator
impertinence
imperviously
impetiginous
imponderable
imposthumate
impressively
imprisonment
impropriator
improvidence
inaccurately
inadequately
inadmissible
inadvertence
inadvertency
inapplicable
inapplicably
inappositely
inarticulate
inartificial
inauspicious
incalculable
incandescent
incapacitate
incautiously
incendiarism
incidentally
incineration
incommodious
incomparable
incomparably
incompatible
incompatibly
incompetence
incompetency
incompletely
inconclusive
inconsequent
inconsistent
inconsolable
inconsolably

inconstantly
incorporeity
incorrodible
incorruption
increasingly
incurability
indebtedness
indecisively
indeclinable
indecorously
indefeasible
indefensible
indefinitely
indelibility
independence
indicatively
indifference
indigestible
indirectness
indiscreetly
indiscretion
indisputable
indissoluble
indoctrinate
ineffaceable
inefficiency
inelasticity
ineradicable
ineradicably
inexpedience
inexpediency
inexperience
inexpertness
inexplicable
inextricable
infectiously
infelicitous
infiltration
infinitively
inflectional
infrequently

infringement
infundibular
infusibility
inhabitation
inhospitable
innutritious
inosculation
insalubrious
insecureness
insolubility
inspectorate
inspissation
installation
instructress
instrumental
insufferable
insufferably
insufflation
insurrection
integumental
intellection
intellective
intellectual
intelligence
intemperance
intercession
interconnect
intercurrent
interdiction
interdictory
interdigital
interference
interfemoral
interglacial
interjection
interlineary
interlocutor
intermeddler
intermediacy
intermediary
intermediate

interminable
interminably
intermission
intermittent
intermixture
intermundane
internuncial
interoceanic
interorbital
interpellate
interpleader
interruption
interruptive
interstitial
intertexture
intervention
intervocalic
intimidation
intolerantly
intoxication
intoxicating
intransigent
intransitive
intrenchment
introduction
introductive
intromission
intussuscept
invalidation
inveiglement
invertebrate
investigable
invisibility
involucellum
invulnerable
irascibility
ironicalness
irrationally
irredeemable
irredeemably
irreflective

irrefragable
irregularity
irremediable
irremediably
irremissible
irrepealable
irreprovable
irresistence
irresistible
irresistibly
irresolution
irresolvable
irrespective
irrespirable
irresponsive
irreverently
irreversible
irreversibly
irritability
johannisberg
journalistic
jurisconsult
jurisprudent
juvenescence
kaleidoscope
kindergarten
kleptomaniac
lachrymatory
laemmergeier
laemmergeyer
languishment
laryngoscope
lasciviously
laticiferous
laudableness
laureateship
legitimately
legitimation
leiotrichous
lenticularly
leptocardian

lexicography
lexicologist
libidinously
libidinosity
licentiously
lifelessness
ligniperdous
likeableness
liquefacient
liquefaction
listlessness
lithographer
lithographic
lithological
lithophagous
liturgiology
localization
lomentaceous
lonesomeness
longitudinal
loquaciously
lugubriously
lukewarmness
luminiferous
luminousness
machicolated
macrobiotics
macropterous
mademoiselle
magnetically
magnetizable
magnificence
magniloquent
maidenliness
maintainable
majestically
malevolently
malformation
malleability
maltreatment
malversation

manifestable
manifestible
manipulation
manipulative
manipulatory
manslaughter
manufacturer
marlinespike
marriageable
marvellously
materialness
mathematical
mechanically
mediatorship
meditatively
megalosaurus
melodramatic
menstruation
merchantable
mercifulness
mercurialize
meretricious
meridionally
metempirical
meteorograph
methodically
metropolitan
mezzorilievo
microbiology
microgeology
microphonous
microscopist
minicomputer
ministration
ministrative
miraculously
mirthfulness
misapprehend
misbelieving
miscalculate
misdemeanant

misdemeanour
misdirection
misinterpret
misplacement
mispronounce
misrepresent
misstatement
mistranslate
mitrailleuse
mobilization
modification
modificatory
moireantique
monastically
monetization
monodelphian
monographist
monomaniacal
monometallic
monomorphous
monopetalous
monophyllous
monseigneurs
monumentally
morphologist
mournfulness
mucilaginous
mucopurulent
mulligatawny
multicostate
multifarious
multiformity
multilateral
multipliable
multiplicand
multiplicity
multitasking
multitubular
municipalize
mysteriously
mythographer

namelessness
narcotically
naturalistic
navigability
nectocalyces
needlessness
neglectfully
neologically
nevertheless
nidification
noctambulist
nomenclature
nominatively
nonagenarian
nonchalantly
northernmost
notification
nutritiously
obdurateness
obligatorily
obligingness
obliteration
obliterative
obscurantism
obscurantist
obsequiously
obsolescence
obsoleteness
obstreperous
occidentally
oceanography
octogenarian
octopetalous
oleomargarin
omnipotently
omnipresence
omnisciently
onomatopoeia
onomatopoeic
ophiophagous
opinionative

oppressively
oratorically
organization
organography
ornamentally
ornithomancy
ornithoscopy
orographical
orthognathic
orthographer
orthographic
ossification
ostentatious
osteodentine
osteographer
osteomalacia
outmanoeuvre
outrageously
overestimate
paedobaptist
palaeobotany
palaeography
palaeolithic
palingenesis
palpableness
panhellenism
pantisocracy
papistically
paracentesis
paradisiacal
paragraphist
paralipomena
paramilitary
parasiticide
parenchymous
paridigitate
parisyllable
parochialism
parochialize
paronomastic
parsimonious

participator
partisanship
partizanship
pathetically
pathological
patriarchate
patriarchism
peacefulness
pellucidness
pentagonally
perambulator
perceptivity
peregrinator
peremptorily
perfidiously
pergameneous
pericarditis
periosteitis
peripherical
perivisceral
permeability
perpetration
perplexingly
perquisition
perseverance
persistently
perspicacity
perspiration
perspiratory
persuasively
pertinaceous
perturbation
pervicacious
pestilential
petrifaction
petrifactive
petrographer
pettifoggery
phanerogamic
pharmacology
pharyngotomy

philanthropy
philharmonic
philhellenic
philistinism
philosophism
philosophize
phlebotomist
phonetically
phosphoresce
photogravure
phraseologic
phrenologist
phylogenesis
phylogenetic
physiocratic
physiography
phytogenesis
phytophagous
pisciculture
pitiableness
pitilessness
placableness
planispheric
pleasantries
plebiscitary
plenipotence
plenipotency
pleuronectes
pluriliteral
plurilocular
pneumatology
pollutedness
polyanthuses
polymorphism
polyphyllous
polyspermous
polysyllable
polysyndeton
polytechnics
populousness
pornographic

portableness
portentously
positiveness
possessively
post-feminist
powerfulness
practicality
practitioner
preceptorial
preciousness
precipitable
precisianism
precociously
precognition
predestinate
preferential
prelatically
premaxillary
preoccupancy
preponderate
presbyterial
presbyterian
prerequisite
prescription
prescriptive
presentation
presidential
presumptuous
prevailingly
pridefulness
priestliness
primigenious
primogenitor
principality
probationary
proclamation
prodigiously
professorate
profoundness
prolegomenon
proletariate

prolificness
prolongation
promulgation
propagandism
propenseness
propitiation
propitiously
proportional
proscription
proscriptive
proselytizer
prosopopoeia
prosperously
prostitution
protestation
prothonotary
protoplasmic
protractedly
protuberance
proverbially
providential
prudentially
pseudonymous
psychologist
psychrometer
pterodactyle
pugnaciously
pulveraceous
pulverizable
purblindness
purification
putrefaction
pyrometrical
pyrotechnist
quadragesmia
quadrangular
quadraphonic
quadrinomial
quadrophonic
quadrumanous
qualmishness

quantitative
quaquaversal
querimonious
questionable
questionably
quinquennium
ramification
ratification
readjustment
readmittance
reannexation
reappearance
reassumption
rebelliously
recalcitrant
recapitulate
recensionist
receptacular
receptionist
reciprocally
recklessness
recollection
recommitment
reconcilable
reconveyance
recordership
recrudescent
recuperation
recuperative
recuperatory
redintegrate
redistribute
reflectively
refractorily
refreshingly
refutability
regardlessly
regeneration
regenerative
regeneratory
registration

rehabilitate
reilluminate
reimposition
reinspection
reinstalment
reinvestment
reinvigorate
rejuvenation
relationship
relativeness
relentlessly
reliableness
religionless
relinquisher
remembrancer
reminiscence
remonstrance
remorsefully
removability
remuneration
remunerative
renewability
renouncement
renunciation
reparability
repercussion
repercussive
reprehension
repressively
reproachable
reproachably
reproduction
reproductive
republicates
requiescence
residentiary
resiniferous
resistlessly
resoluteness
resolutioner
resolvedness

resourceless
respectfully
respectively
resplendence
resplendency
respondentia
responsively
restaurateur
restrainable
restrainably
resurrection
resuscitable
resuscitator
reticulation
retractation
retrenchment
retrievement
retrocession
revengefully
reverberator
rhinoplastic
rhizophagous
rhododendron
rhodomontade
rhombohedral
rhombohedron
rhythmically
ridiculously
romantically
ruthlessness
sacerdotally
sacramentary
sacrilegious
sacrosanctly
saleableness
salubriously
salutariness
salvationist
sanguiferous
sanguineness
sanguinolent

saponifiable
saprophagous
sarcophagous
sarsaparilla
satisfaction
satisfactory
scandalously
scandinavian
scarificator
scarlatinous
scenographic
schoolmaster
schorlaceous
sclerodermic
scornfulness
scoundrelism
scripturally
scrofulously
scrophularia
scrupulosity
scrupulously
sculpturally
scurrilously
scutelliform
secessionism
secessionist
secretariate
sectarianism
sectarianize
sedulousness
segmentation
seignioralty
seismologist
selenography
semeiography
seminiferous
sempervirent
senatorially
sensibleness
sensifacient
separability

separateness
septennially
septuagenary
septuagesima
sequestrator
seraphically
serial-killer
serpentiform
shakspearean
shamefacedly
shamefulness
sheepishness
shrewishness
shudderingly
siderography
significator
simoniacally
simultaneity
simultaneous
single-market
skateboarder
slanderously
slaughterous
slipperiness
slovenliness
sluggishness
sluttishness
snappishness
snobbishness
snowboarding
socratically
solicitation
solicitously
solidifiable
solisequious
solitariness
somnambulate
somnambulism
somnambulist
sonorousness
sophisticate

soporiferous
southernmost
spaciousness
specialities
specifically
spectrometer
spectroscope
spectroscopy
spell-checker
spermatozoon
sphenography
sphragistics
sphygmograph
spiritedness
spiritlessly
spiritualism
spiritualist
spirituality
spiritualize
spitefulness
spokesperson
sporadically
spotlessness
spuriousness
stalwartness
stanniferous
statistician
steatopygous
stenographic
stepdaughter
stereography
stereophonic
stereopticon
stereotypist
sternutation
sternutative
sternutatory
stockbroking
straightness
strawberries
strengthener

stridulation
stubbornness
studiousness
stupefacient
stupefactive
stupefaction
stupendously
stylographic
subcommittee
subcutaneous
subdivisible
subepidermal
subfeudatory
subjectively
subjectivity
sublineation
submaxillary
submissively
suboccipital
subscription
subsequently
subservience
subserviency
subsidiary
substantiate
substantival
substitution
substruction
substructure
subterranean
succedaneous
successfully
successional
successively
succinctness
sudoriferous
sufficiently
suffruticose
suggestively
suitableness
sulphuration

sulphuretted
superannuate
superciliary
supercilious
supereminent
supermundane
supernacular
supernaculum
supplicatory
suppressible
supramundane
supraorbital
surfboarding
surmountable
surprisingly
surrealistic
surrejoinder
surveillance
surveyorship
survivorship
susceptivity
suspiciously
sustentation
sycophantish
sycophantism
syllabically
symbolically
synantherous
synarthrosis
synonymously
synoptically
systematical
tabernacular
tachygraphic
talismanical
tamelessness
tangentially
tangibleness
tastefulness
technologist
technomaniac

telautograph
telegraphist
teleological
temperaments
temporalness
tenuirostral
tercentenary
terebinthine
tergiversate
terribleness
terrifically
tetrapterous
thallogenous
thankfulness
thanksgiving
theatrically
theocratical
theorematist
theosophical
therapeutics
therapeutist
thickskinned
thievishness
thitherwards
thoroughfare
thoughtfully
thriftlessly
ticklishness
titaniferous
topographist
torrefaction
torricellian
tortuousness
toxicologist
traditionist
traducianism
traitorously
tranquillize
tranquillity
transferable
transference

transfusible
transgressor
transhipment
transitional
transitively
transitorily
translatable
translucency
transmigrate
transmission
transmutable
transmutably
transparence
transparency
transpicuous
transplanter
transpontine
transporting
transposable
transudation
transudatory
transumptive
transversely
transvestism
transvestite
trend-spotter
triadelphous
triangularly
tricentenary
trichiniasis
trichomatose
tricuspidate
tridactylous
trigrammatic
tripartitely
triphthongal
triumphalism
triumphalist
triumphantly
tropological
truncheoneer

truthfulness
tuberculated
tuberculosis
tumultuously
tunnel-vision
tyrannically
ubiquitously
ultramontane
umbrageously
unacceptable
unaccustomed
unacquainted
unadulterate
unanswerable
unanswerably
unappealable
unappeasable
unaspiringly
unassailable
unbecomingly
unbreathable
unchallenged
unchangeable
uncharitable
uncharitably
uncommercial
uncovenanted
unctuousness
uncultivated
undeceivable
undeclinable
underclothes
undercurrent
understratum
underwriting
undeservedly
undetermined
undiscerning
undischarged
unexpectedly
unfaithfully

unfathomably
unfavourable
unfavourably
unfranchised
unfrequented
unfruitfully
ungenerously
ungovernable
ungovernably
ungracefully
ungraciously
ungratefully
unhandsomely
unhesitating
unhistorical
unimportance
unimpugnable
uninstructed
uninterested
unitarianism
universalism
universalist
universities
universology
unkindliness
unlawfulness
unlikelihood
unlikeliness
unmanageable
unmarketable
unmercifully
unmistakable
unobservedly
unobstructed
unparalleled
unpatronized
unpleasantly
unpleasingly
unpoetically
unpopularity
unprejudiced

unpreparedly
unpretending
unprincipled
unprivileged
unproductive
unprofitable
unpropitious
unprosperous
unquenchable
unquenchably
unquestioned
unreasonable
unreasonably
unreconciled
unregeneracy
unregistered
unreservedly
unrestrained
unrestricted
unsanctified
unsatisfying
unscriptural
unscrupulous
unsearchable
unseemliness
unstableness
unsteadiness
unstratified
unsuccessful
unsuppressed
unsuspecting
unsuspicious
unsystematic
untenantable
unthinkingly
untowardness
untrammelled
untruthfully
unwieldiness
unwontedness
unworthiness

uproariously
user-friendly
vainglorious
valetudinary
valuableness
vanquishable
vaporization
variableness
vaticination
velocipedist
vendibleness
verification
vernacularly
versificator
verticillate
victoriously
vigorousness
vilification
villainously

vindictively
viscountship
visitatorial
vitalization
vitreousness
vitrifaction
vitrifacture
vitriolation
vituperation
vituperative
viviparously
vocabularies
vocalization
vociferation
vociferously
voluminously
voluptuaries
voluptuously
warehouseman

watchfulness
wellingtonia
whencesoever
wherethrough
whimsicality
whisperingly
whortleberry
womanishness
worshipfully
wranglership
wrathfulness
wretchedness
xylobalsamum
youthfulness
zincographic
zoochemistry
zoophytology

13-Letter Words

absorbability
accessibility
accidentalism
acclimatation
accommodating
accommodation
accommodative
accompaniment
accoutrements
acetabuliform
acetification
acidification
acquisitively
acrimoniously
admeasurement
administrator
admirableness
admissibility
adumbratively
adventurously
advertisement
advisableness
aesthesiology
aesthetically
affirmatively
afforestation
agglomeration
agglutination
agglutinative
aggravatingly
agreeableness
agriculturist
alcoholometer
algebraically
allegorically
allowableness
alternatively
aluminiferous

ambassadorial
ambidexterity
amplification
amplificative
amplificatory
anachronistic
anagrammatist
anaphrodisiac
andropetalous
anglo-american
anglo-catholic
animadversion
animalization
annexationist
antaphroditic
anthropolatry
anthropologic
anthropometry
anthropopathy
anthropophagy
anthroposophy
antiarthritic
antiasthmatic
antichristian
anticorrosive
antiephialtic
antiepiscopal
antilogarithm
antimonarchic
antimonianism
antinephritic
antiscorbutic
antispasmodic
antitypically
aphanipterous
apogeotropism
apostolically
appellatively

appendiculate
applicability
apportionment
apprehensible
appropriately
appropriation
approximately
approximation
approximative
arbitrariness
arboriculture
archaeologist
archaeopteryx
archbishopric
archidiaconal
archimandrite
architectural
argentiferous
argumentation
argumentative
arithmetician
arundinaceous
ascertainable
ascertainment
ascriptitious
assassination
assiduousness
associateship
assyriologist
asthmatically
astonishingly
atheistically
atrociousness
attainability
attentiveness
attributively
audaciousness
authentically

authoritative
autobiography
autochthonous
availableness
axiomatically
baccalaureate
backwardation
ballast-heaver
ball-cartridge
balsamiferous
barefacedness
beatification
beautifulness
beginningless
believability
belles-lettres
bessemer-steel
bibliographer
bibliological
bibliothecary
biodegradable
blackguardism
blamelessness
blasphemously
blindman's-buff
blood.relation
bloodshedding
blood-spilling
blotting-paper
boarding-house
bombastically
booking-office
boundlessness
bountifulness
breech-loading
breviloquence
brevirostrate
broken-hearted
brotherliness
bumptiousness
burglariously

burning-mirror
burnt-offering
butcher's-broom
calcification
calico-printer
callisthenics
calorifacient
campanologist
campeachy-wood
camphoraceous
candidateship
capaciousness
carboniferous
carbonization
carnification
carpet-bedding
carrier-pigeon
carte-de-visite
cartilaginous
castle-builder
casualization
catastrophism
catechistical
categorematic
categorically
cat-o'-nine tails
causelessness
cauterization
cephalo-thorax
cerebro-spinal
ceremoniously
certification
chalcographer
challengeable
chancel-screen
changeability
changefulness
characterless
chartographic
cheerlessness
cheiropterous

cheval-de-frise
chimney-corner
chopping-knife
chorepiscopal
chrematistics
christmas-rose
christmas-tree
chromatophore
chronographer
chrysanthemum
chuck-farthing
churchmanship
church-service
chylification
chymification
cicatrization
cinchonaceous
cinematograph
cinnamon-stone
circumambient
circumduction
circumference
circumfluence
circumjacence
circumjacency
circumspectly
circumvallate
circumvention
circumventive
clamorousness
clandestinely
clarification
clearing-house
cleistogamous
climatography
clincher-built
cloister-garth
coadjutorship
coarse-grained
cobelligerent
cochleariform

coessentially

coextensively

collaboration

collaborateur

collectedness

colloquialism

colloquialist

combativeness

commandership

commemorative

commensurable

commensurably

commiseration

commiserative

communicative

commutability

commutatively

communication

companionable

companionably

companionless

companionship

comparatively

compassionate

compatibility

compendiously

complainingly

complaisantly

complementary

complimentary

comprehension

comprehensive

concatenation

concavo-convex

conceitedness

concentration

concentrative

conceptualism

conceptualist

concomitantly

concretionary

concupiscence

condescending

condescension

conditionally

conduciveness

confabulation

confabulatory

confectionary

confectionery

confederation

confederative

confessionary

confessorship

confidingness

configuration

conflagration

confraternity

confrontation

congratulator

conjecturable

conjecturally

conjugational

conjunctional

conjunctively

consanguinity

conscientious

consciousness

consecutively

consentaneous

consequential

conservatoire

considerately

consideration

consolidation

conspicuously

conspiratress

constableship

constellation

consternation

constrainable

constrainedly

consumptively

contabescence

contamination

contaminative

contemplation

contemplative

contentedness

contentiously

contortionist

contrabandism

contrabandist

contractility

contradiction

contradictive

contradictory

contrapuntist

contrate-wheel

contravention

contributable

controversial

controvertist

convalescence

convalescency

conventionary

conventionist

conversazione

convexo-convex

convocational

convulsionary

copartnership

coralliferous

corollifloral

correlatively

correspondent

corresponding

corresponsive

corroboration

corroborative

corroboratory

corrodibility

corrosiveness

corruptionist
corymbiferous
cosmopolitism
cotton-spinner
cotton-thistle
counteraction
counteractive
counterchange
countercharge
counterfeiter
counter-motion
counter-poison
counter-signal
counter-stroke
counterweight
courteousness
coxcombically
craftsmanship
cranioscopist
creditability
credulousness
cross-breeding
cross-gartered
crosshatching
cross-question
crotchetiness
crustaceology
cryptographer
cryptographic
customariness
cylindrically
dactylioglyph
daddy-longlegs
daguerreotype
dancing-master
dangerousness
dastardliness
daughter-in-law
dauntlessness
dead-reckoning
death-struggle

deceitfulness
deceptiveness
decomposition
deconcentrate
decortication
decrepitation
decriminalize
defectiveness
defencelessly
defensibility
deferentially
defervescence
defervescency
defibrination
deliciousness
deliquescence
delirifacient
deliriousness
demonstration
demonstrative
denationalize
denticulately
denticulation
deodorization
deontological
dephosphorize
deprecatingly
dermatologist
dermo-skeleton
descriptively
desirableness
destructively
desultoriness
deterioration
determinately
determination
determinative
detrimentally
deuterogamist
developmental
dexterousness

dialectically
dialogistical
diamesogamous
diametrically
diaphragmatic
diathermanous
dichlamydeous
dichotomously
dictatorially
differentiate
diffusibility
diffusiveness
digestibility
diphthongally
dipsomaniacal
disappearance
disciplinable
discoloration
disconnection
discontinuity
discontinuous
discreditable
discreditably
discretionary
discriminator
disembarkment
disengagement
disestimation
disfiguration
disfigurement
disgracefully
dishonourable
dishonourably
disintegrable
disinterested
disjunctively
dismemberment
disnaturalize
disobediently
disobligement
disobligingly

disparagingly
disparagement
dispassionate
displantation
dispossession
disproportion
disrespectful
dissemination
dissimilarity
dissimilation
dissimilitude
dissimulation
dissolubility
dissoluteness
distastefully
distinctively
distinguished
distressfully
distressingly
distributable
distrustfully
diversifiable
domestication
domiciliation
double-dealing
double-hearted
double-tongued
draggle-tailed
drawing-master
dressing-table
drill-sergeant
drink-offering
dwelling-house
dynamo-machine
dysmenorrhoea
earthly-minded
eccentrically
echinodermata
economization
educationally
effectiveness

effervescence
effervescible
efficaciously
efflorescence
egotistically
egpytological
elaborateness
electrifiable
electrocution
electro-magnet
electrometric
electromotive
electrophorus
elephantiasis
embarrassment
embellishment
embryological
emigrationist
encomiastical
encompassment
encouragement
encouragingly
encyclopaedia
encyclopaedic
encyclopedism
encyclopedist
endurableness
energetically
enigmatically
enlightenment
entertainment
entomological
entomophagous
entomophilous
entozoologist
environmental
epigrammatist
epigrammatize
epiperipheral
equestrianism
equidifferent

equidistantly
equilibration
equiponderant
equiponderate
equisetaceous
equitableness
equivocalness
erysipelatous
establishment
estimableness
eucharistical
evangelically
everlastingly
exanthematous
exceptionable
exceptionally
excitableness
exclusiveness
excommunicate
excortication
excusableness
expansibility
expansiveness
expectoration
expectorative
expeditionary
expeditiously
expensiveness
experimentist
expostulation
expostulatory
expropriation
exquisiteness
exsanguineous
extemporarily
extensibility
extensiveness
extermination
exterminatory
exterritorial
extrajudicial

extraofficial
extraordinary
extratropical
extravagantly
extravasation
extrinsically
facetiousness
falsification
fantastically
farinaceously
faultlessness
featherweight
ferociousness
fertilization
filibusterism
flashing-point
flesh-coloured
floccillation
floricultural
foolhardiness
foraminiferal
foreknowledge
forementioned
forgetfulness
formulization
fortification
fossiliferous
fossilization
fractiousness
frequentative
fridge-freezer
frightfulness
frivolousness
frumentaceous
funambulation
fundamentally
galvanization
galvanoplasty
gasteropodous
gastrocnemius
generalissimo

gentlemanlike
geometrically
gesticulation
gesticulatory
glorification
glossographer
glossological
goodnaturedly
gracelessness
graminivorous
grammatically
grandiloquent
grandmotherly
grappling-iron
graticulation
gratification
grossulaceous
grotesqueness
gubernatorial
guiltlessness
gymnastically
gymnospermous
haemaglobulin
hairsplitting
hallucination
hallucinatory
harbour-master
harmonization
healthfulness
heartbreaking
heartlessness
helminthology
hemimetabolic
hemispherical
hermaphrodism
hermaphrodite
hermeneutical
herpetologist
heterocarpous
heterodactyle
heterogeneity

heterogeneous
heterogenesis
heteromorphic
heteroplastic
heteropterous
hieroglyphist
holometabolic
homoeopathist
homosexuality
horizontality
horripilation
horticultural
housebreaking
hundredweight
hydrocephalus
hydrodynamics
hydrokinetics
hydrometrical
hymenopterous
hypercritical
hypermetropia
hypochondriac
hypophosphite
hypothecation
hysteranthous
iatrochemical
ichthyologist
ideographical
idiomatically
idiosyncratic
ignominiously
illegibleness
illustriously
immaterialism
immaterialist
immovableness
immutableness
imparipinnate
impartibility
impassibility
impassionable

impassiveness
impeccability
impecuniosity
imperfectness
imperiousness
impersonality
impersonation
impertinently
imperturbable
impetuousness
implacability
importunately
impossibility
impracticable
impracticably
impressionist
impressionism
improbability
impropriation
improvability
improvisation
improvisatory
inadvertently
inappreciable
inappropriate
inattentively
incandescence
incarceration
incognoscible
incombustible
incompetently
inconceivable
inconceivably
incondensable
incongruously
inconsequence
inconsiderate
inconsistence
inconsistency
inconspicuous
incontestable

incontestably
incontinently
inconvenience
inconvertible
inconvincible
incorporation
incorporeally
incorrectness
incorruptible
incorruptibly
incredibility
incredulously
incurableness
indefatigable
indefatigably
independently
indescribable
indeterminate
indifferently
indispensable
indispensably
indisposition
indissociable
indissolvable
individualism
individuality
individualize
individuation
industrialism
industriously
ineffectively
ineffectually
inefficacious
inefficiently
ineligibility
inexhaustible
inexhaustibly
inexpediently
inexpensively
inexperienced
inexpressible

inexpressibly
infallibilism
infallibilist
inferentially
infinitesimal
inflexibility
inflorescence
influentially
infundibulate
ingeniousness
inhospitality
injudiciously
inobservantly
inoffensively
inopportunely
inquisitional
inquisitively
inquisitorial
insatiability
insectivorous
insensibility
insidiousness
insignificant
insinuatingly
inspectorship
instantaneous
instinctively
institutional
instructively
insubordinate
insufficiency
insupportable
insupportably
insusceptible
intangibility
integumentary
intelligencer
intelligently
intemperately
intensiveness
intentionally

intercalation
intercellular
intercolonial
interdigitate
interestingly
interlacement
interlinearly
interlocution
interlocutory
intermarriage
intermediator
intermittence
intermuscular
international
interosculate
interpolation
interposition
interpretable
interrelation
interrogation
interrogative
interrogatory
interruptedly
intersidereal
interspersion
interstellary
interstratify
intertropical
intraparietal
intratropical
intrinsically
introspection
introspective
intrusiveness
inventorially
investigation
investigative
invidiousness
invincibility
inviolability
invisibleness

involuntarily
irascibleness
irrationality
irreclaimable
irrecoverable
irrecoverably
irreligiously
irrepressible
irrepressibly
irresponsible
irresponsibly
irretrievable
irretrievably
jollification
judiciousness
jurisprudence
justification
justificative
justificatory
kaleidoscopic
knickerbocker
labyrinthodom
lackadaisical
languishingly
laryngoscopic
laughableness
lecherousness
lepidodendron
lepidopterous
lethargically
leucocythemia
lexicographer
lexicographic
librarianship
lichenography
lickerishness
lightsomeness
lignification
lipogrammatic
lithofracteur
lithoglyphics

litigiousness
loathsomeness
logarithmical
ludicrousness
luxuriousness
lyencephalous
machicolation
magisterially
magnanimously
magnetization
magnificently
magniloquence
malacostracan
maliciousness
malleableness
manifestation
manufacturing
marsipobranch
martyrologist
masculineness
materfamilias
materialistic
mathematician
matriculation
matrimonially
mediatorially
mediterranean
megacephalous
mellifluently
mellifluously
melodiousness
melodramatist
membranaceous
mensurability
mercenariness
mercilessness
meritoriously
mesencephalon
mesocephalous
metalliferous
metamorphosis

metaphysician
metempiricism
meteorologist
methodistical
metonymically
microcomputer
micrometrical
microscopical
mineralogical
ministerially
misadvertence
miscegenation
miscellaneous
mischievously
misconception
miserableness
misgovernment
mismanagement
misunderstand
moderatorship
mohammedanism
mollification
momentariness
momentousness
monarchically
monochromatic
monocotyledon
monogrammatic
monographical
monometallism
monometallist
monothalamous
monotrematous
monstrousness
morphinomania
mortification
mountainously
multangularly
multicapsular
multinational
multinucleate

multiplicator
multipresence
multisyllable
multitudinous
mummification
mystification
necessitarian
necessitously
negotiability
neighbourhood
nickeliferous
niggardliness
noiselessness
nonconforming
nonconformist
nonconformity
nonsensically
notoriousness
nullification
objectionable
objectionably
objectiveness
obliviousness
obnoxiousness
observational
obstinateness
obstructively
occidentalize
odontoglossum
odoriferously
offensiveness
officiousness
operas bouffes
ophiomorphous
ophthalmology
ophthalmotomy
opportuneness
oppositionist
opprobriously
orchestration
organogenesis

organological
ornamentation
ornithichnite
ornithologist
orthoepically
orthognathous
ostensibility
ostreiculture
outsettlement
overflowingly
overstatement
overvaluation
ovoviviparous
palaeocrystic
palaeographic
palaeontology
palaeotherium
palaeozoology
palatableness
pandiculation
panegyrically
panspermatism
pantheistical
papaveraceous
parabolically
paradoxically
paragraphical
parallelogram
paraphernalia
parasitically
parenthetical
parliamentary
participation
participially
particoloured
particularist
particularist
particularity
particularize
paterfamilias
pathognomonic

patrimonially
patriotically
patronizingly
peaceableness
pedestrianism
pendulousness
penetrability
penetratingly
penitentially
pennilessness
pentadelphous
pentapetalous
pentaphyllous
pentastichous
penuriousness
perambulation
peregrination
perfectionism
perfectionist
perfunctorily
perichondrium
peripatetical
perishability
perpendicular
perscrutation
perseveringly
personalities
perspectively
perspicacious
perspicuously
pestiferously
petrochemical
phanerogamous
pharisaically
pharmaceutics
pharmaceutist
pharmacopoeia
phenomenalism
philanthropic
philhellenism
philomathical

philosophical
philosophizer
phonautograph
phonographist
phosphuretted
photometrical
phraseologist
phrenological
phylacterical
phylacterical
phyllophagous
physiognomist
physiological
picturesquely
piscicultural
plaintiveness
platitudinous
platycephalic
plausibleness
plectognathic
plenteousness
plethorically
pluralization
pneumatically
pneumatometer
pneumogastric
pococurantism
poisonousness
polliniferous
polychromatic
polycotyledon
polydactylism
polysynthetic
polythalamous
ponderability
ponderousness
porcellaneous
porphyraceous
possessionary
post-modernism
post-modernist

powerlessness
practicalness
pragmatically
prayerfulness
precautionary
precentorship
precipitantly
precipitately
precipitation
precipitously
preconception
predestinator
predicability
predicamental
predicatively
predominantly
prefiguration
prefigurement
prejudication
prejudicially
preliminarily
prematureness
premeditation
preoccupation
preordination
preparatively
preponderance
prepositional
prepossessing
prepossession
presbytership
prescientific
prescriptible
presidentship
pressirostral
presumptively
pretentiously
pretermission
preternatural
preterperfect
prevarication

primitiveness
primogeniture
prismatically
privateersman
privatization
probabilities
problematical
proconsulship
procrastinate
professoriate
prognosticate
progressional
progressively
proleptically
promiscuously
pronounceable
pronouncement
pronunciation
propaedeutics
prophetically
proportionate
propositional
proprietorial
prospectively
protectionism
protectionist
protectorship
proterandrous
protestantism
protestantize
proverbialist
provincialism
provisionally
psychological
pulmoniferous
pulverization
punctiliously
puritanically
pusillanimity
pusillanimous
pyrheliometer

pyrotechnical
quadragesimal
quadraphonics
quadrifoliate
quadrilateral
quadriliteral
quadrilocular
quadripartite
quadrophonics
quadruplicate
qualification
qualificative
qualitatively
querulousness
quincentenary
quinquagesima
quinquangular
rapaciousness
ratiocination
ratiocinative
ratiocinatory
rationalistic
readjournment
realistically
reappointment
rearrangement
receivability
reciprocation
recommendable
reconcilement
recrimination
recriminative
recriminatory
recrudescence
recrudescency
rectangularly
rectification
rectilineally
reduplication
reflexibility
refrigeration

refrigerative
refrigeratory
registrarship
regurgitation
reimbursement
reimportation
reinforcement
reinstatement
reinterrogate
reinvestigate
rejuvenescent
religiousness
remissibility
remonstrative
remonstratory
remorselessly
replenishment
reprehensible
reprehensibly
representable
reproachfully
reprobateness
republication
repulsiveness
resistibility
resolvability
respirability
respirational
resplendently
restrictively
resuscitation
retentiveness
retrogression
retrogressive
retrospection
retrospective
reunification
reverberation
reverberatory
reverentially
reversibility

revolutionary
revolutionism
revolutionist
revolutionize
rhapsodically
rhizomorphous
rhopalocerous
righteousness
rollercoaster
russophobists
saccharometer
saccharimeter
sacerdotalism
sacramentally
sacrosanctify
sagaciousness
salaciousness
sanctimonious
sarcastically
scarification
scepticalness
schizomycetes
scholasticism
scintillation
scripturalism
scripturalist
sculpturesque
secondariness
secretaryship
secretiveness
sedentariness
sedimentation
seditiousness
seismographic
seneschalship
senselessness
sensitiveness
sententiously
sentimentally
separableness
septisyllable

septuagesimal
sequestration
sesquilateral
shamelessness
shapelessness
shortwindedly
sightlessness
sigillography
significantly
signification
significative
significatory
singularities
skateboarding
solemnization
solicitorship
solidungulate
somnambulator
somniloquence
sophistically
sophisticator
sorrowfulness
spasmodically
specification
spectroscopic
speculatively
spermatorrhea
splanchnology
splenetically
spontaneously
sportsmanship
sprightliness
squeamishness
squeezability
stalactitical
stalagmitical
stalworthness
staminiferous
staphylopaphy
statesmanlike
statesmanship

statistically
steadfastness
steganography
stenographist
stercoraceous
stereographic
stethoscopist
stoloniferous
strangulation
strategetical
strategically
stratigraphic
strengthening
structuralism
structuralist
structureless
subdeaconship
subordinately
subordination
subordinative
subpiritoneal
substantially
substantively
subtilization
successionist
suffraganship
suffumigation
sulphureously
superabundant
superaddition
superannuated
superdominant
supereminence
superfetation
superficially
superfluities
superfluously
superfortress
superlatively
superposition
supersaturate

supersensible
superstitious
supplantation
supplementary
suppositional
suprascapular
surreptitious
survivability
syllogistical
symmetrically
sympathetical
symptomatical
synchronously
synecdochical
synecphonesis
syntactically
synthetically
syphilization
talkativeness
tantalization
tastelessness
teachableness
telecommuting
telegraphical
televangelist
temperateness
tempestuously
temporalities
temporization
tenaciousness
tergiversator
terminational
terpsichorean
terrestrially
territorially
tetrasyllable
thalamifloral
thaumaturgist
thaumaturgics
theanthropism
theatricality

theologically
theoretically
theriomorphic
thoughtlessly
threateningly
tintinnabular
tolerableness
topographical
toxicological
tracklessness
traditionally
tranquillizer
transatlantic
transcendence
transcendency
transcription
transcriptive
transgression
transientness
transitionary
translucently
transmigrator
transmissible
transmittable
transmittance
transmutation
transparently
transpiration
transportable
transposition
transpositive
transversally
tremulousness
triangularity
triangulation
tripinnatifid
troublesomely
typographical
umbelliferous
unaccompanied
unaccountable

unapostolical
unappreciated
unassimilated
uncertainties
uncomfortable
uncomfortably
uncomplaining
unconditional
unconditioned
uncomfortable
uncomfortably
unconquerable
unconquerably
underclothing
undergraduate
underestimate
understanding
undiscernible
undisciplined
undissolvable
undisturbedly
undiversified
unembarrassed
unenlightened
unfamiliarity
unfashionable
unfashionably
unfortunately
ungrammatical
unguardedness
unimpassioned
unimpeachable
unimpressible
uninhabitable
uninstructive
uninteresting
unintermitted
uninterrupted
unjustifiable
unjustifiably
unmentionable

unmindfulness
unnecessarily
unneighbourly
unobtrusively
unperceivable
unphilosophic
unprecedented
unpresentable
unrecompensed
unrepresented
unrighteously
unsavouriness
unserviceable
unsightliness
unskilfulness
unsubstantial
unsurpassable
unsusceptible
unsymmetrical
unthriftiness
untrustworthy

unwarrantable
unwarrantably
unwillingness
unworkmanlike
unworldliness
vegetarianism
venerableness
ventriloquial
ventriloquism
ventriloquist
ventriloquize
ventriloquous
vermiculation
vernacularism
versicoloured
versification
vexatiousness
videocassette
video-recorder
violoncellist
visionariness

vitrification
vivaciousness
volatilizable
volumenometer
voluntariness
voraciousness
vulcanization
vulnerability
wearisomeness
wheeler-dealer
whistleblower
whithersoever
wholesomeness
wonderfulness
word-processor
worthlessness
xerophthalmia
xylographical
yachtsmanship
yellowishness
zygodactylous

14-Letter Words

abominableness
abstemiousness
abstractedness
acceptableness
accomplishable
accomplishment
accountability
accountantship
acknowledgment
administration
administrative
adscititiously
advantageously
adventitiously
affectionately
aforementioned
aggrandizement
aggressiveness
alphabetically
amphibological
anagrammatical
antaphrodisiac
anthropography
antidepressant
antiphlogistic
antiquarianism
antithetically
apheliotropism
aphoristically
apologetically
apophthegmatic
apprehensively
apprenticeship
arboricultural
archaeological
archdeaconship
archiepiscopal

arithmetically
asset-stripping
astrologically
astronomically
attainableness
attractiveness
augmentatively
aurora-borealis
auspiciousness
authentication
autobiographer
autobiographic
bacteriologist
barometrically
beautification
believableness
billiard-marker
biographically
bird-of-paradise
bituminiferous
blithesomeness
boa-constrictor
boarding-school
boisterousness
bouleversement
brachycephalic
branchiostegal
breathlessness
bristol-diamond
britannia-metal
brobdingnagian
calcographical
capitalization
capriciousness
cardinal-flower
carline-thistle
cartridge-paper

castrametation
catadioptrical
catechetically
catherine-wheel
censoriousness
censurableness
centralization
chalcographist
chancellorship
changeableness
characteristic
chargeableness
charitableness
chicken-hearted
chorographical
circuitousness
circumambiency
circumambulate
circumferentor
circumgyration
circumlittoral
circumlocution
circumlocutory
circumnavigate
circumnutation
circumspection
circumstantial
circumvolution
classification
coessentiality
cognoscibility
colourableness
colour-sergeant
commensurately
commensuration
commentatorial
commissaryship

commodiousness
composing-stick
comprehensible
comprehensibly
concavo-concave
conceivability
concentrically
concessionaire
conclusiveness
condensability
conditionality
confidentially
congloberation
congeutination
conglutinative
congratulation
congratulatory
congregational
consanguineous
conscriptional
constitutional
constitutively
constructional
constructively
consubstantial
consuetudinary
contagiousness
contemptuously
contiguousness
continentalist
continentalism
continuousness
contractedness
contradictable
contradictious
contraindicate
contraposition
controllership
controvertible
controvertibly
contumaciously

contumeliously
convalescently
conventionally
conversational
convertibility
convexo-concave
co-ordinateness
copper-bottomed
copper-fastened
corolliflorous
correspondence
correspondency
corruptibility
cosmopolitical
cotemporaneous
counsellorship
counterbalance
courageousness
creditableness
cross-reference
crystallizable
crystallomancy
cucurbitaceous
dactylioglyphy
deceivableness
dechristianize
decolorization
deconsecration
decorativeness
definitiveness
degenerateness
deliberateness
delightfulness
demobilisation
democratically
demonetization
demoralization
denominational
denominatively
deplorableness
depolarization

derogatoriness
descendibility
despicableness
despitefulness
destructionist
detestableness
diabolicalness
diaheliotropic
dicotyledonous
diffusibleness
digestibleness
diminutiveness
diphthongation
diplomatically
disaggregation
disappointedly
disappointment
disappropriate
disapprovingly
disarrangement
disciplinarian
disconsolately
discontentedly
discontentment
discontinuance
discountenance
discouragement
discouragingly
discourteously
discretionally
discriminately
discriminating
discrimination
discriminative
discursiveness
disdainfulness
disembarkation
disemboguement
disembowelment
disenchantment
disenchantress

disencumbrance
disengagedness
disenthralment
disgustfulness
disillusionize
disinclination
disincorporate
disinformation
disingenuously
disinheritance
disintegration
disinvestiture
disjointedness
disorderliness
disquisitional
disrespectable
dissertational
distemperature
distensibility
distinguishing
distractedness
distributively
divertissement
dodecasyllable
doublebreasted
ecclesiastical
ecclesiologist
educationalist
effeminateness
electioneering
electrobtology
electrodynamic
electrokinetic
electrolytical
elementariness
eleutheromania
emblematically
empyreumatical
encyclopaedist
enharmonically
enterprisingly

enthronization
enthusiastical
entoperipheral
epigrammatical
equiponderance
ethnographical
etymologically
eulogistically
evangelicalism
evangelization
excommunicable
excrementitial
excruciatingly
experimentally
expressionless
expressiveness
extemporaneous
extinguishable
extinguishment
extortionately
extraparochial
extrinsicality
faintheartedly
fallaciousness
fantasticality
farsightedness
fastidiousness
favourableness
fibrocartilage
figurativeness
flagitiousness
floriculturist
foraminiferous
foreordination
forisfamiliate
fortidableness
fortuitousness
fraternization
freespokenness
friendlessness
fringillaceous

frolicsomeness
fructification
gastrovascular
genealogically
generalization
geocentrically
geographically
goodhumouredly
grandiloquence
gregariousness
groundlessness
guillotinement
gyrencephalate
handicraftsmen
harmoniousness
helminthagogue
hemispheroidal
heresiographer
hermaphroditic
heteroclitical
heteromorphous
heterophyllous
hieroglyphical
hippopotamuses
histrionically
honourableness
horticulturist
hydrographical
hyperaesthesia
hyperbolically
hypercriticism
hypocritically
hypostatically
hypothetically
ichnolithology
ichthyological
ichthyophagous
ichthyophagist
identification
idiopathically
illegitimately

illustratively
imparidigitate
impassableness
imperyiousness
implacableness
impoverishment
impressibility
impressionable
impressiveness
improvableness
improvisatrice
inalienability
inapprehension
inarticulately
inartificially
inauspiciously
incapacitation
incautiousness
incommensurate
incommunicable
incompressible
inconclusively
inconsiderable
inconsiderably
inconsistently
inconveniently
incorporeality
indecipherable
indecomposable
indecorousness
indefiniteness
indestructible
indestructibly
indeterminable
indifferentism
indiscreetness
indiscriminate
indisposedness
indistinctness
indiyisibility
indoctrination

inexpressibles
infectiousness
inflexibleness
inharmoniously
inordinateness
inquisitionary
insatiableness
inseparability
insignificance
insignificancy
institutionary
instrumentally
insufficiently
insuperability
insuppressible
insurmountable
insurrectional
intangibleness
intellectually
intercessional
intercommunion
intercommunity
interdependent
interjectional
interlineation
intermaxillary
intermediately
intermediation
intermigration
interpellation
interpenetrate
interplanetary
interpretation
interpretative
intractability
intransitively
intransmutable
invariableness
invincibleness
inviolableness
irrationalness

irrecognizable
irreconcilable
irreconcilably
irremovability
irreparability
irreproachable
irreproachably
irresoluteness
irrespectively
jurisdictional
knickerbockers
lamellirostral
lapidification
latitudinarian
leucocythaemia
libertarianism
libidinousness
licentiousness
lieutenantship
longitudinally
macadamization
macrocephalous
magniloquently
mathematically
mensurableness
meretriciously
metaphorically
metaphysically
metempsychosis
metensomatosis
meteorological
metropolitical
mettlesomeness
microcephalous
microprocessor
mineralization
ministerialist
miraculousness
misanthropical
misapplication
miscalculation

misinformation
mismeasurement
multifariously
multiplication
multiplacative
mysteriousness
mythologically
naturalization
neurohypnotism
neurohypynlogy
neuropathology
neutralization
obligatoriness
obsequiousness
obstreperously
obstructionist
ophthalmodynia
ophthalmoscope
ophthalmoscopy
opinionatively
opisthocoelous
opisthographic
oppressiveness
ornithodelphia
ornithodelptic
ornithologicai
orthographical
ostentatiously
outrageousness
overpoweringly
pachydactylous
pachydermatous
palaeographist
papilionaceous
paragrammatist
parallelepiped
parallelopiped
paraphrastical
parenchymatous
parsimoniously
passionateness

pathoeogically
pentadactylous
perceptibility
perfectibility
perfidiousness
peripateticism
periphrastical
perishableness
perissopactyle
permissibility
perniciousness
perspirability
persuasiveness
pertinaciously
pestilentially
phantasmagoric
phantasmagoria
pharmaceutical
pharmacologist
pharmacopolist
phelloplastics
philanthropist
phonographical
phraseological
physiognomical
phytogeography
phytopathology
pisciculturist
plectognathous
pleonastically
pleurapophysis
pneumatologist
polysyllabical
polytheistical
popularization
practicability
prebendaryship
precariousness
precociousness
preconcertedly
predestinarian

predestination
predeterminate
preferentially
preponderation
preposterously
presumptuously
procrastinator
procuratorship
productiveness
professionally
prognosticator
prohibitionist
proletarianism
propaedeutical
propitiatorily
propitiousness
proportionable
proportionably
proprietorship
procencephalon
prosperousness
providentially
quadragenarian
quadridigitate
quadrisyllable
quantification
quantitatively
quermioniously
quinquepartite
ranunculaceous
reasonableness
recalcitration
recapitulation
recapitulatory
receivableness
recommendation
recommendatory
reconciliation
reconnaissance
reconstruction
rectilinearity

recurvirostral
redintegration
redistribution
reflectiveness
refractoriness
regardlessness
regenerateness
rehabilitation
reimprisonment
reintroduction
rejuvenescence
relentlessness
relinquishment
reminiscential
remonetization
remorsefulness
remunerability
reorganisation
reprehensively
requisitionist
resistibleness
resolvableness
respectability
respirableness
responsibility
responsiveness
retrogradation
revengefulness
revivification
rosicrucianism
sabbatarianism
sacchariferous
sacramentarian
sacrilegiously
sanctification
sanguinivorous
satisfactorily
scandalousness
scholastically
scientifically
scrupulousness

scurrilousness
seasonableness
secularization
sensationalism
sensationalist
sentimentalism
sentimentalist
sentimentality
sentimentalize
sesquipedalian
sesquialterate
simplification
simultaneously
slatternliness
solidification
somnambulation
somnambulistic
sophistication
specialization
spectroscopist
speechlessness
sphaeristerium
stationariness
stenographical
stigmatization
stratification
stupendousness
subarborescent
subconsciously
subinfeudation
submissiveness
substantiality
substantialize
substantiation
sufferableness
superabundance
superannuation
supercelestial
superciliously
supereminently
supererogatory

superficiality
superincumbent
superintendent
supernaturally
superscription
supersensitive
superphosphate
superstructure
supposititious
supramaxillary
susceptibility
suspiciousness
synchronically
systematically
tabularization
tatterdemalion
tautologically
teleologically
telescopically
terminological
tetradactylous
thoughtfulness
thriftlessness
tintinnabulary
traditionalism
transcendental
transitoriness
transmigratory
transverberate
tridimensional
tripersonalist
tumultuousness
ultramontanist
ultramontanist
unacknowledged
unappropriated
unconscionable
unconscionably
uncontrollable
uncontrollably
undecomposable

understatement
undiscoverable
unfaithfulness
unfruitfulness
ungracefulness
ungratefulness
unincorporated
unintelligible
unintelligibly
unintermitting
unipersonalist
unmercifulness
unostentatious
unpremeditated

unprepossessed
unpresumptuous
unprosperously
unquestionable
unquestionably
unrecognizable
unreliableness
unrestrainedly
unsatisfactory
unscripturally
unscrupulously
unsociableness
unsuccessfully
unsuitableness

untranslatable
valetudinarian
villainousness
vindictiveness
vituperatively
viviparousness
volatilization
vulnerableness
weightlessness
wonderstricken
zincographical
zingiberaceous
zinziberaceous
zoroastrianism

Words Liable to be Confused

Some words with totally different meanings are liable to be confused, often, but not always, because they are pronounced in a similar way or have similar spellings. Below is a list of words which are often confused, together with short examples of usage to help you to differentiate them.

accept	accept a gift	allusion	make no allusion to recent events
except	everyone except Mary		
		delusion	under the delusion that he is immortal
access	access to the building; access to computer data	illusion	an optical illusion
excess	an excess of food at the picnic	altar	praying at the altar
		alter	alter the dress
adapter	the adapter of the novel for TV	alternately	feeling alternately hot and cold
adaptor	an electrical adaptor	alternatively	we could drive there – alternatively we could walk
addition	an addition to the family	amend	amend the law
edition	a new edition of the book	emend	emend the text before printing
adverse	an adverse reaction to the drug	angel	heavenly angels
averse	not averse to the idea	angle	a triangle has three angles; a new angle to the story
advice	seek legal advice		
advise	We advise you to go	annex	annex a neighbouring country
affect	badly affected by the news	annexe	build an annexe to the house
effect	the effects of the drug		
		antiquated	antiquated attitudes
alley	a bowling alley	antique	valuable antique furniture
allay	allay the child's fears		

261

arisen	a problem has arisen	**base**	at the base of the
arose	a problem arose today		pillar; base the
			argument on facts
ascent	the ascent of Everest	**bass**	sing bass; fishermen
assent	he gave his assent to		catching bass
	the proposal		
		bath	lie soaking in the bath;
astrology	believers in astrology		bath the baby
	read horoscopes	**bathe**	bathe in the sea; bathe
astronomy	astronomy involves the		a wound
	scientific study of the		
	stars and the planets	**baton**	the conductor's baton;
			a relay baton
ate	we ate bread and cheese	**batten**	secure the broken
eaten	we have eaten too much		door with wooden
			battens; batten down
aural	an aural impairment		the hatches
	requiring a hearing aid; an		
	aural comprehension test	**beach**	building sand castles
oral	both oral and written		on the beach
	language exams; oral	**beech**	beech and oak trees
	hygiene recommended		
	by the dentist	**been**	having been famous
		being	being poor scared her
bad	bad men arrested by		
	the police	**beat**	beat them at tennis;
bade	We bade him farewell		beat the dog with a
bail	the accused was		stick
	granted bail	**beet**	sugar beet; soup made
bale	a bale of cotton; bale		with beet
	out; bale out water;		
	bale out of an aircraft	**beat**	we should beat them
		beaten	we should have beaten
ballet	practising ballet steps		them
ballot	voting by means of a		
	secret ballot	**became**	she became famous
		become	he wants to become a
bare	bare feet		doctor
bear	bear the pain; bear		
	children; bears looking	**beer**	a pint of beer
	for food	**bier**	a funeral bier

began	the child began to cry	**born**	babies born in hospital
begun	it had begun to rain	**borne**	I could not have borne the pain; water-borne diseases
belief	have belief in his son's abilities		
believe	believe that his son could succeed	**bouquet**	a bouquet of roses
		bookie	place a bet with a bookie
beside	the bride stood beside the groom	**bow**	take a bow after the performance; bow to the queen
besides	besides, he has no money; who, besides your mother, was there	**bough**	the bow of a tree
bit	the dog bit the postman	**boy**	boys and girls
		buoy	a mooring buoy in the bay
bitten	he was bitten by a rat	**breach**	a breach of the peace; breach the enemy's defences
blew	the wind blew; the hat blew away	**breech**	the breech of a gun; a breech delivery of a baby
blown	the wind had blown fiercely; the papers have been blown away	**bread**	bread and butter
		bred	born and bred
bloc	the African bloc of countries	**break**	break an arm
block	a block of flats; a block of wood; block a pipe	**brake**	failure of the car's brakes; brake suddenly on seeing the dog in the road
boar	shooting wild boar		
bore	the speaker is a bore		
		breath	take a deep breath
boast	boast about his achievements	**breathe**	breathe deeply
boost	give a boost to the economy	**bridal**	the bridal party going to the church
		bridle	the horse's bridle
bonny	a bonny little girl with beautiful hair	**broke**	the watch fell and broke
bony	the man's bony knees	**broken**	the watch was broken

brooch	wear a silver brooch
broach	afraid to broach the subject
buffet	[buffit] heavy waves regularly buffet the cliffs
buffet	[boofay] serve a cold buffet at the party; the station buffet
but	he was dead, but his family did not know
butt	butt in rudely to the conversation; the goat will butt you; a cigarette butt
calf	a cow and her calf; the calf of the leg
calve	hoping the cow would calve soon
callous	a cruel, callous tyrant
callus	the callus on her finger
came	they came late
come	they promised to come
cannon	soldiers firing cannons
canon	the canons of the cathedral; the canons and principles of the Christian church
canvas	a bag made of canvas; the canvas painted by a local artist
canvass	canvass for votes
carton	a carton of milk
cartoon	children laughing at TV cartoons

cast	the whole cast came on stage; cast a quick glance; a cast in the eye
caste	the caste system in india
censor	appoint a film censor; censor letters
censure	censure the child's unruly behaviour
cereal	cereal crops; breakfast cereal
serial	a magazine serial
chafe	tight shoes will chafe your heels; chafe at the delay
chaff	separate the wheat from the chaff
chartered	a chartered surveyor; a chartered boat
charted	the charted areas of the region
cheap	buy cheap clothes at the market
cheep	birds beginning to cheep
check	check the addition; check the tyre pressure; act as a check on her extravagance
cheque	pay by cheque
checked	a checked tablecloth
chequered	a chequered career

choose	you may choose a cake	compulsive	a compulsive gambler
chose	she chose a peach from the fruit dish	compulsory	compulsory to wear school uniform
chosen	you have chosen well; the chosen few	concert	an orchestral concert
		consort	the queen's consort
chord	a musical chord; strike a chord	confident	confident of success
cord	the cord of a dressing gown; spinal cord; vocal cord	confidant	he was the king's trusted confidant
		confidante	she was the queen's closest confidante
coarse	made of some coarse material; a coarse sense of humour	conscience	suffering from a guilty conscience
course	taking a French course; a golf course; in due course	conscious	he was knocked out but is conscious now; conscious that she was all alone; a conscious decision
coma	the patient is still in a coma	conservative	wear conservative clothes; a conservative, rather than radical, approach
comma	put a comma instead of the full stop	Conservative	the Conservative Party in British politics
commissionaire	the hotel commissionaire		
commissioner	a police commissioner	consul	he was British consul in Rome then
compliment	embarrassed at being paid a compliment	council	she was elected to the town council
complement	a full complement of staff; the complement of a verb	counsel	counsel for the defence; seeking professional counsel
complimentary	complimentary remarks; complimentary tickets	contemptible	a contemptible act of cowardice; a contemptible fellow
complementary	complementary medicine; a complementary amount; complementary angles	contemptuous	contemptuous of the achievements of others; contemptuous of the law

continual	disturbed by continual interruptions; in continual pain	currant	a currant bun
continuous	a continuous line of cars; a continuous roll of paper	current	unable to swim against the strong current
coop	a hencoop	cygnet	a swan and her cygnets
coup	a military coup	signet	a signet ring
corps	an army corps; the corps de ballet	cymbal	banging the cymbals
corpse	a corpse found in a shallow grave	symbol	a symbol of purity; a mathematical symbol
councillor	a town councillor	dairy	milk from the dairy
counsellor	a bereavement counsellor	diary	writing in her diary every night
courtesy	treat the visitors with courtesy	dear	dear friends; clothes which are too dear
curtsy	curtsy to the queen	deer	hunting deer
credible	a credible story	dependant	trying to provide for his wife and other dependants
creditable	a creditable performance	dependent	dependent on her family for personal care
credulous	credulous enough to believe anything	deprecate	strongly deprecate the behaviour of the gang of youths
crevasse	a crevasse in the glacier	depreciate	depreciate in value
crevice	a crevice in the rock	desert	camels in the desert; He deserted his wife and family
cue	a billiards cue; an actor famous for missing his cue	dessert	have chocolate cake for dessert
queue	the bus queue	detract	detract from his reputation as an actor
curb	curb their extravagance	distract	try not to distract the driver
kerb	cars parked by the kerb		

device	a device designed to save water	**discomfit**	the question seemed to discomfit her
devise	devise a rescue plan	**discomfort**	living in great discomfort
devolution	the population voted for the devolution of power from the government to the assembly	**discriminating**	discriminating in their choice of wines
evolution	the theory of evolution was first proposed by Charles Darwin	**discriminatory**	discriminatory against women
dew	the morning dew	**discus**	throwing the discus
due	payment is due now; in due course	**discuss**	discuss the matter
did	you did enough; He did steal the money	**distinct**	see a distinct improvement; a style quite distinct from others
done	you have done enough	**distinctive**	the distinctive markings of the zebra
die	very ill and likely to die	**draft**	a first draft of a report
dye	about to dye her fair hair black	**draught**	there was a draught in the room from the open window; a draught of cold beer
died	the poet died young		
dyed	he dyed his white shirt blue	**dragon**	a dragon breathing fire
		dragoon	the dragoon guards; We dragooned her into helping us
dinghy	a dinghy capsizing in the storm		
dingy	a dingy basement flat		
		drank	we drank some white wine
disadvantageous	disadvantageous to one of the teams; disadvantageous, rather than favourable, circumstances	**drunk**	to have drunk too much; a drunk woman staggering down the street
disadvantaged	disadvantaged people in society	**drunken**	a drunken, violent man; a drunken brawl

drew	the child drew a picture
drawn	he has drawn a picture of a house
driven	we were driven home by my father
drove	we drove home after midnight
dual	serve a dual purpose
duel	fight a duel
economic	a country facing economic disaster; charging an economic rent for the flat
economical	the economical use of resources; an economical car to run; economical with the truth
eerie	in the eerie atmosphere of a thick mist
eyrie	the eagle's eyrie
elder	Mary has two brothers and James is the elder
eldest	John has three sisters and Jill is the eldest
elicit	elicit information
illicit	an illicit love affair
eligible	eligible for promotion; an eligible bachelor
legible	scarcely legible handwriting
elude	elude capture by the police
allude	allude to facts which he had concealed

emigrant	emigrants weeping for their native land
immigrant	illegal immigrants to the country
emigration	the poor standard of living led to mass emigration from the country
immigration	anxious to reduce the extent of immigration into the country
emission	the emission of poisonous gases
omission	the omission of her name from the invitation list
emotional	an emotional person; an emotional reaction
emotive	an emotive subject
employee	hiring several new employees
employer	asking their employer for an increase in salary
enormity	the enormity of the crime
enormousness	the enormousness of the elephant
envelop	she wanted to envelop the child in her arms; Mist began to envelop the mountains
envelope	a brown envelope
enviable	an enviable affluent lifestyle
envious	envious of other people's wealth

epitaph	carve an epitaph on a gravestone	expand	expand the business; metals expanding in the heat
epithet	King Alfred was given the epithet 'great'	expend	expend a great deal of energy
equable	an equable climate; an equable temperament	expansive	his knowledge of literature was expansive
equitable	an equitable system	expensive	spending a lot of money on expensive meals
erotic	erotic picture of naked women		
erratic	an erratic driver; impulsive, erratic behaviour	expedient	politically expedient
		expeditious	a parcel sent by the most expeditious method
ewe	a ewe and her lambs		
yew	the yew tree in the graveyard	extant	old customs which are still extant in some areas
exceedingly	exceedingly beautiful	extinct	an endangered species that is likely to be extinct soon; a volcano that has been extinct for centuries
excessively	excessively fond of alcohol		
exceptional	a singer of exceptional talent; an exceptional amount of rain	faint	feel faint; a faint noise
		feint	a feint in fencing
exceptionable	find their behaviour exceptionable	fair	a fair result; fair hair; sideshows at a fair
executioner	bring the condemned man to the executioner	fare	bus fare; How did you fare in the exam?
executor	an executor of a will	fate	suffer a terrible fate; by a strange twist of fate
exercise	physical exercise; an English exercise		
exorcise	exorcise evil spirits	fête	a fête in aid of charity
		fearful	fearful of being left behind; what a fearful smell
exhausting	an exhausting climb		
exhaustive	an exhaustive search	fearsome	see a fearsome sight

feat	perform a brave feat	**flour**	flour to make bread
feet	sore feet	**flower**	pick a flower from the garden
fiancé	Jill and her fiancé		
fiancée	Jim and his fiancée	**flout**	flout the new school rule
		flaunt	flaunt her long legs
final	a final warning		
finale	all the cast took part in the final	**font**	babies christened at the font
		fount	printed in a small size of fount
flair	have a flair for languages		
flare	send up a flare as a signal for help; make the fire flare up; a skirt with a slight flare	**forbade**	she forbade them to leave
		forbidden	she was forbidden to leave
flammable	clothes made of flammable material	**foresaw**	we foresaw trouble
inflammable	highly inflammable substances such as petrol	**foreseen**	the problem could not have been foreseen
		forgave	we forgave them
		forgiven	we have forgiven them
flea	bitten by a flea		
flee	people beginning to flee from the burning houses	**forgot**	we forgot about the party
		forgotten	I had forgotten the event
fleshy	fleshy upper arms; a fleshy fruit	**formally**	formally dressed
fleshly	fleshly pleasures	**formerly**	formerly the president of the club
flu	suffering from flu	**fort**	soldiers defending the fort
flue	cleaning the flue		
		forte	tact is not his forte
flew	the bird flew away		
flown	the bird has flown away	**foul**	commit a foul on the football pitch; a foul smell
floe	an ice floe	**fowl**	a chicken is a type of fowl
flow	the flow of water		

found	they found the missing child	**goal**	score a goal
founded	their grandfather founded the firm	**gaol**	escape from gaol
freeze	freeze the vegetables; freeze to death	**gone**	he has gone
frieze	a decorative frieze	**went**	she went yesterday
froze	we froze the meat immediately	**gorilla**	a gorilla in the zoo
frozen	frozen vegetables; have frozen to death	**guerrilla**	guerrillas fighting in the mountains
funeral	mourners at the funeral	**grate**	a fire burning in the grate
funereal	solemn funereal music	**great**	a great improvement; a great man
gaff	blow the gaff		
gaffe	a social gaffe	**grew**	the plants grew well
gamble	decide to gamble on a horse in the next race	**grown**	the plant had grown tall
gambol	lambs beginning to gambol about	**grief**	weeping from grief
		grieve	time to grieve for her dead husband
gate	shut the gate	**grill**	put the meat under the grill
gait	a shuffling gait	**grille**	a metal grille on the window
gave	he gave money to the poor	**grisly**	the grisly sight of a decaying body
given	we had been given some money	**grizzly**	a grizzly bear
		hail	a hail storm; a hail of bullets; hail a taxi
gentle	a gentle touch; a gentle breeze	**hale**	hale and hearty
genteel	a genteel tea party	**hair**	cut off her hair
		hare	a running hare
glacier	a glacier beginning to melt	**half**	a half of the apple
glazier	a glazier mending the window	**halve**	halve the apple

hangar	an aeroplane hangar	**idle**	too idle to work
hanger	a clothes hanger	**idol**	the pop star as teenage idol; worshipping an idol
hanged	they hanged the murderer	**imaginary**	the child's imaginary friend
hung	they hung the pictures	**imaginative**	an imaginative story; an imaginative person
heal	the wound began to heal	**immoral**	wicked and immoral
heel	a blister on the heel	**immortal**	no one is immortal
hear	hear the news	**inapt**	an inapt remark
here	here and there	**inept**	an inept attempt
hereditary	a hereditary title	**incredible**	find the story incredible
heredity	part of his genetic heredity	**incredulous**	incredulous enough to believe anything
heron	a heron catching fish	**industrial**	an industrial estate
herring	fishermen catching herring	**industrious**	studious and industrious
		ingenious	an ingenious plan
hid	we hid the treasure	**ingenuous**	an ingenuous young person
hidden	they have hidden the treasure		
		its	a dog wagging its tail
hoard	a hoard of treasure	**it's**	it's raining
horde	a horde of invaders		
		jam	strawberry jam; a traffic jam; the machine seemed to jam
honorable	an honorable gentleman; honorable deeds		
honorary	the honorary post of secretary	**jamb**	a door jamb
		jib	jib at the high price
hoop	jump through a hoop	**jibe**	ignore the nasty jibe
whoop	a whoop of delight		
		judicial	a judicial enquiry into the accident
human	a human being		
humane	the humane killing of the injured animal	**judicious**	a judicious choice of words

junction	a road junction	licence	have a driving licence
juncture	at this juncture we went home	license	to license the sale of alcohol
key	a door key	lifelong	a lifelong ambition
quay	the boat tied to the quay	livelong	the livelong day
knead	knead the bread dough	lighted	a lighted match
kneed	he kneed his attacker in the stomach	lit	we lit the fire; we have lit the fire
		lightening	lightening the load
knew	we knew him slightly	lightning	struck by lightning; a lightning decision
know	we did not know him		
known	if I had known		
knight	a knight in shining armour	liqueur	an after-dinner liqueur
night	a stormy night	liquor	strong liquor such as whisky
laid	we laid the patient on the bed; they laid a new carpet	liquidate	liquidate a debt; liquidate an asset; liquidate an enemy
lain	he had lain injured for days	liquidize	liquidize the soup
		literal	a literal translation
lair	the animal's lair	literary	literary and artistic tastes
layer	a layer of dust		
		literate	people who are scarcely literate
laterally	moving laterally; thinking laterally	loath/loth	loath/loth to join in
latterly	latterly she was very ill	loathe	I loathe him
lath	a lath of wood	local	the local shops; drinking at his local
lathe	using a lathe in the factory	locale	a perfect locale for a rock concert
lead	pipes made of lead		
led	he led the group	loose	loose clothing
		lose	lose your luggage; lose weight
leak	a leak in the pipe		
leek	a leek to make soup		

loot	the thieves' loot	**mediate**	mediate between the rival groups
lute	playing the lute	**meditate**	meditate to relax
		melted	the ice cream melted; melted chocolate
lumbar	lumbar pain	**molten**	molten lava
lumber	to lumber along awkwardly		
		metal	chairs made of metal
luxuriant	luxuriant vegetation	**mettle**	a test of the football team's mettle
luxurious	a luxurious lifestyle		
		meter	read the gas meter
magnate	a shipping magnate	**metre**	a metre of silk
magnet	a fridge magnet		
		miner	a coal miner
mail	deliver the mail	**minor**	a minor incident; legally still a minor
male	male and female		
		missal	members of the congregation carrying missals
main	the main reason		
mane	the lion's mane		
		missile	hit by a missile
maize	grow maize		
maze	get lost in the maze		
		mistaken	a case of mistaken identity; we were mistaken
manner	a friendly manner		
manor	a manor surrounded by beautiful gardens		
		mistook	I mistook him for you in the dark
masterful	she prefers masterful men		
masterly	a masterly performance	**model**	a model of a ship; a fashion module
		module	a space module; a software module; a study module
mat	a door mat		
matt, matte	matt/matte paint		
		momentary	a momentary lapse of memory
meat	meat such as beef		
meet	meet a friend		
		momentous	a momentous decision
medal	a gold medal		
meddle	meddle in the affairs of others		

moral	the moral of the story; a person with no morals	**oar**	the boat's oars
		ore	iron oar
morale	morale was low in the firm	**observance**	the observance of school rules
		observation	keep the patient under observation
motif	decorated with a motif of roses		
motive	a motive for murder	**of**	made of gold; tired of working; a glass of wine
muscle	strain a muscle	**off**	run off; switch off; badly off
mussel	eat fresh mussels		
naturalist	a naturalist interested in local flowers	**official**	an official report; official duties; council official
naturist	naked people on a naturist beach	**officious**	upset at the officious manner of the hotel receptionist
naval	a naval cadet		
navel	your navel is in the middle of your abdomen	**organism**	an organism found in the water supply
		orgasm	to reach orgasm
negligent	negligent parents		
negligible	a negligible amount of money	**outdoor**	an outdoor sport
		outdoors	playing outdoors
net	caught in a net	**overcame**	we overcame the enemy
net, nett	net, nett profit		
		overcome	an enemy difficult to overcome
niceness	appreciate the old lady's niceness		
nicety	the nicety of the distinction	**overtaken**	he had overtaken the other runners
		overtook	they overtook the car in front
notable	a notable figure in the town	**pail**	a pail of water
noticeable	a noticeable improvement	**pale**	looking pale; a pale colour
nougat	nougat is a sweet		
nugget	a nugget of gold; a nugget of information	**pain**	suffering from pain
		pane	a pane of glass

pair	a pair of gloves	**pendant**	wearing a silver pendant
pare	he began to pare his toenails	**pendent**	pendent lights lighting up the room
pear	an apple and a pear		
		perceptible	a perceptible improvement
palate	the soft palate		
palette	an artist's palette	**perceptive**	a perceptive remark
pallet	a straw pallet		
		perpetrate	perpetrate a crime
passed	she passed the exam; we passed the other car; the feeling passed	**perpetuate**	perpetuate the myth
		persecute	persecute members of other religions
past	past times; in the past; walking past the church; a mile past the village	**prosecute**	prosecute thieves
		personal	a personal letter; a personal assistant
pastel	pastel colours	**personnel**	the person in charge of office personnel
pastille	sucking a throat pastille		
		phase	the next phase of the development; phase in the changes
pâté	chicken liver pâté on toast		
patty	a small meat patty	**faze**	nothing seems to faze her
peace	warring nations now at peace	**pigeon**	a pigeon looking for food
piece	a piece of cake	**pidgin**	pidgin English
peak	a mountain peak; talent at its peak	**place**	a sunny place; get a place at university
peek	peek through the window	**plaice**	plaice and chips
peal	the bells began to peal	**plain**	a plain carpet; rather a plain girl; corn growing on the plain
peel	peel an orange		
pearl	a pearl necklace	**plane**	a plane taking off; the plane used by the joiner; writing on a different plane from other crime writers
purl	knit two, purl two		
pedal	pedal the bike		
peddle	peddle their wares		

plaintiff	evidence on behalf of the plaintiff	**premier**	a meeting of European premiers; one of the country's premier actors
plaintive	a plaintive cry		
plate	the food on the plate	**première**	the premiere of the film
plait	wearing her hair in a plait	**premises**	seek new office premises
plum	eating a plum	**premise**	based on a mistaken premise
plumb	plumb straight; plumb in the middle; plumb the depths; plumb-in the bath		
		prescribe	prescribe antibiotics for the disease
		proscribe	proscribe the carrying of dangerous weapons
politic	not politic to ask any questions		
political	political parties	**principal**	the college principal
		principle	a person of principle; the principle of the steam engine
pour	pour water		
pore	pore over the book; a clogged pore		
		prise	prise open the lid of the tin
practice	go to football practice		
practise	to practise dance steps	**prize**	win a prize
pray	pray to God		
prey	the fox's prey; prey on one's mind	**program**	a computer program
		programme	a theatre programme
precede	the leader who preceded the present one; precede them into the room	**proof**	no proof of his guilt
		prove	able to prove her innocence
proceed	You may proceed; proceed to cause trouble	**prophecy**	the gift of prophesy; her prophecy came true
		prophesy	prophesy that there would be a war
precipitate	rash, precipitate action; precipitate economic panic	**prostate**	the prostate gland
		prostrate	lying prostrate on the ground
precipitous	a precipitous slope		

purposely	leave the book behind purposely
purposefully	walk purposefully into the room
quash	quash a rebellion; quash a conviction
squash	squash the tomatoes; squash the insect with his foot
quiet	a quiet child; a quiet time of day
quite	quite good; quite right
racket	the noisy children made quite a racket; a drugs racket; tennis racket
racquet	tennis racquet (variant spelling)
rain	get wet in the rain
reign	in the reign of the last king
rein	a horse's reins
raise	raise one's arm; raise a family
raze	raze the whole street to the ground
ran	they ran away
run	he started to run; She had run away
rang	they rang the bell
rung	they had rung the bell
rap	rap at the window
wrap	wrap the presents

rapt	with rapt attention
wrapped	we wrapped the presents
read	I read the book last week
red	a red dress
real	made of real leather; a real friend
reel	a reel of thread; dance a reel
refuge	seek refuge from the storm
refugee	a political refugee
regal	a regal wave of the hand
regale	regale them with his adventures
relief	bring relief from pain
relieve	relieve the pain
rest	rest after work
wrest	wrest the knife from his hand
retch	feel sick and begin to retch
wretch	the poor wretch
review	the review of the play; the annual salary review
revue	a musical revue
rhyme	children reciting a rhyme; cook rhymes with book
rime	rime on the grass on a cold morning

ridden	she had ridden the horse home	**rye**	grow rye and barley
rode	he rode a fine stallion	**wry**	a wry smile; a wry sense of humour
right	the right person for the job; the right to be free; the right hand	**sail**	the sail of a boat; go for a sail
rite	a religious rite	**sale**	an end-of-season sale
write	write in pencil	**salon**	a hair-dressing salon
		saloon	a saloon car; a saloon bar
risen	the sun had risen		
rose	the sun rose		
		sang	they sang a song
road	the road through the town	**sung**	we had sung a song earlier
rode	the child rode her bicycle		
		sank	the ship sank
roe	cod roe	**sunk**	the ship has sunk
row	a row of green beans; row a boat	**sunken**	a sunken wreck
		saviour	the saviour of the organization; Christ the saviour
role	play the role of Hamlet; the parental role		
roll	a roll of carpet; a ham roll; roll a ball	**savour**	savour the delicious food
rote	learn the answers by rote	**saw**	we saw him go
wrote	he wrote a letter	**seen**	I have seen the film before
rough	a rough material; rough weather		
ruff	a lace ruff at the neck	**sawed**	we sawed the wood
		sawn	all the wood has been sawn
rout	rout the enemy		
route	the shortest route to the town	**scared**	scared of the dark
		scarred	scarred for life in the accident
rung	the bottom rung of the ladder; we had rung the bell		
		scene	a scene in the play; the scene of the accident
wrung	she wrung her hands in grief	**seen**	have seen the play

scent	the scent of roses	series	a series of disasters; a TV series
sent	she sent a letter		
		serious	a serious matter; looking serious
sceptic	a sceptic arguing with the believers		
septic	a septic wound; a septic tank	sew	sew new curtains
		sow	sow seeds
scraped	he scraped the car on the gate	sewed	she sewed tiny stitches
scrapped	they scrapped their original plans	sewn	the dress which she had sewn
sculptor	a statue by a famous sculptor	shaken	she was shaken by the accident
sculpture	carve a piece of sculpture	shook	he shook the child angrily
		shear	to shear sheep
seam	sew the seam of a dress; a seam of coal	sheer	a sheer slope; sheer impertinence; sheer silk
seem	they seem familiar		
seasonal	seasonal hotel work	shelf	put the book on the shelf
seasonable	seasonable weather for spring	shelve	shelve the plan
seasoned	a seasoned dish of stew; seasoned travellers	shoe	a high-heeled shoe
		shoo	shoo the dog away
secret	a secret hideout; their engagement was a secret	showed	we showed them the house
secrete	secrete the money under the floorboards	shown	he has shown me the book
		shrank	the child shrank back in fear; the dress shrank in the wash
see	I see a light		
sea	boats sailing on the sea	shrunk	the child had shrunk from the angry man; the dress had shrunk
sensual	a sensual mouth		
sensuous	the sensuous feel of the silk sheets		

sight	the sight of the woman crying	spoke spoken	she spoke with feeling he has spoken to the parents
site	the battle site; a building site		
		sprang sprung	he sprang to his feet the lion had sprung over the fence
singeing	singeing a blouse with an iron		
singing	singing a song		
		stair stare	a stone stair stare into space
slay	slay an enemy in battle		
sleigh	a sleigh ride in the snow		
		stake	a stake missing from the fence; stake a claim
slow	at a slow pace	steak	eat a large steak
sloe	a ripe sloe		
soar	soar up high	stalk	the stalk of the flower
sore	a sore finger	stock	a large stock of goods; stocks and shares
solder	to solder metal		
soldier	a soldier in the British army	stank stunk	he stank of beer the room had stunk for days
sole	the sole reason; the sole of the foot; a dish of sole	stationary stationery	the car was stationary a shop stocking stationery
soul	body and soul; a poor old soul	statue	stone statues in the grounds of the house
some	some people	statute	pass a new statute
sum	the sum total		
		steal	steal money from the till
son	a son and two daughters	steel	tools made of steel
sun	lie in the sun on the beach		
soot	soot falling down the chimney	stile	climb over the stile
suit	an evening suit	style	dress with style; a style of writing
sped	the car sped away into the night	stimulant	athletes taking illegal stimulants
speeded	we speeded up to pass the car in front	stimulus	the stimulus of a valuable prize

storey	the top storey of the house	summary	a summary of the report; his summary dismissal
story	tell a story	summery	sunny, summery weather
straight	a straight road; a straight answer	sundae	an ice cream sundae
strait	the Bering Strait	Sunday	have a rest on Sunday
straightened	she had her teeth straightened	surplice	the priest's surplice
straitened	in straitened circumstances	surplus	a surplus of food at the party
strategy	the team's winning strategy; devise a strategy to counteract bullying	swam	we swam in the river
		swum	he has swum across the river
stratagem	devise a stratagem to mislead the enemy	swingeing	a swingeing blow; swingeing cuts
		swinging	a swinging gate; the swinging sixties
strewed	they strewed flowers	swollen	her eye has swollen up; swollen glands
strewn	flowers were strewn	swelled	her injured ankle swelled
strife	quarrelling and strife		
strive	strive to overcome the difficulty	swore	they swore they would find the killer
striven	we haven striven to succeed	sworn	he has sworn to get revenge
strove	they strove to win	tail	the dog's tail
suede	a jacket made of real suede	tale	tell a tale
swede	cutting up a swede for dinner	taken	she has taken the book
		took	she took the book
suit	wearing a smart suit; a law suit; a suit of cards	taper	a lighted taper; The road seems to taper there
suite	a three-piece suite; a suite of rooms; a ballet suite	tapir	a tapir is a pig-like animal

taught	he taught us maths	**thyme**	flavour the sauce with thyme
taut	a taut rope; a face taut with concentration	**time**	what time is it?; not enough time
tea	a cup of tea		
tee	a golf tee	**tic**	a nervous tic
		tick	the tick of the clock; the dog bitten by the tick; in a tick; a tick at a correct answer
team	a football team		
teem	the town will teem with tourists		
tear	wipe away a tear	**timber**	a house made of timber
tier	one tier of the wedding cake	**timbre**	the timbre of his voice
		tire	runners beginning to tire
teeth	have two teeth extracted	**tyre**	change a car tyre
teethe	the child has begun to teethe		
		to	go to town
		too	she wants to go too
temporal	temporal, not spiritual	**two**	two or three times
temporary	a temporary post		
		toe	injure a toe
their	their home	**tow**	tow the broken-down car
there	stay there		
they're	they're quarrelling again		
		tomb	the tomb of the Egyptian king
thorough	a thorough cleaning		
through	pass through	**tome**	struggling to read a legal tome
thrash	thrash the youth with a belt		
thresh	thresh the corn	**topi**	wear a topi in the hot sun
		toupee	a bald man wearing a toupee
threw	he threw the ball		
through	go through the door		
		tore	she tore her dress
threw	he threw the ball	**torn**	she has torn her dress; a torn dress
thrown	he had thrown the ball		
throes	in the throes of studying for exams	**trait**	dishonesty is an unpleasant trait
throws	he throws the ball	**tray**	tea served on a tray

treaties	signing treaties to end the war	**unwanted**	unwanted guests
treatise	write a treatise on company law	**unwonted**	speak with unwonted enthusiasm
		urban	prefer urban to rural life
trod	she trod on the cat's tail	**urbane**	an urbane young man
trodden	she had trodden on some mud	**vacation**	go on vacation to America
troop	a troop of soldiers; troop out of school	**vocation**	have a vocation to be a priest
troupe	a troupe of actors	**vain**	a vain young woman; a vain attempt
turban	hair hidden by a turban	**vane**	a weather vane
turbine	a turbine engine	**vein**	inject the drug into a vein; a vein of pessimism in the novel
tycoon	a business tycoon		
typhoon	a ship damaged in a typhoon	**vale**	the Vale of Evesham
		veil	a hat with a veil; draw a veil over the incident
unaware	unaware of what had happened		
unawares	taken unawares by the attack	**veracity**	doubt the veracity of the account
		voracity	the voracity of the youth's appetite
unconscionable	an unconscionable delay		
unconscious	knocked unconscious by the blow; unconscious of the recent event	**vertex**	the vertex of a cone
		vortex	the swimmer was caught in a vortex of water and drowned
undid	they undid all the damage		
undone	the damage could not be undone	**vigilant**	be vigilant because of pickpockets
		vigilante	the thief was caught by a vigilante
unexceptional	a disappointing, unexceptional performance	**wafer**	an ice cream wafer; a Communion wafer
unexceptionable	unnecessary complaints about unexceptionable behaviour	**waver**	begin to waver about the decision

waif	a starving waif	**went**	they went quite suddenly; She went pale
waive	waive the extra charges	**gone**	he has gone home; She had gone deaf
wave	wave to their departing guests		
		wet	a wet day; wet the floor
waist	a leather belt round the waist	**whet**	whet the appetite
waste	liquid waste from the factory; a waste of food	**whit**	not care a whit
		wit	find his wit amusing; a person of wit and intelligence
want	want more money; for want of enough money		
wont	she was wont to arrive late	**whole**	the whole group
		hole	dig a hole
warden	the warden of the hostel	**withdrawn**	he has withdrawn from the election; a shy, withdrawn child
warder	a prison warder	**withdrew**	he withdrew from the election
ware	kitchen ware; stallholders selling their wares	**wittily**	he spoke wittily after dinner
wear	wear a skirt; show signs of wear	**wittingly**	she wittingly told a lie
way	the quickest way home; the correct way to do it	**woe**	sadness and woe
		woo	woo her and marry her
weigh	weigh the apples		
		woke	she woke early
weak	invalids too weak to get out of bed	**woken**	she had woken early
week	go to the supermarket every week	**wore**	he wore the shoes
		worn	he had worn the shoes; an old, worn carpet
weakly	weakly children who did not survive		
weekly	look forward to their weekly visit	**would**	we knew she would go
		wood	a pine wood

wove	he wove the material	**wrote**	she wrote the letter
woven	he has woven the material	**written**	she has written the letter
weaved	the cyclist weaved in and out of the line of traffic		
		yoke	the yoke of a dress; the yoke of a plough
		yolk	egg yolk
wreak	wreak vengeance; wreak havoc		
wreck	wreck the car; wreck their plans	**yore**	in days of yore
		your	your house
		you're	you're wrong
wreath	a holly wreath		
wreathe	mist had begun to wreathe the mountain peaks